FUN Skills

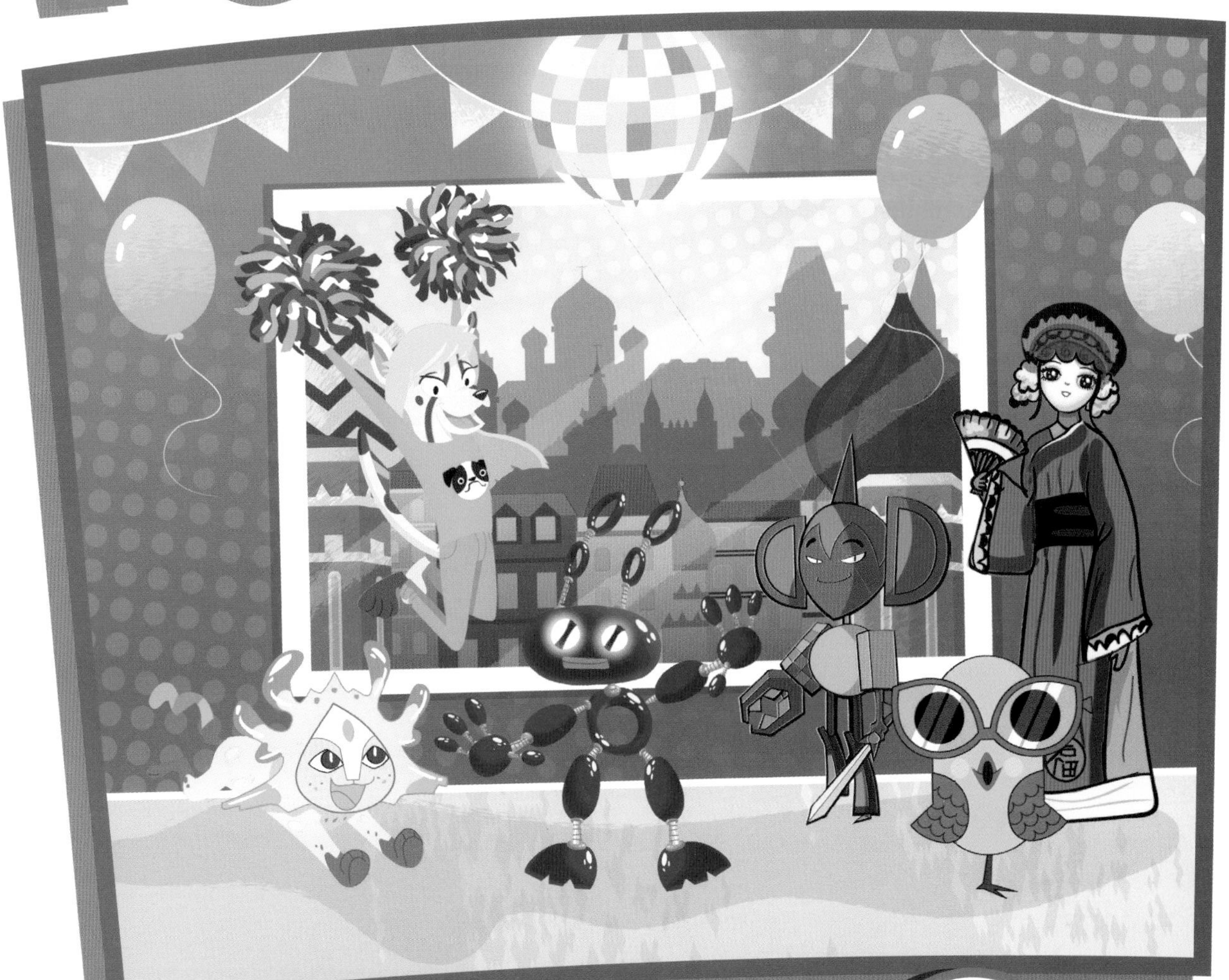

Student's Book 4

Bridget Kelly • David Valente

Cambridge University Press
www.cambridge.org/elt

Cambridge Assessment English
www.cambridgeenglish.org

Information on this title: www.cambridge.org/9781108563673

First published 2020

20 19 18 17 16 15 14 13 12 11 10 9

Printed in Malaysia by Vivar Printing

A catalogue record for this publication is available from the British Library

ISBN 978-1-108-56367-3 Student's Book and Home Booklet with Online Activities

Contents

Map of the book

Unit	Topic	Skills focus	Can do	
1 **About me** page 6	Personal details	**Reading and Writing** Copy the correct names next to their descriptions	Read and understand simple descriptions of pictures and familiar topics	Song
2 **Routines** page 10	Regular activities	**Reading and Writing** Choose the correct answer to a question from three possible answers	Understand basic questions	Chant
		Review Units 1–2 *page 14*		
3 **All about town** page 16	Places around town	**Listening** Listen for words, names and detailed information Match words heard and pictures **Speaking** Talk about trips to places in town	Understand simple spoken descriptions Describe a regular activity	Chant
4 **Are you sporty?** page 20	Sports	**Speaking** Understand the beginning of a story Continue the story based on a series of pictures **Reading and Writing** Complete gaps in a text using words provided	Tell a very simple story with the help of pictures Complete sentences using the context to identify the correct word	
		Review Units 3–4 *page 24*		
5 **My dream school** page 26	School facilities	**Reading and Writing** Complete sentences Respond to questions Write sentences	Read and understand short texts about familiar topics with the help of pictures	Song Think Big
6 **Food around the world** page 30	International food	**Listening** Listen for words, colours and specific information Colour items according to instructions heard **Speaking** Suggest a picture that is different and explain why	Understand simple spoken descriptions Give simple spoken descriptions of objects, pictures and actions	Think Big
		Review Units 5–6 *page 34*		

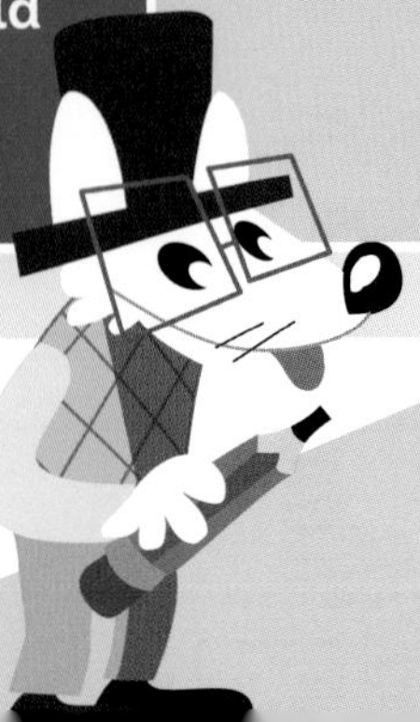

1 About me

Hi, my name is Lily. I'm 10 years old. I live with my grandparents in a village near a big national park in the jungle. I love watching the animals through the telescope on our balcony. I can see parrots in the trees and sometimes elephants.
I can also hear the birds and the waterfall at night when I'm in bed. My grandma says I'm very brave because I'm never scared of the animal sounds.

On Saturday afternoons, I go to the town centre with my grandpa. Our favourite places are the shopping centre and the roller disco. Roller skating is really, really, really fun! My grandpa is great at roller skating and his favourite drink is lychee milkshake. Lychees are his favourite fruit.

I don't have a pet, but a bat visits our balcony at night. I call him Charlie and he can hang upside down! Guess what Charlie likes to drink... Yes, that's right, lychee milkshake, the same as grandpa!

1 Meet Lily. Look at the pictures and read the questions below. Don't read the text yet. Guess the answers with a friend.

1 How old is Lily? ______

2 Who does she live with? ______

3 What does she like doing at home? ______

4 What does she do at the weekends? ______

2 Now read Lily's description and check your guesses. Write your answers on the lines above.

3 Check your answers with your friend.

TIP!

How old? = circle the numbers.
Who? = circle names of family members.
What? = underline names of activities.

4 Lily wants to know about you! Write your answers below.

1 Are you afraid of the dark? ______________________

2 What can you hear outside your window at night? ______________________

3 Can you buy lychees in your shops? ______________________

4 What is your favourite milkshake? ______________________

5 02 **Listen to the three children singing Lily's song. Say the words in your head.**

6 03 **Sing Lily's song in groups of three. Take turns to be A, B and C. Do the actions, click your fingers and be rappers!**

1 **Look and read about Lily's friends from around the world. Choose the correct names and write them on the lines. There is one example.**

Emma

Michael

Katy

Holly

George

Sarah

Harry

David

This is me with my uncle on our farm. I love helping him with the animals! *Emma*

2 This is me with my mum, dad and little brother. He's 6 years old. ____________

4 This is me on my mum's back! And my sister is on my dad's back! We're playing games. ____________

1 I have no brothers or sisters. I'm watching TV with my parents on the sofa. ____________

3 This is me with my aunt. We're in the garden, and we really love flowers! ____________

5 I live with my grandparents, just like Lily! They are my favourite people! ____________

2 Talk about the two extra pictures with your friend. Write about the two children.

3 Ask and answer the questions with four friends. Tell them two true things and two false things about you. Write your friend's answers in the table.

Friend's **NAME**	What do you do at **HOME?**	What do you do at the **WEEKEND?**

4 Look at your friends' answers. What is true and what is false? Tell the class all the funny false things about your friends.

2 Routines

1 **Look at all the pictures. Guess which pet belongs to who. Tell a friend.**

2 **Read what the children say to check your guesses.**

Julia

Bruno is my pet parrot and he's a brilliant dancer! Every Sunday afternoon we go samba dancing. Every morning before school, Bruno and I practise our samba moves. We go to a big dance competition once a year. **What do you do before school?**

Chi

My pet lizard, Hong, really likes swimming. On Saturday mornings, we go to a huge pool near my house. There are lots of slides and diving boards. Hong is the best diver. **What do you do at weekends?**

Emma

Ramona is my pet rabbit and her favourite food is strawberry pancakes. Every morning for breakfast Ramona eats strawberry pancakes and is VERY fat! We have a picnic with my family on Sunday afternoons. Ramona always comes to our picnics and guess what she eats? STRAWBERRY PANCAKES! **What do you usually have for breakfast?**

Asim

My pet donkey, Azzizi, lives with my aunt and uncle, but I visit him every Friday afternoon. We sometimes go water skiing on the river and Azzizi is SO good at water skiing! In the evenings, we watch comedies on TV and laugh a lot! **What do you usually watch on TV?**

3 **Check your answers with your friend. Did you guess right?**

4 Read the sentences below and choose which is correct. Work with a friend. There is one example.

TIP!

Read carefully – read slowly and check each fact.

Bruno

(A) He is a great dancer.

B He is a terrible dancer.

1 **Azzizi**

A They go water skiing on Sundays.

B They go water skiing on Fridays.

2 **Bruno**

A He dances in a TV competition every year.

B He dances in a samba competition every year.

3 **Ramona**

A She eats a lot of pancakes.

B She doesn't eat any pancakes.

4 **Hong**

A She is scared of diving.

B She isn't scared of diving.

5 **Bruno**

A They usually practise their dances before school.

B They usually practise their dances after school.

6 **Azzizi**

A They watch funny shows on TV.

B They watch football games on TV.

5 Do a class survey. Talk to four friends. Write their names and ask questions about their routines. Make short notes.

	Friend 1	Friend 2	Friend 3	Friend 4
What do you do before school?				
What do you do at weekends?				
What do you usually have for breakfast?				
What do you usually watch on TV?				
What do you do after school?				
What do you eat on your birthday?				

1 Work with three friends. Write a chant about a dream pet and their amazing routines. Choose one word from each list. Think of a pet name with your friend. There is one example.

Animals
dolphin
kangaroo
penguin
snail
shark
whale

Fun activities
ice skating
roller skating
skateboarding
playing in a band
texting friends
playing the piano

Places
funfair
farm
sports centre
swimming pool
supermarket
zoo

When
always
before school
after school
every day
every weekend

My pet *dolphin* **is called** *Alfonso* **.**
It loves *ice skating* **at the** *sports centre*
after school **. My pet is so cooooooool!**

Our Amazing Pets Chant!

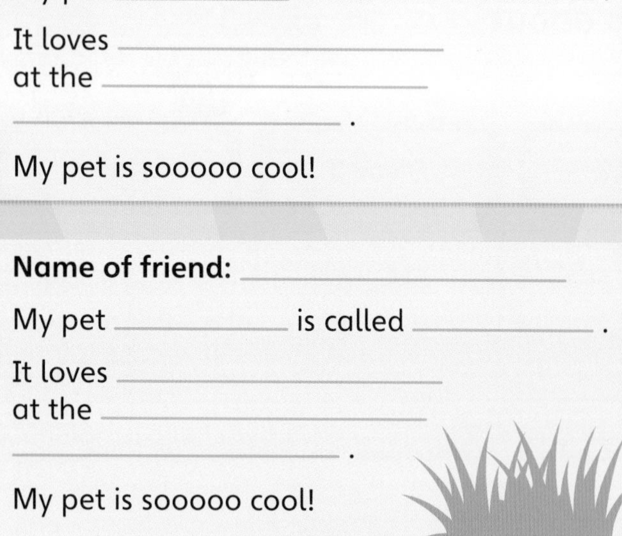

Me

My pet ____________ is called ____________ .

It loves ______________________
at the ______________________
______________________ .

My pet is sooooo cool!

Name of friend: ______________________

My pet ____________ is called ____________ .

It loves ______________________
at the ______________________
______________________ .

My pet is sooooo cool!

Name of friend: ______________________

My pet ____________ is called ____________ .

It loves ______________________
at the ______________________
______________________ .

My pet is sooooo cool!

Name of friend: ______________________

My pet ____________ is called ____________ .

It loves ______________________
at the ______________________
______________________ .

My pet is sooooo cool!

2 04 Listen to the chant on page 66. Then practise the chant with your group. Click your fingers and keep the rhythm. Then, say your chant for your class.

3 Read each question and circle the best answer. There is one example.

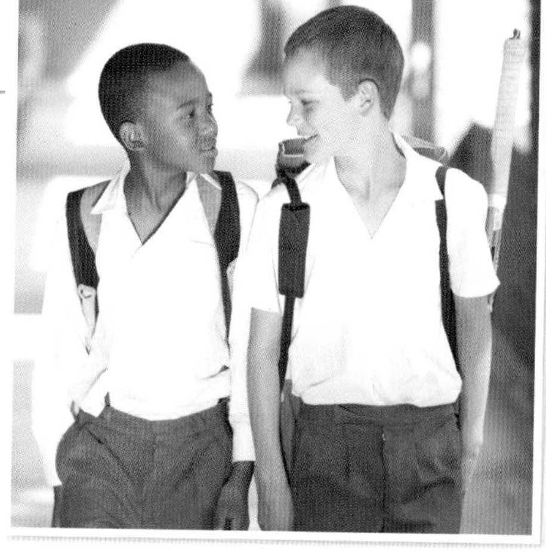

Jim: What did you do on Sunday morning?
Fred: **A** I'll see you about 10 o'clock.
(**B**) I had pancakes at Grandma's.
C I don't get up early.

1 **Jim:** Can you come to my house next weekend?
Fred: **A** Me too!
B Great idea!
C Well done!

2 **Jim:** What time can you come to my house?
Fred: **A** Yes, I can.
B I enjoy travelling by train.
C On Friday evening, I think.

3 **Jim:** Would you like to play my new computer game with me?
Fred: **A** Yes, you gave it to them.
B No, this is the best one.
C OK, let's do that.

4 **Jim:** When do you play computer games?
Fred: **A** Every day.
B That's right.
C Very carefully.

TIP!

Read the question twice.
Read A, B and C before you circle an answer.

4 Work with your friend. Ask and answer questions about imaginary pets from task 1.

5 Tell your class who has an amazing pet!

Review Unit 1

Skills: Listening and Speaking

1 Talk to a friend about each picture. Write the words under the pictures.

A parrot
B balcony
C waterfall
D jungle
E town centre
F roller skates
G milkshake
H village
I shopping centre

Mark: ___ / 10

2 05 **Listen. Who is talking? Say why!**

Lily's grandpa

Charlie the bat

3 06 **Listen again. Tick the correct boxes. There is one example.**

What does Lily do on the balcony?

1 What do they do on Saturdays?

2 Where do Lily and her grandpa go on Saturdays?

3 What milkshake does Lily's grandpa like best?

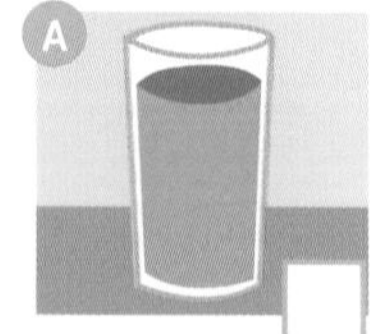

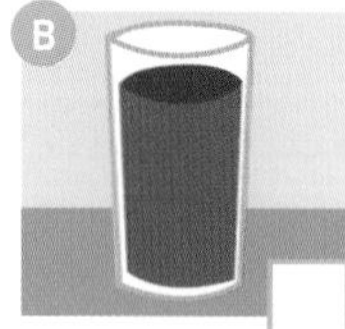

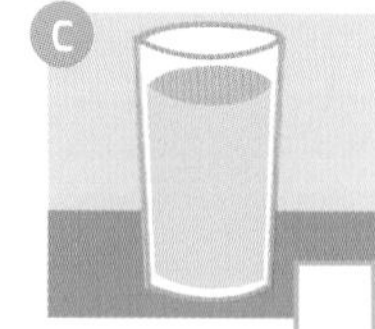

4 What does Charlie do on the balcony?

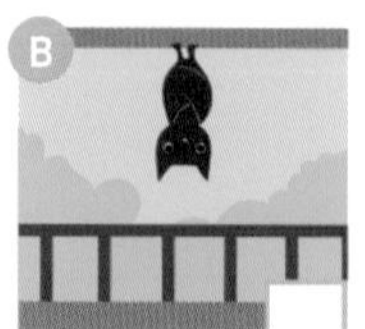

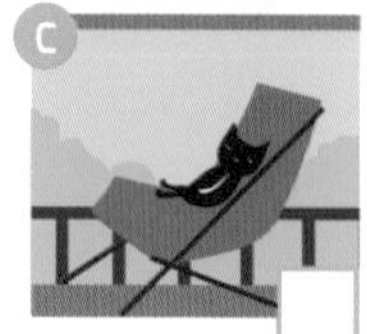

Mark: ___ / 4

Total: ___ / 14

Skills: Listening and Speaking

1 07 **Who is speaking? Is it Asim, Julia, Chi or Emma? Listen and circle A, B, C or D. After you listen, check with a friend.**

A 

B 

C 

D 

Mark: ___ / 1

2 08 **Listen again and write in the calendar. After you listen, check with your friend. There is one example.**

	Fridays	Saturdays
mornings	1 *take the bus*	4
afternoons	2	5
evenings	3	6

Mark: ___ / 5

3 **Complete YOUR weekend calendar. Write the names of your weekend days. Then write your routine.**

My Weekend		
mornings	1	4
afternoons	2	5
evenings	3	6

Mark: ___ / 6

4 **Ask your friend about their weekend routine. Write their answers in the orange calendar.**

My Buddy's Weekend		
mornings	1	4
afternoons	2	5
evenings	3	6

Mark: ___ / 6

5 **Who has the best weekend?**

Mark: ___ / 2

Total: ___ ___ / 20

3 All about town

pet shop
lake
park

1 Look at the map and label the places with the correct words.

supermarket library sports centre funfair cinema
market square train station hospital

2 09 Where did they go? Draw lines on the map. Use a red pencil for Kim and a blue pencil for Ben. Listen and check.

Kim: I parked in the car park in my small, red car,
Then I went to the hospital to see my sick grandma
Then I bought a bag of apples in the market square
And last of all I met my friends at the big funfair!

Ben: I arrived at the station on a new orange train
Then I went to the cinema to watch a film called *Rain*.
Then I went to the New Café to drink a cup of tea.
And last of all I read some comics in the library.

3 Now say the chant yourselves.

4 Which words have sounds that rhyme? Draw lines.

1 car grandma

2 square funfair

3 train rain

4 tea library

5 Look at the pictures, choose places on the map on page 16 and write the third verse for the chant in task 2. Try to use sounds that rhyme at the ends of the sentences.

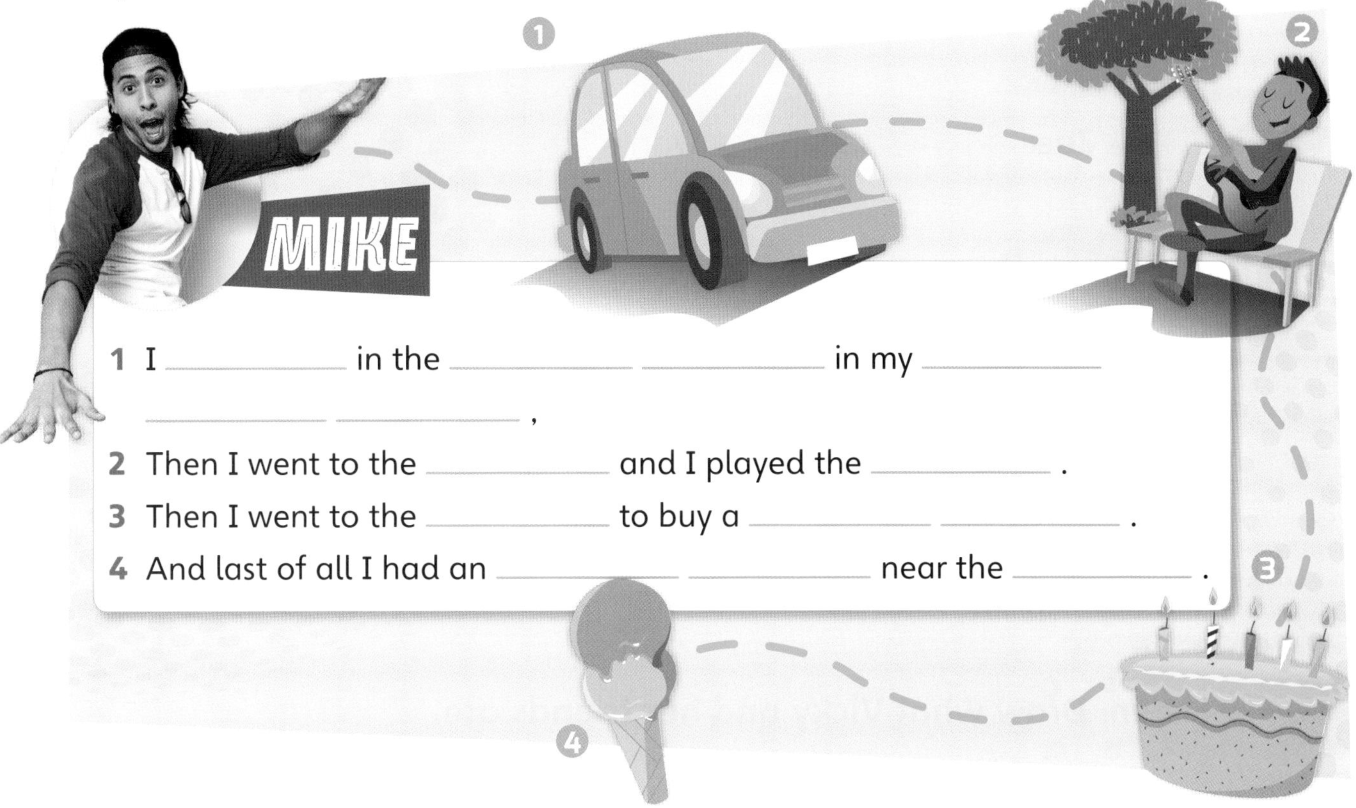

1 I ________ in the ________ ________ in my ________
________ ________ ,

2 Then I went to the ________ and I played the ________ .

3 Then I went to the ________ to buy a ________ ________ .

4 And last of all I had an ________ ________ near the ________ .

6 Now think of some places in town and write a verse about you. Try to make it rhyme.

I ________________________________ .

Then I ________________________________ .

Then I ________________________________ .

And last of all I ________________________________ .

1 10 **Which places did each person go to? Write names next to the places.**

TIP!
You will hear about the people in a different order to the photos on the page.

bookshop ______	market ___Vicky___
library ______	shopping centre ______
park ______	sports centre ______
pet shop ______	supermarket ______

2 11 **Listen. Draw what Vicky and her friends ate.**

3 Look at the pictures below. Where can you buy each thing?

4 12 Listen. Write the letters by the person in task 1 who bought each item. There is one example.

A

B
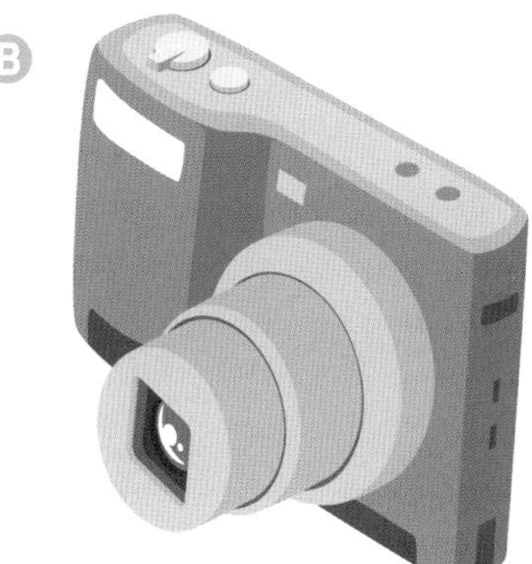

C
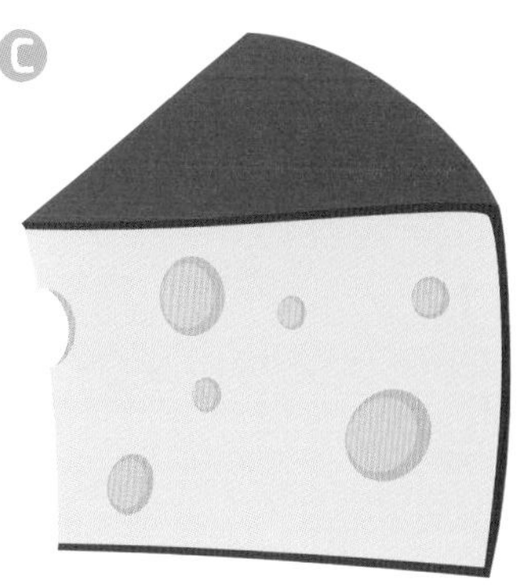

D

E

F
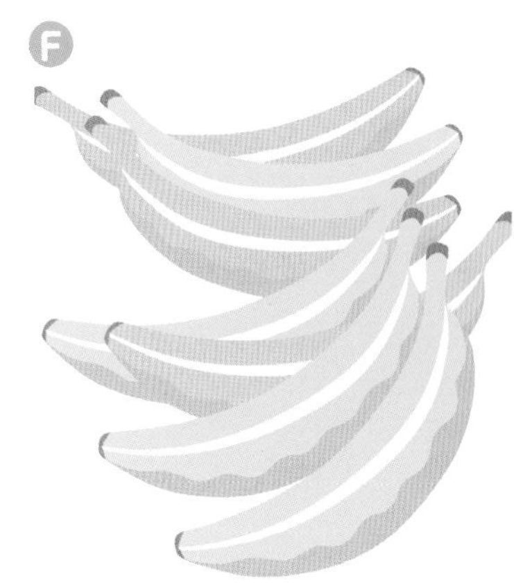

5 Write the names of two places on a piece of paper. Talk to your friend about when you go to those places.

I go to the lake to fly my kite after school.

4 Are you sporty?

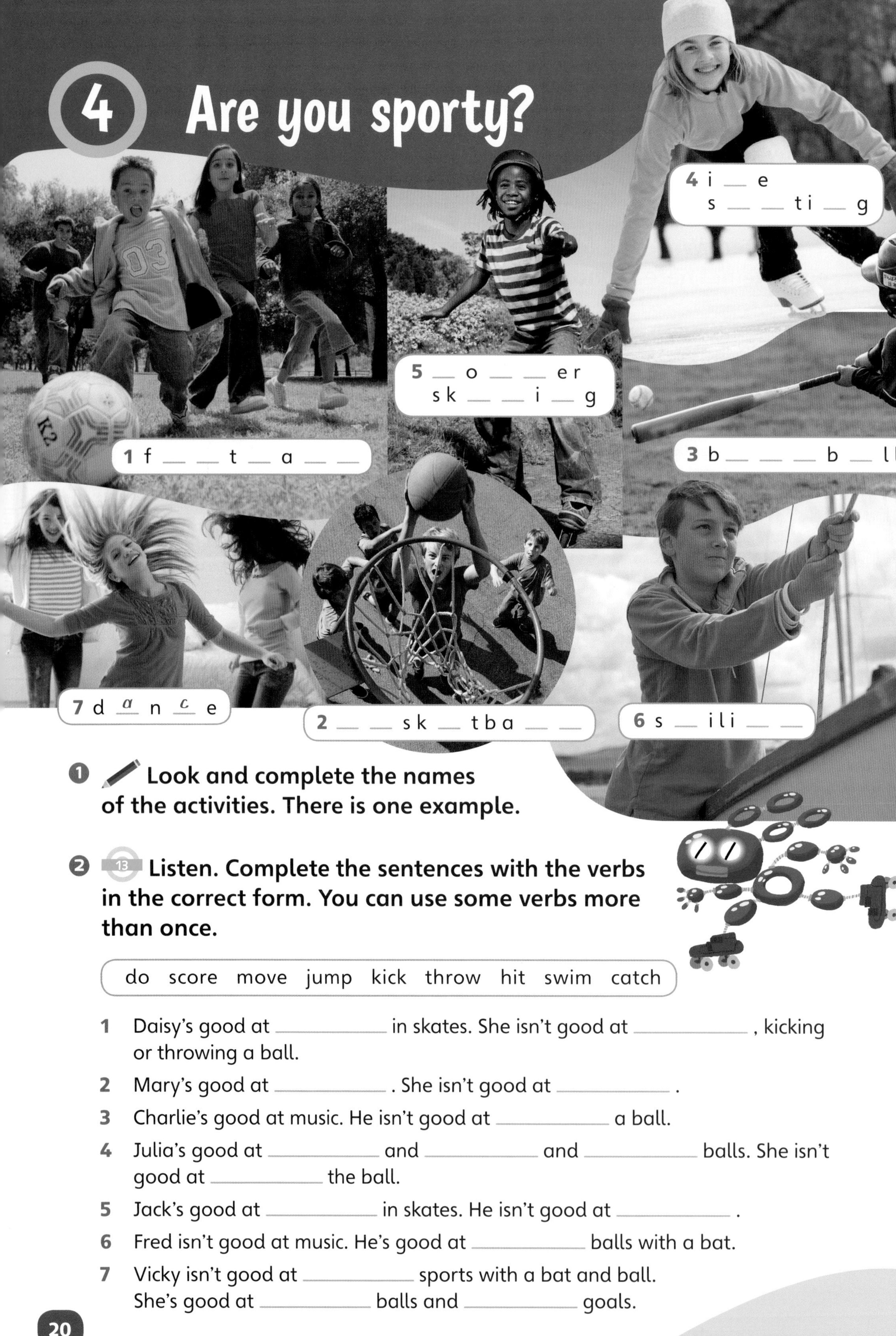

❶ **Look and complete the names of the activities. There is one example.**

❷ 13 **Listen. Complete the sentences with the verbs in the correct form. You can use some verbs more than once.**

do score move jump kick throw hit swim catch

1 Daisy's good at ____________ in skates. She isn't good at ____________ , kicking or throwing a ball.
2 Mary's good at ____________ . She isn't good at ____________ .
3 Charlie's good at music. He isn't good at ____________ a ball.
4 Julia's good at ____________ and ____________ and ____________ balls. She isn't good at ____________ the ball.
5 Jack's good at ____________ in skates. He isn't good at ____________ .
6 Fred isn't good at music. He's good at ____________ balls with a bat.
7 Vicky isn't good at ____________ sports with a bat and ball. She's good at ____________ balls and ____________ goals.

3 **Are you sporty? Ask a friend and circle the answers. Count their answers.**

1 What do you enjoy doing most?
A playing tennis B walking C playing video games
2 How often do you do sport?
A every day B one or two days a week C never
3 What do you enjoy doing most?
A doing sport B watching sport C reading a book
4 Which one are you really good at?
A running quickly B running slowly C sitting down

2–3 As: You're really sporty. You love moving and you don't like sitting down all day.

2–3 Bs: You're a little sporty, but you don't want to do sport all the time.

2–3 Cs: You're not sporty at all. You really like using computers and reading books.

4 **Read about Jane and circle the best words.**

Jane is **really sporty / a little sporty / not sporty at all**.

Jane's Blog

I enjoy doing sport, but I only do it one or two days a week. I'm good at running and jumping, so I like playing basketball. I'm not good at hitting a ball with a bat, so I don't like playing baseball. I enjoy watching sport on TV and I really like walking in the countryside.

5 **Now write four sentences about you. What sports do you like / not like? What sports are / aren't you good at?**

A picnic on the lake

1 **Look at picture 1. Listen and write T (true) or F (false).**

1. Alice and Luis are brother and sister. ____________
2. It's a beautiful morning. ____________
3. They are sailing on the sea. ____________

2 **Work with your friend. Tell the story for pictures 2, 3 and 4.**

3 **Read this dialogue. Which picture is it?**

Alice: Here you are! You can have my sandwich.

Luis: Thanks, Alice!

4 **Write a short dialogue for one of the pictures.**

5 **Read your dialogue to a friend. Which picture is it?**

6 What sports do the photos show?

1 ______________________

2 ______________________

3 ______________________

4 ______________________

7 Read the text. Choose the right words and write them on the lines.

near these making ~~in~~ have cleverest

Sheep live ____in____ many countries in the world. There are many kinds of sheep. Most sheep are white, but some are white with black faces and some **1** ____________ black faces and bodies.

Sheep live in fields **2** ____________ farms or in the mountains. They are good at walking up mountains. They like grass and eat a lot of it every day. Farmers get milk from **3** ____________ animals and in some places, people like **4** ____________ cheese from this milk. Sheep also give us meat.

Some people say that sheep aren't the **5** ____________ animals in the world, but I don't think this is correct. What do you think?

Review Unit 3

Skills: Reading and Speaking

1 Read about Fred's day in town and number the places in order.

A 

B 

C 

D 

E 

F 

First, I took the bus to a very big shop that sells lots of different things like food, toys and sometimes clothes. I bought a birthday cake there to give to my sister. Second, I walked to one of my favourite places to read a book. I like it because it's very quiet. The next place I went wasn't quiet at all! There were lots of people there having fun! I went on some exciting rides and I had an ice cream.

After that, I walked to the big square in the centre of town to buy some fruit. Farmers sell food there every day. Then I went for a swim and played table tennis with my friends. There's a great place where you can do that near the train station. In the evening, I saw my sister Amy because it was her birthday. We watched a film and ate birthday cake. It was a fun day!

Mark: ___ / 6

2 Choose a place and say what you did there. Can your partner guess the place?

pet shop   station   hospital   shopping centre   café

I went there to buy a puppy.

Was it the pet shop?

Mark: ___ / 6

Total: ___ ___ / 12

Skills: Listening and Writing

1 15 **Listen and draw lines from Sofia to the things she needs.**

Mark: ___ / 4

2 **Plan a sports holiday and write a list.**

My sports holiday

Day / time	sport	What to take
Monday afternoon	football	

Mark: ___ / 8

Total: ___ ___ / 12

CHECKLIST

I used capital letters for the days of the week. ☐

I checked my spelling. ☐

My handwriting is clear. ☐

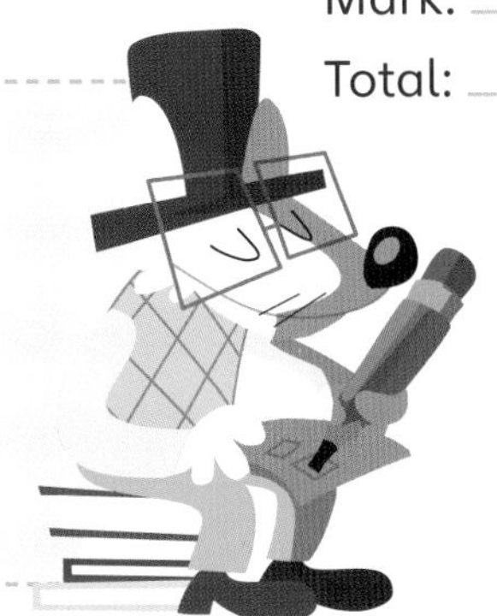

5 My dream school

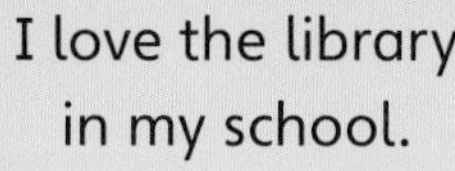
I love the library in my school.

1 ASYA, Turkey

2 FILIP, Poland

We are lucky – we have a swimming pool at my school!

3 ANDRES, Mexico

We have big windows in my class. They are great.

4 KANYA, Thailand

We have 10 new computers at my school.

1 Meet four more new friends. Which school would you like to visit? Talk to your friend.

2 Four dream schools! Finish the sentences and answer the questions.

Asya

Asya's dream school is in a *cinema*.

What's the teacher wearing? Superhero *clothes*.

Filip

1 Filip's dream school is in the ______.

2 Where's the classroom? ______.

Andres

3 Andres' dream school is in a ______.

4 What are they drinking? ______.

Kanya

5 Kanya's dream school is in a ______.

6 What are they reading? ______.

3 Read about the children's dream schools. Write *A*, *B*, *C* or *D*.

A Asya B Filip C Andres D Kanya

1 In my dream school, the older children teach us English. Our classroom is in a fantastic café and we wear baseball caps. We sometimes play speaking games in our English lessons and drink purple milkshakes. YUM! ________

2 My dream school is in a big circus and our teachers are clowns. We laugh a lot because we read English comics and sing songs. Everyone wears funny circus clothes. GREAT! ________

3 My dream school is brilliant! We have English lessons in a cinema. We wear superhero clothes and read e-books! My dream school is exciting because my teachers are superheroes. My English lessons are always FUN! ________

4 My dream school is the best! Our English lessons are in the jungle and the classrooms are in tree houses. We wear pirate clothes and my English teacher is a pirate too! The lessons are never boring. WOW! ________

4 Read about the children's dream schools again. Work with your friend and write in the table.

TIP!

Underline the answers in the bubbles. Copy the spellings correctly!

Our dream school!

Name	Where is the classroom?	Who are the teachers?	What do the children wear?
Filip	*in a tree house*	*pirates*	*pirate clothes*
Andres	1 ________	2 ________	3 ________
Kanya	4 ________	5 ________	6 ________
Asya	7 ________	8 ________	9 ________

5 Which dream school do you like best? Why? Tell your friend!

1 16 **Listen to the song. Write the missing words with your friend. There are two examples.**

Asya

My dream school is really ___brilliant___!
Our classroom is in a ___cinema___.
We use e-books to learn English.
It's like you are on Mars!!

Filip

My dream school is in the **1** ________. There's always lots to see and do. We are **2** ________ who look for **3** ________. Our classroom really is the best.

Andres

My dream school is so fantastic! Our classroom is in a cool **4** ________. We drink **5** ________ and wear **6** ________ ________. Visit my dream school today.

Kanya

My dream school is like a wonderland. Our teachers here are all great **7** ________. We read comics and we sing **8** ________ songs. Come inside and have a look around my dream **9** ________.

2 17 **Listen to the song again and check your answers.**

3 **Write about your dream school! Choose ONE word from each list.**

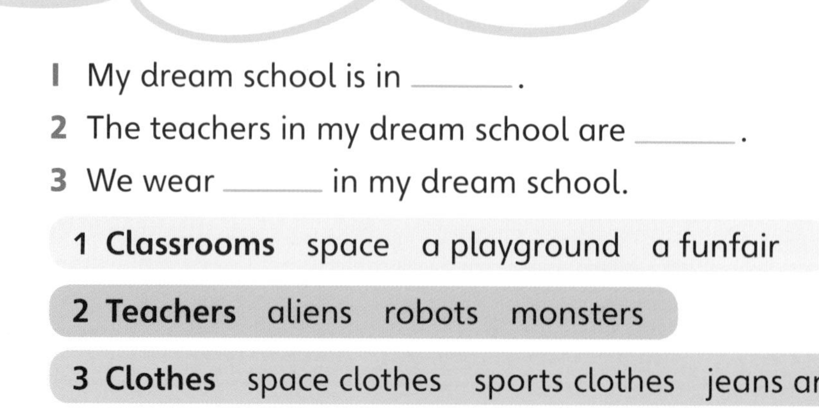

My dream school!

1 My dream school is in ______.
2 The teachers in my dream school are ______.
3 We wear ______ in my dream school.

1 Classrooms space a playground a funfair

2 Teachers aliens robots monsters

3 Clothes space clothes sports clothes jeans and T-shirts

4 Use your answers from task 3. Ask your friends if anyone has the same dream school.

Where are the classrooms in your dream school?

Who are the teachers in your dream school?

What do you wear in your dream school?

5 Tell the class about your dream schools!

THINK BIG

Think about the rest of your dream school! Then read the questions and write the answers with a friend.

1 What do you do in your English lessons?
2 What special things are in the school building?
3 What is most fun about your dream school?

6 Food around the world

Jenny, USA.

We have delicious burgers and fries.

Stefano, Italy.

We have great pasta and fantastic pizza.

Chanchai, Thailand.

My favourite food is noodles with chicken.

Sebastian, Mexico.

We have lots of fresh fruit like mangoes.

Ayako, Japan.

We love fresh fish, we don't cook it!

6 Matiana, Peru.

My family love a typical dinner of fish cooked in fruit juice.

1 Read and match the countries with the foods.

1 Japan 2 Mexico 3 Thailand 4 Italy 5 USA 6 Peru

A pizza B fresh fruit C fish in fruit juice D fresh fish

E burgers F noodles

2 18 Listen and colour the food.

3 Which is your favourite food? Write the numbers: 1–6. 1 = your favourite.

fish sushi ____
fresh fruit ____
noodles ____
pizza ____
burgers ____
fish in fruit juice ____

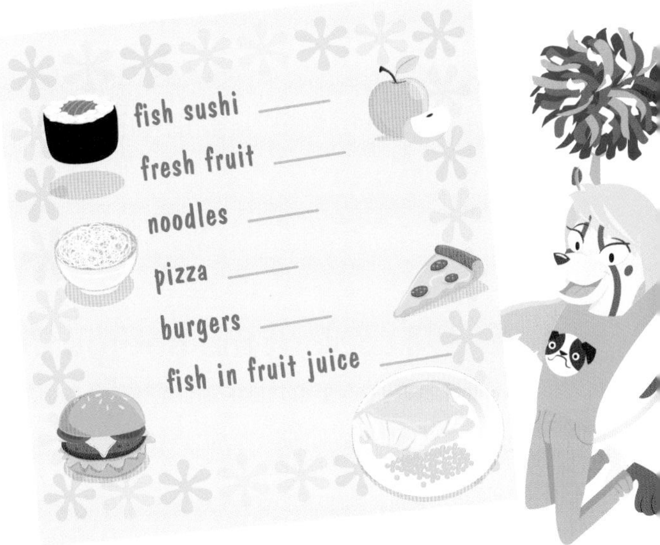

4 Compare with a friend.

> My favourite is noodles because I eat them with lots of cheese.

> My least favourite is...

5 Look at the picture. Match the food words from basket A with the words in basket B. There is one example.

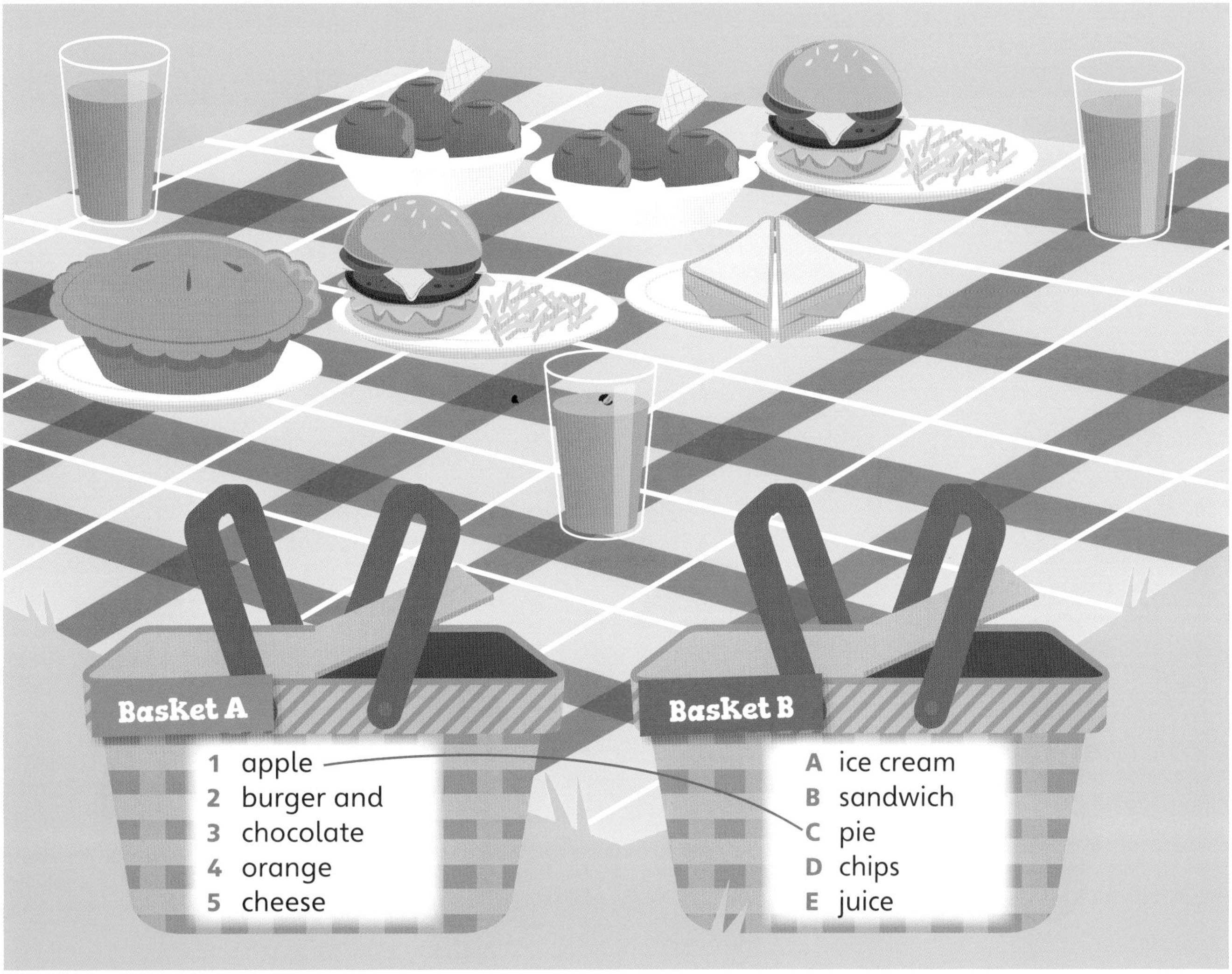

Basket A
1 apple
2 burger and
3 chocolate
4 orange
5 cheese
Basket B
A ice cream
B sandwich
C pie
D chips
E juice

6 19 Listen and point to the food.

7 20 Listen to the children again. In your group, take turns to dance when you hear the food you like.

I think the third one is different because it's a drink and the cake, fruit and biscuits are food. You eat them!

1 Look at the photos. Tell a friend which one is different. There is one example.

1

2

3

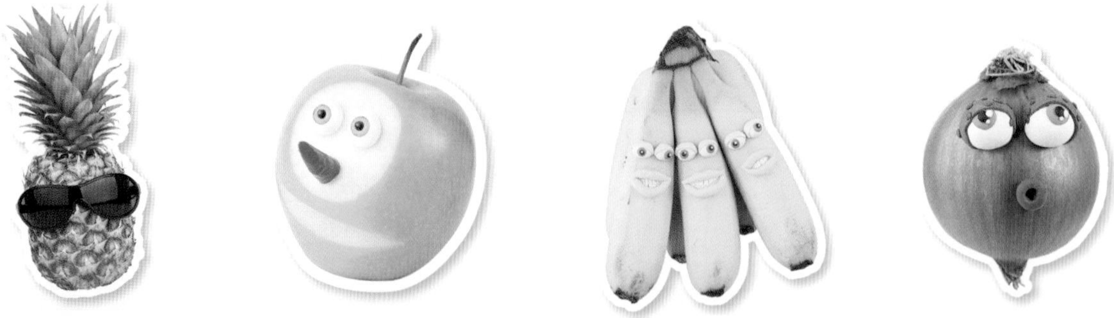

4

2 Choose words from the picnic baskets to make crazy combinations! Write five questions in the table.

beans	onions
honey	peas
coconut	pineapple
ice cream	coffee

pasta	cake
pancakes	chips
salad	rice
meatballs	noodles

	friend 1	friend 2	friend 3	friend 4
1 Do you like ________ on your ________?	☐	☐	☐	☐
2 Do you like ________ on your ________?	☐	☐	☐	☐
3 Do you like ________ on your ________?	☐	☐	☐	☐
4 Do you like ________ on your ________?	☐	☐	☐	☐
5 Do you like ________ on your ________?	☐	☐	☐	☐

3 Walk around the classroom and interview four friends. Put a tick (✓) for *Yes* and a cross (✗) for *No*. Answer their questions.

Do you like ice cream on your meatballs?

Yes, I do!

No, I don't!

4 Then tell your class who likes the best crazy combinations.

THINK BIG

Think about food from around the world. Answer the questions with a friend.

1 What food from other countries do you like?
2 What food from other countries can you find in your town / city?

Review Unit 5

Skills: Listening and Speaking

1 21 **Listen to Masha from Russia and Chang from China. Circle the answers to the questions.**

MASHA

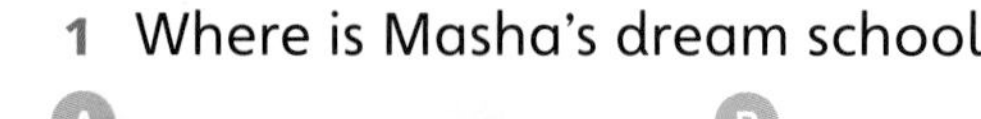

1 Where is Masha's dream school?

A  B  C 

2 What does she wear?

A  B  C 

3 Who are her teachers?

A  B  C 

CHANG

1 Where is Chang's dream school?

A  B  C 

2 Who are his teachers?

A  B  C 

3 What does he wear?

A  B  C 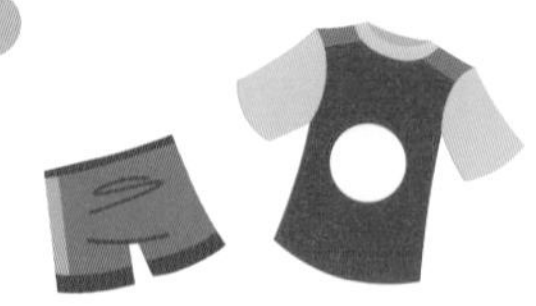

Mark: ___ / 6

2 **Talk to four friends. Ask and answer the questions.**

1 Do you like Chang's or Masha's dream school best? Why?
2 Do you like your school? Why or why not?
3 What do you wear at school?
4 Who is your dream teacher? Why?

Mark: ___ / 4
Total: ___ / 10

Skills: Reading and Speaking

1 Read about Masha, Chang and Yigit and colour their foods.

What's your favourite food, Masha?

MASHA, Russia

I really love beetroot soup. It is famous in Russia. Beetroot is a red vegetable and the soup is red too. My dad cooks the best beetroot soup with orange carrots, white onions, yellow potatoes and brown sausage. I am hungry now!

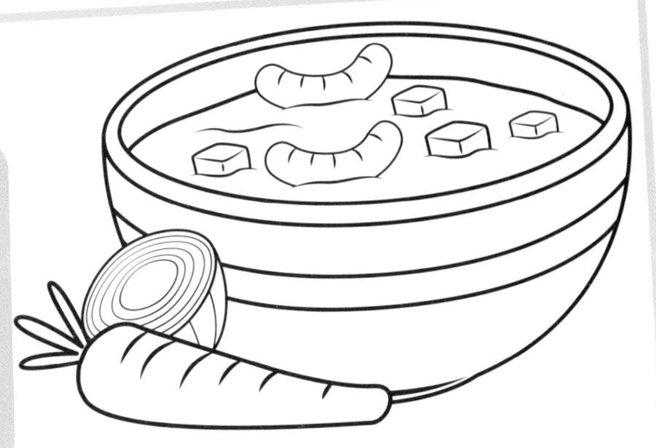

What do you often eat at home, Chang?

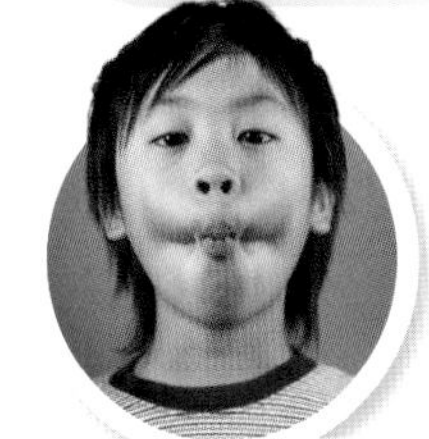

CHANG, China

My family likes to eat Chinese food called dim sum. My aunt and I make chicken feet dim sum. They are an orange colour and are my favourite! We often eat dim sum with red rice and green vegetables called bok choy at home.

What do Turkish children like to eat at parties, Yigit?

YIGIT, Turkey

My classmates and I go to the café near my school for birthday parties. They have the best meatballs and chips in my town! The meatballs are brown and the chips are yellow. We eat them with red tomatoes and white rice.

Mark: ___ / 12

2 Talk to four friends. Ask and answer the questions.

1 Whose food do you want to try? Masha's, Chang's or Yigit's? Why?
2 What's your favourite food from other countries?
3 What do you often eat at home?
4 What do you like to eat at parties?

Mark: ___ / 4
Total: ___ / 16

7 Sunny or cloudy?

WEATHER DIARY – MOSCOW, RUSSIA

Monday: Today the weather was very cold. There were clouds in the morning and there was snow in the afternoon. The snow was beautiful.

HOT ☐ COLD ☐

WEATHER DIARY – CAIRO, EGYPT

Monday: The weather was hot and sunny today! But in the evening it was very windy and we had to stay inside.

HOT ☐ COLD ☐

1 Look at the weather diaries. Tick (✓) the correct icons.

2 Write the missing nouns and adjectives.

3 **Look at the pictures in task 4 and write the number and letter. There is one example.**

rain <u>2A</u> **1** cloud ____ **2** rainbow ____
3 snow ____ **4** ice ____ **5** wind ____ **6** sun ____

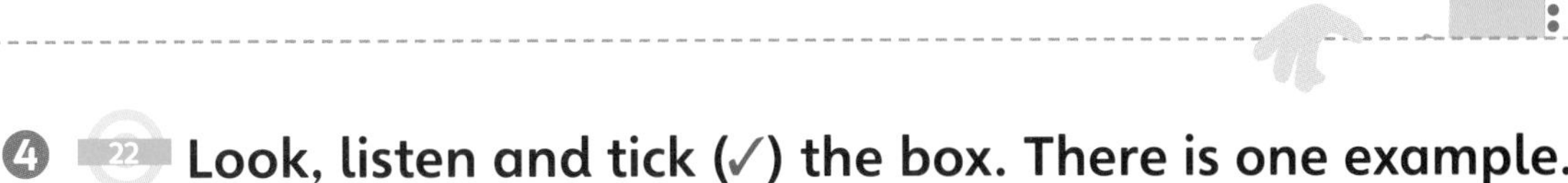

4 22 **Look, listen and tick (✓) the box. There is one example.**

1 Which T-shirt is Tom's?

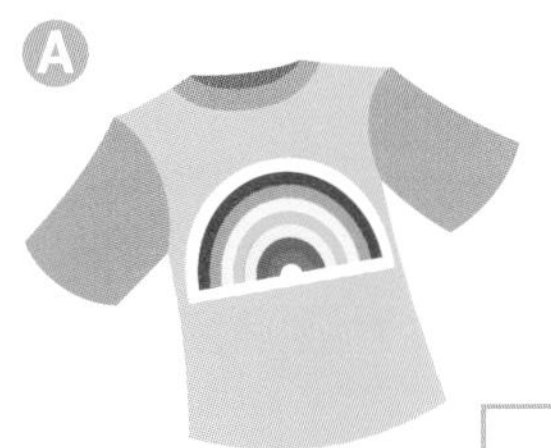

2 What was the weather like on Tuesday?

3 What is the weather like now?

4 What would Sarah like to do today?

5 **Choose words from task 2 to complete the sentences.**

1. There was a lot of ____________ today. Now everything is white.
2. It was grey and ____________ all morning, but it didn't rain.
3. It was very ____________, so we flew our kite.
4. The ____________ was very hot today, so I stayed inside.

6 **Make a weather diary for this week.**

1 23 **Read and listen to the text.**

Clouds

What are clouds?

Watching clouds is fun, but did you know this? They have lots of very small drops of water in them? When it's very cold, clouds can have small drops of ice or snow in them, too.

When there aren't many clouds in the sky, the weather is often sunny and dry.

When there are a lot of clouds in the sky, the weather is often wet. Grey clouds have a lot more drops of water, ice or snow in them than white clouds.

Did you know there are ten different kinds of clouds? Here are three of them.

A **Cirrostratus** are thin, long clouds. You often see them before it snows.

B **Altostratus** are big, grey clouds. There are often lots of them on wet, rainy days.

C **Cumulus** are white clouds and they can be lots of different shapes. You often see them on hot, sunny days.

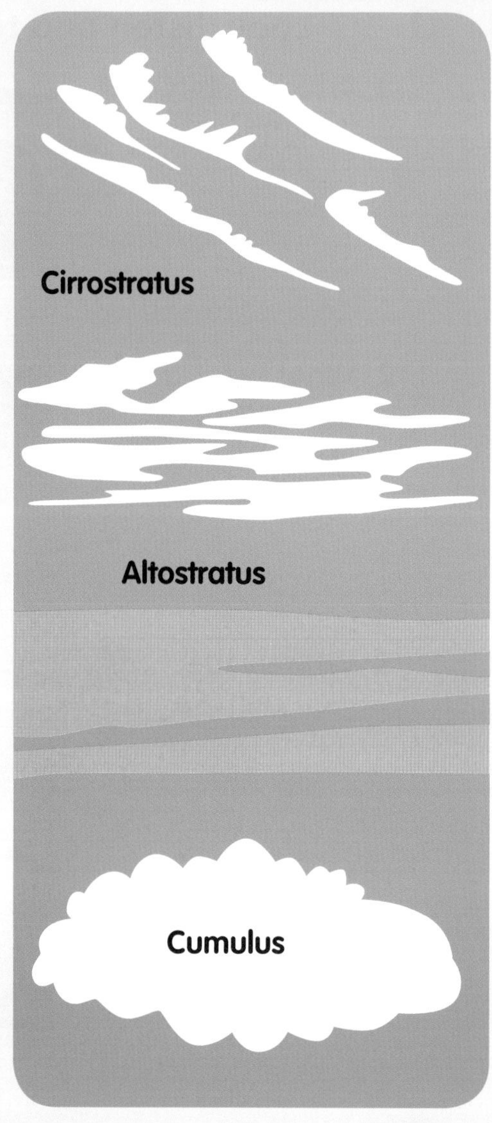

2 **Read again and answer the questions.**

1 Why are some clouds grey?
______________________________.

2 It's a hot sunny day. What kind of clouds can you see? ______________.

3 It's a rainy day and there isn't any sun. What kind of clouds can you see?
______________.

4 There's a big white cloud in the sky. It's the shape of a rabbit.
What kind of cloud is it? ______________.

5 What kinds of clouds can be very thin? ______________.

3 Look outside. Then answer the questions.

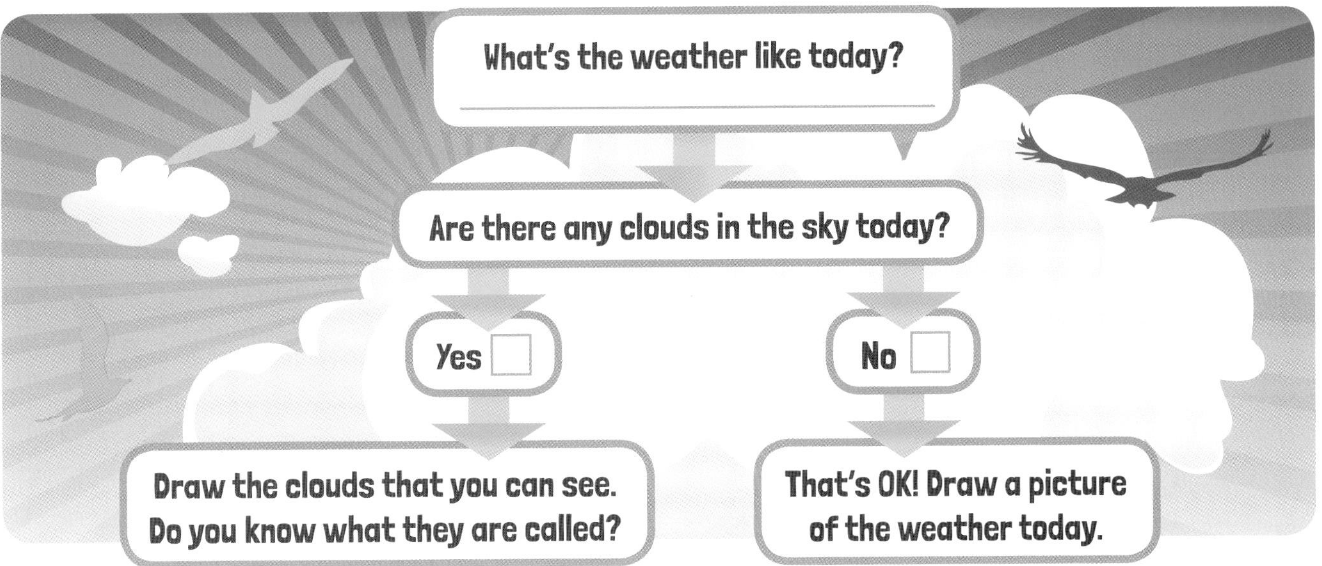

4 Look at the words and fill in the gaps about you. Then ask a friend.

Me

1 When it's rainy, I often ____.

2 When it's sunny, I often ____.

3 When it's windy, I often ____.

4 The last time I saw snow was ____.

5 The last time I saw a rainbow was ____.

6 I like ______________ weather the best.

My friend

1 When it's rainy ______________ often ____.

2 When it's sunny, ______________ often ____.

3 When it's windy, ______________ often ____.

4 The last time ______________ saw snow was ____.

5 The last time ______________ saw a rainbow was ____.

6 ______________ like ______________ weather the best.

What do you do when it's ...?

When was the last time you saw ...?

What weather do you like best?

When it's rainy, I often watch DVDs.

The last time ...

I like ...

1 Look at the photos. What did Zoe do last week?

2 24 Now listen and write the days of the week. There is one example.

~~Monday~~ Tuesday Wednesday Thursday Friday Saturday Sunday

3 25 Listen again and write T (true) or F (false).

1 Zoe had pasta for lunch on Monday. F
2 Zoe didn't like the film called 'Lizard'. ☐
3 Zoe saw her grandma on Wednesday. ☐
4 Zoe's uncle has a horse. ☐
5 Zoe planted a tree at her school on Friday. ☐
6 Zoe never goes shopping on Saturdays. ☐
7 Zoe went to bed before 8 o'clock on Sunday. ☐

4 26 Listen. Does the voice go up or down?

Did you do your homework last week? Yes, I did.

5 **What did Fred do last weekend?**
Colour green for *yes* and red for *no*.

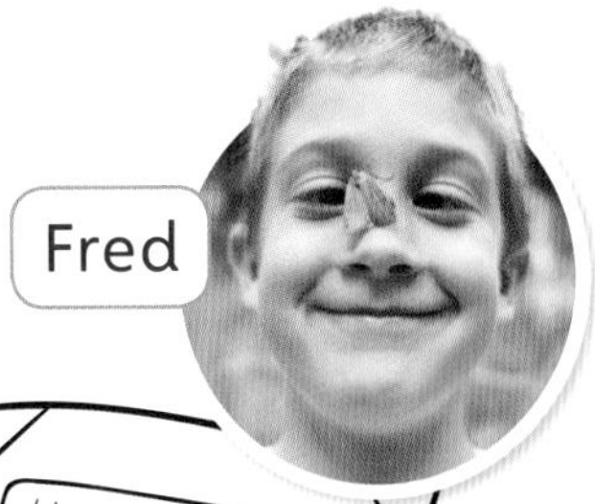

Fred

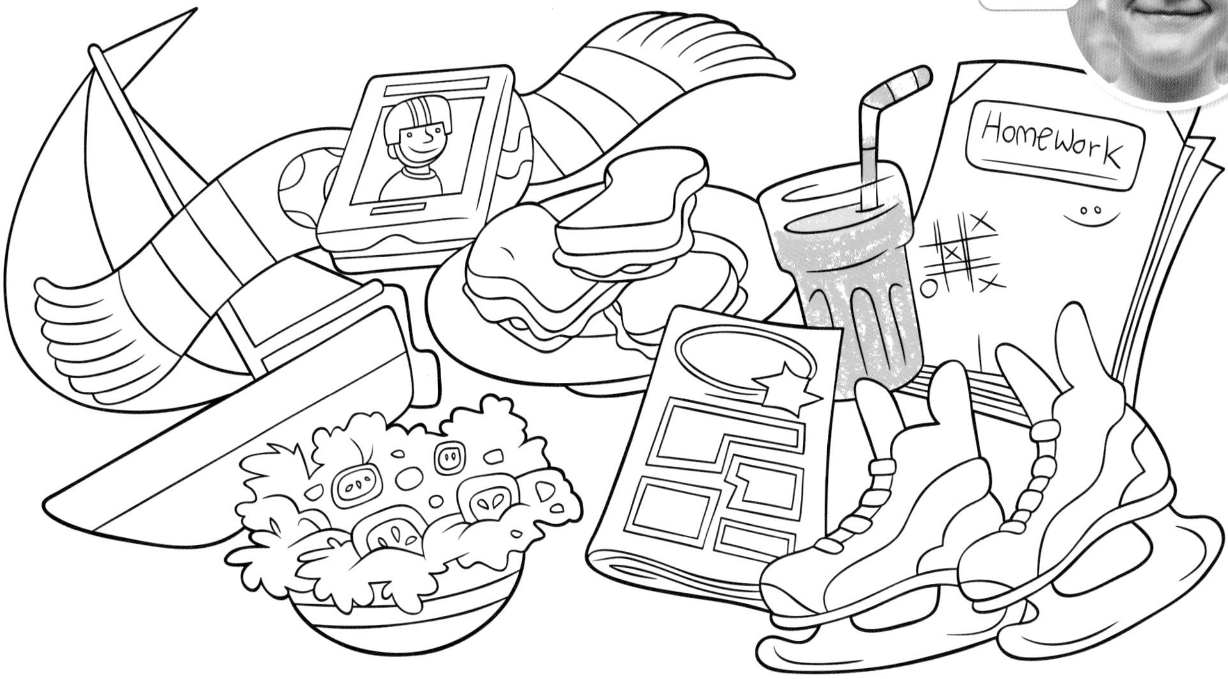

Homework

1 drank a milkshake ✓
2 went sailing ✓
3 watched a DVD ✗
4 bought a scarf ✓
5 learned to ice skate ✗
6 read a comic ✓
7 made a salad ✓
8 did his homework ✓
9 ate some sandwiches ✗

6 **Write four things you did last weekend.**

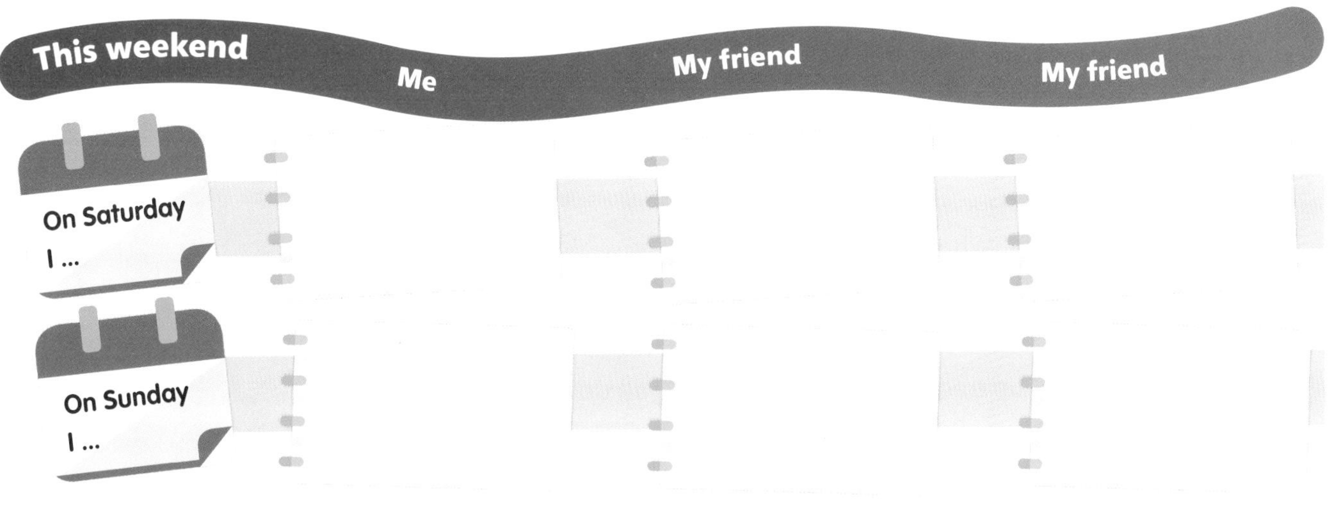

7 **Ask your friends and write in the boxes in task 6.**

What did you do last weekend?

On Saturday, I went to the cinema and I made pancakes. On Sunday, I ...

1 Read the quiz. What do you think 'adventurous' means?

2 Do the quiz with a friend.

Quiz time!

Do you like to try new things? How adventurous are you? Do the quiz and find out.

1. **You're in the park and you see an elephant. What do you do?**
   - a Make friends – elephants are cool!
   - b Run away and hide! Elephants are scary!
2. **You're in a café and there are chocolate and cheese sandwiches for lunch. Do you try them?**
   - a Yes, why not?
   - b Ugh, never!
3. **Your friend invites you to go roller skating, but you don't know how to roller skate. Do you go?**
   - a Yes, I can learn.
   - b No, thanks – I think it's dangerous.
4. **It's very cold and it's snowing. Do you go outside, or stay inside?**
   - a Go outside and play in the snow! It's fun!
   - b Stay inside and watch DVDs. It's too cold!
5. **Your friend lives in a circus and invites you to be a clown one night. Do you do it?**
   - a Yes, I love making people laugh.
   - b No, thanks. I have to do my homework.
6. **You're walking in the countryside and you see a mountain in front of you. What do you do?**
   - a Climb the mountain. It's exciting.
   - b Go home. I'm tired!
7. **You're at the beach and you see an alien. It asks you to help it. What do you do?**
   - a Ask the alien what it wants.
   - b Run away and hide. Aliens are scary!
8. **One day you wake up and you can fly. What do you do?**
   - a Fly around the world. It's brilliant!
   - b Go to the doctor. I don't want to fly.

3 Talk with your friend. Do you think your friend is adventurous? Why? / Why not?

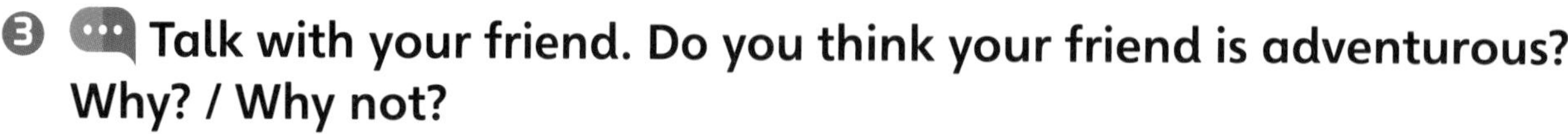

Mostly As - You're adventurous!
Mostly Bs - You're not very adventurous.

4 Read the story about an adventure. Which quiz question does it match?

Last Saturday, I went to the beach. It was very sunny and I wanted to go for a swim. When I got there, I saw a green and purple alien on the beach.

'My name's Tub,' said the alien. 'I can't find my space-car. Can you help me? It's green!'

'Yes, I can help you,' I said.

So we looked for Tub's space-car on the beach.

'I can see it,' I said. 'It's under the sand!'

'Thanks!' said Tub. 'Now I can go home!'

Tub said goodbye and got in the space-car. Then Tub drove up into the sky. Look – here's a photo I took!

5 Read the questions. Then read the story again and underline the answers with the correct colours.

1 When did it happen? Where did it happen?
2 What was the weather like? Why did you go there?
3 Who / What did you see? What did they say? What did you say?
4 What did you do? Then what happened?
5 How did it end?

6 Choose a question from the quiz and plan a story for it. Use the colours to make your plan.

1 *Last* ____________ *I* ____________
2 *It was* ____________ *and I* ____________
3 ____________ ____________ ____________
4 ____________ ____________
5 ____________

7 Now write your story and draw a picture.

5 **Read the song, look at the photos and write the animal words.**

This pretty bird can talk.
It likes fresh fruit and carrots.
It's one of the cleverest birds in the world.
That's right! It's a ___________ !

This cool animal is clever.
It eats cold fish and swims.
It never walks, it loves to play.
That's right! It's a ___________ !

This little beast eats green leaves.
It's small and has no tail.
It's got a shell and two long eyes.
You guessed it! It's a ___________ !

This fish is always hungry.
It's sometimes scary too.
It's got big teeth and it's very fast.
You guessed it! It's a ___________ !

6 33 **Listen to the song and check your answers. Then sing the song.**

7 **Write an animal riddle and find a picture. Show your friends. Can you guess their riddles?**

Review Unit 11 

Skills: Writing and Speaking

1 **Draw and colour a picture of your favourite place. Choose a place that's outside, not inside. Make sure you draw everything that you can see in that place.**

the weather plants building animals sea / lake / river

Now make notes in the column in the table about your favourite place. When there isn't an answer – you can write 'There aren't any.'

Questions	My favourite place	______'s favourite place
1 What's your favourite place? e.g. My grandma's house.		
2 Where is it?		
3 What's the weather like in the picture?		
4 Are there plants? What are they?		
5 Are there buildings? What are they?		
6 Is there water? What is it?		
7 Are there animals? What are they?		
8 Why do you like it?		

2 **Ask and answer with your friend. Fill in the table with their answers.**

What's your favourite place?

It's my grandma's house.

Total: ____ / 16

Skills: Listening and Reading

1 34 **Listen to Aria talk about things that she wants to do and number the pictures in order. There is one example.**

1 ☐ ☐

☐ ☐ ☐

Mark: ___ / 5

2 35 **Listen to Aria again and check your answers.**

3 **What's wrong? Read and think. Can you correct the red phrases so that they are correct?**

This year, Aria wants to do six new things. First, she wants to climb the tree in the park and have **1)** ~~chocolate ice-cream~~ *a picnic lunch* up there. Second, she wants to build a house for the ducks because she thinks that they have **2)** a hot shower at night. Then, Aria wants to learn to make **3)** a picnic lunch for her friends. After that, she wants to look for the treasure. Her sister says that it's in **4)** the sea. Next, Aria wants to swim with dolphins because they love to play in **5)** the forest. Last of all, Aria wants to get really wet and then she wants to have **6)** cold feet.

Mark: ___ / 5

Total: ___ ___ / 10

Songs and chants

Unit 1, page 7

Hey Lily!

Student A: Hey Lily!
Lily: Hey you!
Student A: What can we do in Kota Kinabalu?
Lily: We can watch elephants through my telescope!
Student A: Is that true?
Student B: Hey Lily!
Lily: Hey you!
Student B: What can we do in Kota Kinabalu?
Lily: We can go shopping and roller skating too!
Student B: Is that true?
Student A: Hey Lily!
Lily: Hey you!
Student A: What can we do in Kota Kinabalu?
Lily: We can drink milkshakes with Charlie the bat!
Student A: Is that true?
Lily and Student A and Student B: Yes, it's true!!!

Unit 2, page 12

Our amazing pets

Claire: My pet rabbit's called Daisy.
Claire: It likes pancakes and picnics!

Jim: My pet puppy's called Zoe.
Jim: It loves swimming in our garden pool!

Jane: My pet parrot's called Paul.
Jane: It goes skating on the big lake!

Ali: My pet kitten's called Ahmad.
Ali: It dresses up in funny ties!

Unit 3, page 16

About town

I parked in the car park in my small, red car,
Then I went to the hospital to see my sick grandma,
Then I bought a bag of apples in the market square
And last of all I met my friends at the big funfair!

I arrived at the station on a new orange train,
Then I went to the cinema to watch a film called Rain.
Then I went to the New Café to drink a cup of tea
And last of all I read some comics in the library.

Songs and chants

Unit 5, page 28

My dream school

Girl 1: My dream school is really brilliant!
Our classroom is in a cinema.
We use e-books to learn English.
It's like you are on Mars!!

Boy 1: My dream school is in the jungle.
There's always lots to see and do.
We are pirates who look for treasure.
Our classroom really is the best.

Boy 2: My dream school is so fantastic!
Our classroom is in a cool café.
We drink milkshakes and wear baseball caps.
Visit my dream school today!

Girl 2: My dream school is like a wonderland.
Our teachers here are all great fun.
We read comics and we sing English songs.
Come inside and have a look around
my dream school.

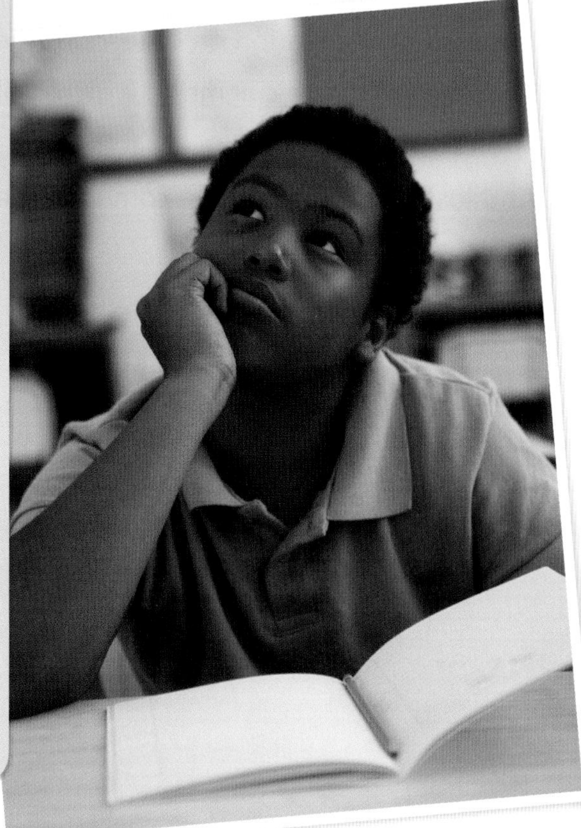

Unit 6, page 31

Food

Apple pie, apple pie
Burger and chips, burger and chips
Cheese sandwich, cheese sandwich
Chocolate ice cream, chocolate ice cream
Orange juice, orange juice!

Unit 12, page 63

Animals

This pretty bird can talk.
It likes fresh fruit and carrots,
It's one of the cleverest birds in the world.
That's right! It's a parrot!

This cool animal is clever,
It eats cold fish and swims,
It never walks, it loves to play!
That's right! It's a dolphin!

This little beast eats green leaves,
It's small and has no tail.
It's got a shell and two long eyes.
You guessed it! It's a snail!

This fish is always hungry.
It's sometimes scary too!
It's got big teeth and it's very fast.
You guessed it! It's a shark!

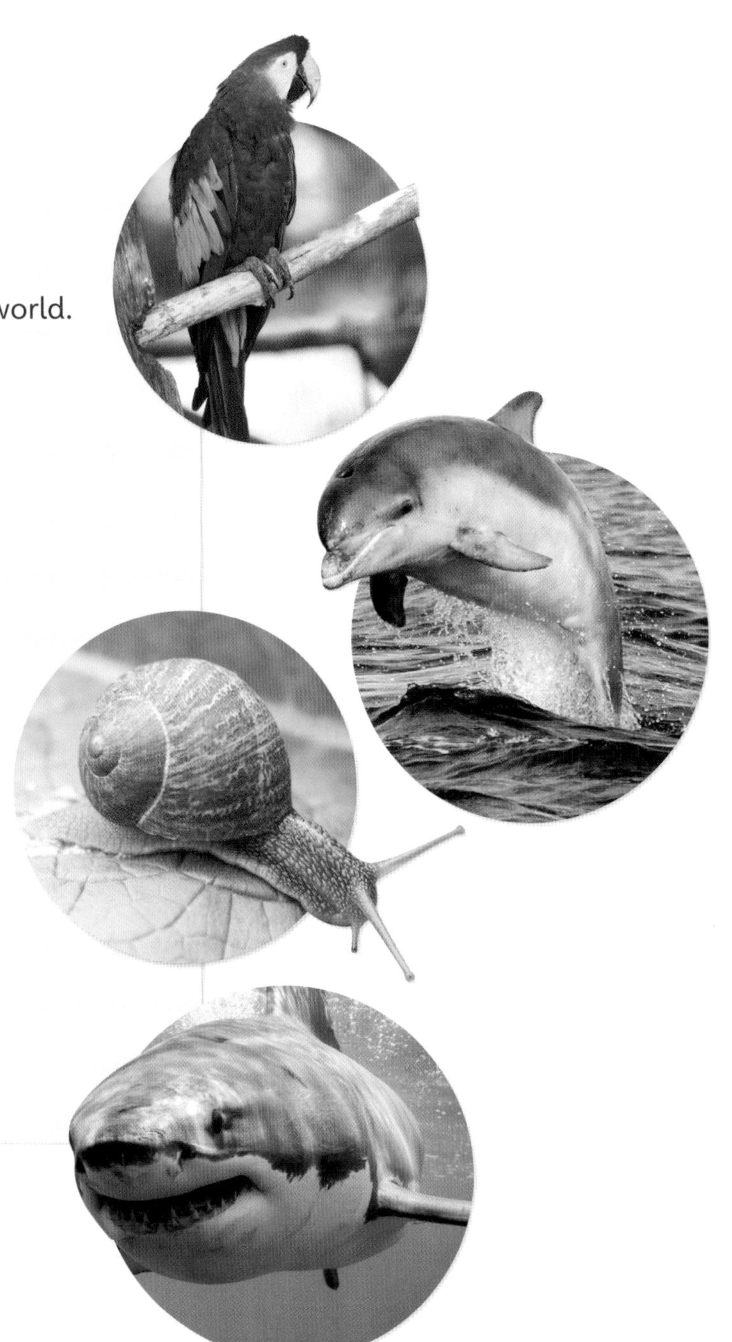

Unit 1

When clauses

I can hear the waterfall at night **when** I'm in bed.
When the teacher talked, we listened.

1 Match the two parts of the sentence.

1 When I go to bed,
2 I put on my coat
3 I hurt my leg
4 When I go to sleep,

A when it's cold.
B I dream.
C when I fell from a tree.
D I get undressed.

2 Correct the sentences. Rewrite them with *when*.

1 he got home, he had his lunch.

______

2 I jumped she shouted.

______

3 they see funny clowns, they laugh.

______

4 we go to bed we're tired.

______

Unit 2

Prepositions of time

Daisy goes for a picnic **on** Monday mornings.
She cleans her teeth **at** 12 o'clock.
She plays with her friends **after** school.
She has breakfast **before** school.

1 Choose the correct words.

1 Let's meet **on** / **at** 3 o'clock.
2 Wash your hands **on** / **before** dinner.
3 Hugo goes shopping **after** / **on** Saturdays.
4 **At** / **Before** lunch, I went ice skating.
5 I did my homework in the morning **after** / **before** school.
6 My mum was tired **on** / **after** work.

2 Complete the conversation with *on*, *at*, *after* or *before*.

Julia: Jim, what did you do (1) ______ school yesterday evening?

Jim: First, I went roller skating. (2) ______ roller skating, I had dinner and went to bed (3) ______ 9 o'clock. And you?

Julia: I had lots of homework to do (4) ______ today, so I went home (5) ______ school. Our teacher always gives us lots of homework (6) ______ Thursdays.

Unit 3

Go + -ing

I **go swimming** on Saturdays.
We **went shopping** yesterday.

1 Look and complete the sentences. Use the correct form of *go* and these words.

fishing skateboarding riding ice skating roller skating

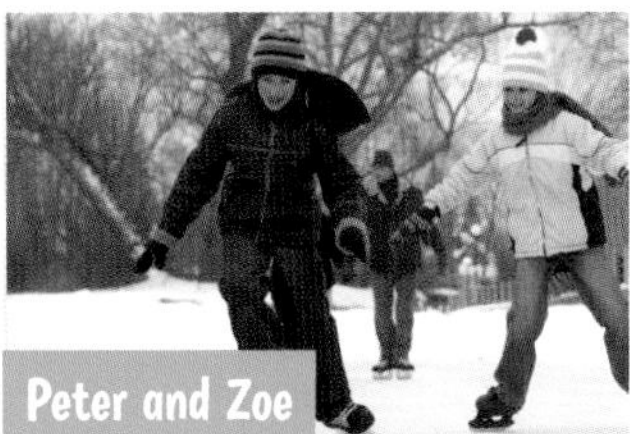

1 Cristina ______________ last week.
2 Arda always ______________ at the weekend.
3 Emma ______________ every morning.
4 Francesca and Hugo ______________ yesterday.
5 Peter and Zoe ______________ last Monday.

Infinitive of purpose

Dan went to the pet shop **to buy a puppy**.

2 Match the two parts of the sentence.

1 I go to bed
2 I dressed up
3 I phoned Charlie
4 I clean my bedroom

A to say hello.
B to sleep.
C to go to the party.
D to help my parents.

3 Complete the sentences with the correct forms of these verbs.

invite buy score go

1 Anna went to town ______________ a new T-shirt.
2 Mary gets up at 7 o'clock ______________ to school.
3 Robert texted Paolo ______________ him to a party.
4 Jane kicked the ball ______________ a goal.

Unit 4

Adverbs of frequency

Jack **never** falls.
He **always** laughs.
He **often** dresses up.
He dances **sometimes**. / He **sometimes** dances. / **Sometimes**, he dances.

1 Write the adverbs.

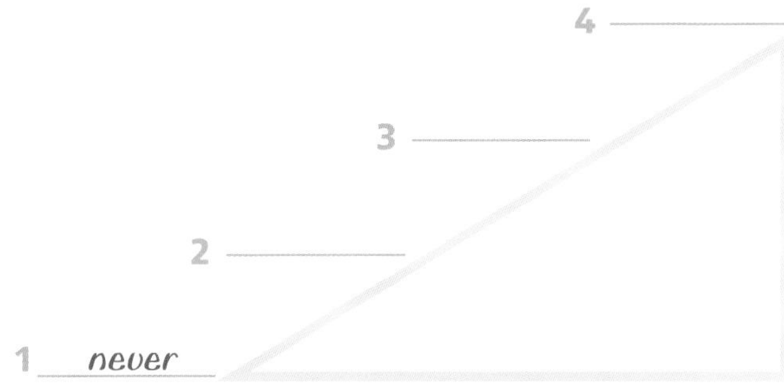

2 Rewrite the sentences using the adverbs.

1 Zoe eats meat. (never)
______________.
2 Vicky rides a bike. (often)
______________.
3 Peter's dog is hungry. (always)
______________.
4 Julio's horse is naughty. (sometimes)
______________.

Unit 5

Be good at + noun

What are you **good at**?
Is he good at singing?
I'm good at English.
Daisy**'s not good at** basketball.
Paul and Charlie **aren't good at** colouring.

'm = am 's = is

1 Put the words in the correct order.

1 good / are / drawing? / at / you

____

2 mum's / at / fishing. / my / good

____

3 at? / good / Fred / what's

____

4 roller skating. / not / he's / at / good

____

2 Complete the sentences about the pictures. Use *good at* (✓) or *not good at* (✗) and these words.

music ice skating football tennis

1 

Peter

________________________. (✓)

2 

Mary

________________________. (✗)

3 

Zoe and Julia

________________________. (✓)

4

Jack and Jim

________________________. (✗)

Unit 6

I think/know ...

I think our teacher's very nice.
I don't think Charlie can drive.
I thought it was funny.

I know his name.
I don't know where he lives.
When the teacher asked the question,
I knew the answer.

1 Complete the sentences with the correct form of *know* or *think*.

1 Matt ________ he's good at skating, but he isn't.

2 I ________ Jack's number, so I couldn't call him.

3 Zoe ________ you're here because she can see you from her window.

4 My friend ________ it was my birthday yesterday. But my birthday is today!

5 They ________ it was a dolphin, but it was a whale.

Unit 7

Verb + infinitive

What would Sarah **like to do** today?
Hugo **started to laugh**.

1 Complete the sentences. Use the infinitive of these verbs.

ride hurt get up send play ~~go~~

1 Jim wants some new roller skates. He needs *to go* shopping.

2 My grandma likes ______ at 5 in the morning.

3 Alice tried ______ a photo, but the internet was too slow.

4 Ben is learning ______ a bike. His sister teaches him every day.

5 At school, Jane chose ______ the guitar, not the piano.

6 I'm sorry! I didn't mean ______ you.

How / what about + noun or *-ing*

How/What about going for an ice cream?
How/What about an ice cream?

2 Complete the sentences. Use these nouns.

this DVD a parrot a pancake

1 A: I'm hungry.
B: How about ______?

2 A: This film's boring.
B: What about ______?

3 A: I'd like a pet.
B: How about ______?

3 Complete the sentences. Use these verbs in the *ing* form.

buy go cook

1 A: I'm hungry.
B: What about ______ some pasta?

2 A: This film's boring.
B: How / What about ______ to the park?

3 A: I'd like a pet.
B: What about ______ a rabbit?

Unit 8

Question words *why*, *when*, *where*, *how*

Why did you go there?
When did it happen?
Where did you go?
How did it end?

1 Match the questions and answers.

1 Why is Sally talking to Kim?
2 When does school start?
3 Where are Mustafa and Miguel?
4 How did you break it?

A At 9 o'clock.
B In the playground.
C I dropped it.
D To practise Spanish.

2 Put the questions in the correct order.

1 where / shopping? / go / you / did

______

2 did / Daisy / hurt / foot? / her / how

______

3 football? / you / play / do/ when

______

4 Jack / silly / hat? / why / wearing / a / is

______

Unit 9

Superlative adverbs

good/well
What do you like **best** about your school?
badly
Everyone sang badly, but Jack sang the **worst**.
slowly, quickly, etc.
Who ran **most** slow**ly**?
Eva ran **most** quick**ly**.
Hugo speaks **most** loud**ly**.
Fred speaks **most** quiet**ly**.

1 Complete the sentences with the superlative adverb.

1 Sally climbed the mountain __________ . (quickly)

2 Jackie sings __________ in our class. (loudly)

3 Ed's good at ice skating, but Clare skates __________ . (well)

4 Who do you think draws __________ at school? (badly)

5 My uncle drives __________ in my family. (slowly)

6 I like lots of food, but I like ice cream __________ . (good)

Unit 10

Adverbs of degree

We laughed **a lot**.
The room was **very** cold.

1 Put the sentences in the correct order.

1 weekends. / a lot / sleeps / at / Julia

____

2 sky / is / today. / very / grey / the

____

3 a lot / dance / you / did / at / party? / the

____

4 very / was / yesterday. / tired / Dan

____

2 Write the sentences with *a lot* or *very* in the correct position.

1 My mother talks.

____________________ .

2 She's good at tennis.

____________________ .

3 My drink wasn't cold.

____________________ .

4 His baby sister grew last year.

____________________ .

Unit 11

Must for obligation

He **must** do his homework.
Your room **mustn't** be too hot or too cold.
Must I feed the cat?

mustn't = must not

1 Match the two parts of the sentence .

1 You mustn't talk — A quiet when the teacher talks.
2 Must I — B get up now?
3 We must be — C to school by 8:30.
4 We must come — D loudly in a hospital.

2 Complete the sentences with *must* and one of the verbs in the box.

be	drive	dress up	bounce	wear	clean

1 You ______ your teeth before you go to bed.
2 People ______ slowly near our school.
3 Boys ______ trousers at our school, not shorts.
4 We ______ to go to the party.
5 When you play basketball, you ______ the ball.
6 When you go roller skating, you ______ careful.

Unit 12

Indirect objects

Give your homework to **the teacher**.
Dad gave it to **me**.

1 Put the sentences in the correct order.

1 drawing / Lily / me. / gave / her / to

______

2 gave / teddy / Jack / the / Molly. / to

______

3 to / Jim / rollers skates / his / her. / gave

______

4 milkshake / gave / Clare / Ben. / her / to

______

2 Look and write sentences.

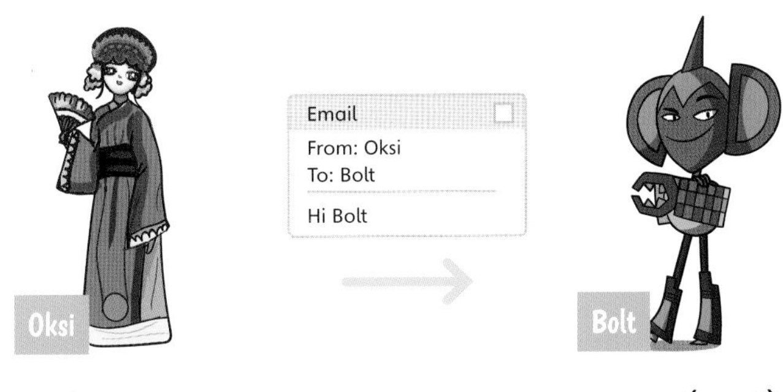

1 ______ . (sent)

2 ______ . (gave)

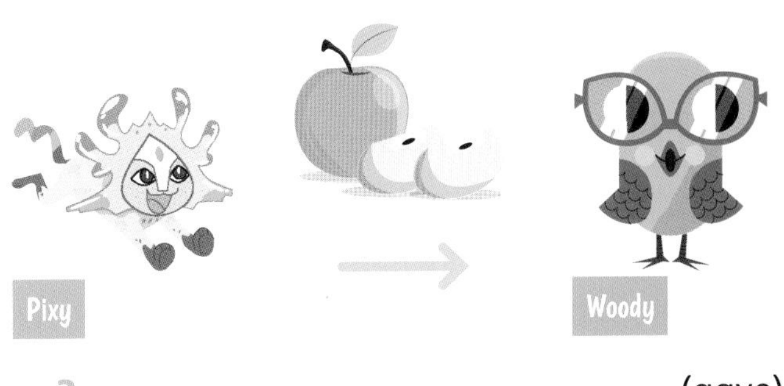

3 ______ . (gave)

Unit 1

When clauses

1 Complete the sentences and ask a friend.

When I'm happy, I smile. And you?
When I'm happy, I sing!

When I'm happy ...	... I eat some food.
When I'm sad ...	... I play a game.
When I'm tired ...	... I laugh.

Unit 3

Go + *ing*

2 Make questions with *Do you like going* and these words. Talk with a friend.

shopping roller skating riding fishing dancing swimming

Do you like going shopping?

Yes, I do.

When do you go shopping?

I go shopping at weekends.

Unit 8

Student A

Question words *why*, *when*, *where*, *how*

3 Complete the sentences. Student B has the information you need. Ask and answer questions.

Student B: look at page 77.

A: *Where did Jack go?*
B: *He went to* the circus.

Jack went to ________ (where?) on ________ (when?). He went by ________ (how?).

Julia travels to school by train because she lives in a different city.

On ________ (when?), Emma went shopping to ________ (why?). The party is at ________ (where?).

Charlie plays football after school on Thursdays. He goes home in his mum's car.

Unit 4

Student A

Adverbs of frequency

4 Complete the table. Student B has the information you need. Ask *How often ...?* Write *never*, *sometimes*, *often* or *always*. Answer your friend's questions.

Student B: look at page 77.

A: *How often does Bolt listen to music?*
B: *He* sometimes *listens to music.*

	How often?	
Bolt	________	listen to music
Milo		play tennis
Pixy	________	watch TV
Oksi		take photos

Grammar fun pairwork!

Unit 3

Infinitive of purpose

5 Complete the sentences with a friend. Check with the class. Who wrote most answers?

We go to school to learn, to have fun, to play ...

We go to school to ...
I went shopping to ...
I phoned my friend to ...
She waved to ...
He made a cake to ...
I got up at 5 am to ...

Unit 8

Student B

Question words *why*, *when*, *where*, *how*

6 Complete the sentences. Student A has the information you need. Ask and answer questions.

Student A: look at page 76.

A: *Where did Jack go?*
B: *He went to* ___the circus___ .

Jack went to the circus on Sunday. He went by bus.

Julia travels to ________ *(where?) by* ________ *(how?) because she* ________ *(why?).*

On Saturday, Emma went shopping to buy a birthday present. The party is at her cousin's house.

Charlie plays ________ *(what?)* ________ *(when?). He goes home* ________ *(how?).*

Unit 4

Student B

Adverbs of frequency

7 Complete the table. Student A has the information you need. Ask *How often ...?* Write *never*, *sometimes*, *often* or *always*. Answer your friend's questions.

Student A: look at page 76.

A: *How often does Bolt listen to music?*
B: *He* ___sometimes___ listens to music.

	How often?	
Bolt	→	listen to music
Milo	________	play tennis
Pixy	→	watch TV
Oksi	________	take photos

Reading & Writing Checklist

Circle  if your answer is Yes!

I am good at spelling words and copying them.	
I know and can spell all seven days of the week.	
I enjoy looking at pictures and answering questions about them.	
I like matching pictures to the correct part of a story.	
I can read and understand short stories with pictures.	
I like reading stories in English in class.	
I can write short sentences about a picture.	
I know and can spell ten words for things in school.	
It's fun to finish a story by filling in gaps.	
I can write two sentences about my routines.	
I can write three sentences about my town in task 6 on page 17.	

How many magic squirrels did you get?

Reading & Writing Checklist

Check your progress, colour the stars!

	OK	Great
I can write a play and act it out.	☆	☆☆
I can match words for things in a town to the correct pictures.	☆	☆☆
I had lots of good ideas and great words to describe my dream school on page 29.	☆	☆☆
I know and can spell some weather words on page 36.	☆	☆☆
I can fill in the story on page 50 with the correct words.	☆	☆☆
I chose the best title for the story on page 50.	☆	☆☆
I can describe where things are using the words in task 5 on page 57.	☆	☆☆
I understand and can solve the riddle on page 62.	☆	☆☆
I enjoyed reading the stories in the book.	☆	☆☆

Listening Checklist

Circle [squirrel] if your answer is Yes!

I can understand a lot when my teacher speaks English. 

I am good at writing words when I hear the spelling. 

I was able to match the correct pictures to Lily's description of her routine in task 3 on page 14. 

I drew a good picture of what Vicky and her friends ate after listening to the story in task 2 on page 18. 

I know and can spell ten words for things in school. 

I know when to spell, write or tick in the listening tasks. 

I filled in the gaps in the song with the correct words in task 1 on page 28. 

I enjoyed matching the right names to the pictures in task 1 on page 46. 

I know which picture to choose when I hear a description. 

I can write two sentences about my routines. 

I filled in the correct information in the gaps in task 3 on page 62. 

I know the colours and like colouring the picture when I listen to the description. 

How many magic squirrels did you get?

Speaking Checklist

Check your progress, colour the stars!	OK	Great
I can tell people about myself in English.		
I interviewed four friends about what they do and guessed their false answers in tasks 3 and 4 on page 9.		
I can ask people to repeat a question if I don't understand what they said.		
I described a place clearly so my friend could guess where it was in task 2 on page 24.		
I can use lots of adjectives to describe pictures.		
I talked about my favourite food with my friend in task 4 on page 31.		
I talked about what I did last weekend in task 6 and 7 on page 41.		
I have lots of good ideas for telling a story.		
I asked and answered questions about classroom jobs in task 3 on page 49.		
I am good at answering questions with more than one or two words, because it is fun to talk in English.		

Word list

Unit 1

afraid *adj* ____________

balcony *n* ____________

bat *n* ____________

buy *v* ____________

farm *n* ____________

grandparent *n* ____________

jungle *n* ____________

milkshake *n* ____________

parrot *n* ____________

roller skating *n* ____________

shopping centre *n* ____________

village *n* ____________

waterfall *n* ____________

Unit 2

band (music) *n* ____________

dance *n+v* ____________

dolphin *n* ____________

fat *adj* ____________

ice skating *n* ____________

kangaroo *n* ____________

laugh *v* ____________

pancake *n* ____________

penguin *n* ____________

picnic *n* ____________

rabbit *n* ____________

shark *n* ____________

snail *n* ____________

supermarket *n* ____________

whale *n* ____________

Unit 3

café *n* ____________

car park *n* ____________

cheese *n* ____________

cinema *n* ____________

comic *n* ____________

cup *n* ______________

film *n* ______________

funfair *n* ______________

hospital *n* ______________

lake *n* ______________

library *n* ______________

map *n* ______________

market *n* ______________

park *n* ______________

puppy *n* ______________

rain *n+v* ______________

sandwich *n* ______________

sick *adj* ______________

square *n* ______________

star *n* ______________

station *n* ______________

tea *n* ______________

train *n* ______________

Unit 4

baseball *n* ______________

basketball *n* ______________

countryside *n* ______________

dance *v* ______________

farmer *n* ______________

field *n* ______________

grass *n* ______________

kick *n* ______________

mountain *n* ______________

sail *n+v* ______________

skates *n* ______________

sport *n* ______________

tennis *adj* ______________

Unit 5

boring *adj* ______________

circus *n* ______________

clown *n* ______________

dream *n+v* ______________

e-book *n* ____________

pirate *n* ____________

teach *v* ____________

treasure *n* ____________

Unit 6

burger *n* ____________

city *n* ____________

cook *v* ____________

fish *n* ____________

fruit *n* ____________

noodles *n* ____________

pasta *n* ____________

pizza *n* ____________

salad *n* ____________

sauce *n* ____________

soup *n* ____________

Unit 7

cloudy *adj* ____________

cold *adj* ____________

DVD *n* ____________

fall *v* ____________

hot *adj* ____________

ice *n* ____________

snow *n+v* ____________

weather *n* ____________

wet *adj* ____________

wind *n* ____________

windy *adj* ____________

Unit 8

climb *v* ____________

dangerous *adj* ____________

scarf *n* ____________

tired *adj* ____________

wake (up) *v* ____________

Unit 9

carry *v* ______________

coat *n* ______________

dentist *n* ______________

dress up *v* ______________

film star *n* ______________

nurse *n* ______________

party *n* ______________

pop star *n* ______________

tractor *n* ______________

vegetable *n* ______________

window *n* ______________

Unit 10

cough *n* ______________

earache *n* ______________

fine *adj* ______________

headache *n* ______________

paint *n* ______________

panda *n* ______________

stomach-ache *n* ______________

temperature *n* ______________

toothache *n* ______________

Unit 11

asleep *adj* ______________

flat *n* ______________

forest *n* ______________

kitten *n* ______________

leaf / leaves *n* ______________

loud *adj* ______________

roof *n* ______________

wave *v* ______________

Unit 12

grow *v* ______________

plant *n+v* ______________

swimsuit *n* ______________

tooth / teeth *n* ______________

In your book ...

Likes: sleeping on the beach, running in the forest, flying in the air

Dislikes: octopuses, sleeping in a cave

Likes: pizza, running, playing football, treats

Dislikes: flying, singing, pancakes

Likes: singing, dancing, flying, fans

Dislikes: watching TV, meat, dogs

Likes: flying very high, fruit

Dislikes: swimming in the sea, vegetables

Likes: meat, skipping

Dislikes: watching TV, going to school

Likes: fresh fish, water, plants

Dislikes: noise, light

... from kids around the world

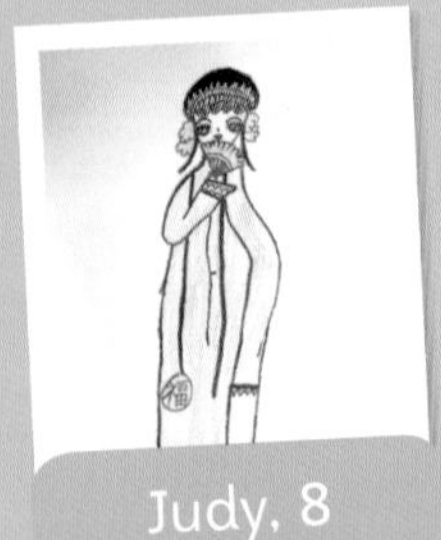

Judy, 8

Mariyam, 10

Nikita, 9

Alejandro, 10

Vaja, 9

Daniel, 9

Checklist buddy

Likes: pizza, apple juice, playing ball

Dislikes: ice cream, burgers, mice, cats

Exam Professor

Likes: science, music, interesting animals, playing basketball

Dislikes: disorder, meat, destruction, black

Think Big Giraffe

Likes: plants

Dislikes: meat

Likes: reading, eating, joking, art

Dislikes: pickles, flies, the dark, cockroaches

Mariya, 8

Mario, 11

Adriana, 7

Edith,11

Author acknowledgements

Bridget Kelly would like to thank Ann-Marie, Lynn and David - she really enjoyed working with them all. And thanks to Colin and little Aedan as always.

David Valente would like to sincerely thank Katherine Bilsborough and Emily Hird for being great sounding boards throughout the writing process.

Publisher acknowledgements

The authors and publishers are grateful to the following for reviewing the material during the writing process:

Lucie Cotterill, Jane Ritter, Khara Burgess: Italy; Muruvvet Celik: Turkey; Nguyen Hoa, Georges Erhard: Vietnam; Roisin O'Farrell: Spain; Gustavo Baron Sanchez: Mexico.

The authors and publishers acknowledge the following sources of copyright material and are grateful for the permissions granted. While every effort has been made, it has not always been possible to identify the sources of all the material used, or to trace all copyright holders. If any omissions are brought to our notice, we will be happy to include the appropriate acknowledgements on reprinting & in the next update to the digital edition, as applicable.

Key: Gr: Grammar; U: Unit.

Photography

The following photographs are sourced from Getty Images. **Gr:** Adie Bush/Image Source; dimid_86/iStock/Getty Images Plus; Glow Images, Inc; MamiEva/RooM; UpperCut Images; **U1:** Morsa Images/DigitalVision; Fabio Lamanna/EyeEm; Westend61; RichVintage/E+; Punnawit Suwuttananun/Moment; andresr/E+; Emilija Manevska/Moment; Slawomir Tomas/EyeEm; yusnizam/iStock/Getty Images Plus; robas/E+; Cherry Tantirathanon/EyeEm; NurPhoto; Daniel Limpi/EyeEm; Avalon/Universal Images Group; **U2:** Fadi Mckean/EyeEm; Karina Mansfield/Moment; EMS-FORSTER-PRODUCTIONS/DigitalVision; Westend61; Sean_Warren/E+; 2A Images; JGI/Jamie Grill; **U3:** SensorSpot/E+; GSO Images/Photodisc; Flashpop/DigitalVision; AFP; Hufton and Crow/Corbis Documentary; Stephen Dorey/Photolibrary; Dave Shafer/Aurora; Tom Sibley/Corbis; Nikada/iStock Unreleased; Eakachai Leesin/EyeEm; drbimages/iStock/Getty Images Plus; **U4:** Jose Luis Pelaez Inc/DigitalVision; Ty Allison/Taxi; Tony Garcia/Image Source; Shoji Fujita/DigitalVision; Mark Hunt; Jupiterimages/Polka Dot/Getty Images Plus; Seb Oliver/Cultura; Compassionate Eye Foundation/Natasha Alipour Faridani/DigitalVision; LifeJourneys/E+; photography by Linda Lyon/Moment; Matthew Ashmore/EyeEm; **U5:** andresr/E+; kali9/E+; Tim Hall/Cultura; Hill Street Studios/DigitalVision; PhotoAlto/Sigrid Olsson; xavierarnau/E+; Alexei Polyansky/EyeEm; Sue Barr/Image Source; **U6:** Maskot; Erick Olvera/EyeEm; Westend61; Indeed; Thiti Sukapan/EyeEm; hadynyah/E+; Massimo Lama/EyeEm; Martin Deja/Moment; Slawomir Tomas/EyeEm; Elizabeth Livermore/Moment; hdere/E+; vinicef/iStock/Getty Images Plus; IngaNielsen/iStock/Getty Images Plus; Steve Lewis Stock/Photographer's Choice; Jose Luis Pelaez Inc/DigitalVision; Nancy Honey/Cultura; Andersen Ross/Stockbyte; Monkey Business Images; FuatKose/E+; real444/E+; CactuSoup/iStock/Getty Images Plus; CactuSoup/E+; JLPH/Cultura; twomeows/Moment; paul mansfield photography/Moment; Luis Alvarez/DigitalVision; Alexei Polyansky/EyeEm; David Sacks/The Image Bank; Jasmin Merdan/Moment; Science Photo Library; **U7:** Per Eriksson; Arata Ishida/EyeEm; **U8:** Andreas Ulvdell/Folio Images; jreika/iStock/Getty Images Plus; Giovanna Graf/EyeEm; Aliraza Khatri's Photography/Moment; Bob Peterson/UpperCut Images; Gerard Puigmal/Moment; amenic181/iStock/Getty Images Plus; Louis Turner/Cultura; Jeff Titcomb/Stone; PeopleImages/E+; Artyom Geodakyan/TASS; Godong/Universal Images Group; Esther Moreno Martinez/EyeEm; Emma Kim/Cultura; **U9:** Compassionate Eye Foundation/DigitalVision; photosindia; Hero Images; Inti St Clair/DigitalVision; **U10:** Hero Images; BananaStock; kwanchaichaiudom/iStock/Getty Images Plus; 1MoreCreative/iStock/Getty Images Plus; Ismailciydem/iStock/Getty Images Plus; Sawitree Pamee/EyeEm; **U11:** Christian Offenberg/EyeEm; Michele Falzone/AWL Images; Rafal Nycz/Moment; FG Trade/iStock/Getty Images Plus; **U12:** Christophe Bourloton/iStock/Getty Images Plus; MakiEni's photo/Moment; John Russell/EyeEm; Will Heap/Dorling Kindersley; Ramn Carretero/EyeEm; Shutter Chemistry/500px Prime; Shutter Chemistry/500px Prime.

The following photograph is sourced from other library.

U4: MARK HICKEN/Alamy Stock Photo.

Front cover photography by Amanda Enright; Jhonny Nunez; Leo Trinidad; Pol Cunyat; Dan Widdowson; Pipi Sposito; Pand P Studio/Shutterstock; Piotr Urakau/Shutterstock

Illustrations

Amanda Enright (Advocate); Leo Trinidad (Bright); Fran Brylewska (Beehive); Pipi Sposito (Advocate); Pablo Gallego (Beehive); Dave Williams (Bright); Collaborate Agency; Wild Apple Design Ltd

Front cover illustrations by Amanda Enright; Jhonny Nunez; Leo Trinidad; Pol Cunyat; Dan Widdowson; Pipi Sposito; Pand P Studio/Shutterstock; Piotr Urakau/Shutterstock

Audio

Audio production by Ian Harker

Songs composition, vocals and production by Robert Lee at Dib Dib Dub Studios, UK.

Chants composition and production by AmyJo Doherty and Martin Spangle.

Design

Design and typeset by Wild Apple Design Ltd
Cover design by Collaborate agency

A1 Movers Mini Trainer

Two practice tests without answers

1

Cambridge University Press
www.cambridge.org/elt

Cambridge Assessment English
www.cambridgeenglish.org

Information on this title: www.cambridge.org/9781108585118

First published 2019

40 39 38 37 36 35 34 33 32 31 30 29 28 27

Printed in Malaysia by Vivar Printing

A catalogue record for this publication is available from the British Library

ISBN 978-1-108-58511-8 A1 Movers Mini Trainer with Audio Download

Acknowledgements

The authors and publishers acknowledge the following sources of copyright material and are grateful for the permissions granted. While every effort has been made, it has not always been possible to identify the sources of all the material used, or to trace all copyright holders. If any omissions are brought to our notice, we will be happy to include the appropriate acknowledgements on reprinting and in the next update to the digital edition, as applicable.

The authors and publishers would like to thank the following contributors:

Page make up, illustration and animations: QBS Learning

Squirrel character illustration: Leo Trinidad

Cover illustration: Dan Widdowson

Author: Trish Burrow

Audio production: DN and AE Strauss Ltd and James Miller

Editor: Alexandra Miller

Contents

A1 Movers

Test 1 Training and Exam Practice

Test 2 Exam Practice

Vocabulary: Movers names

1 Listen to your teacher say the names and point.

Jane Fred Peter Zoe Paul

Clare Jack Charlie Daisy Vicky

Pre-Listening: describing people

2 Look at what the people are doing in Exercise 3. Say two things about the picture.

TIP! In the exam, look quickly at the picture while you listen to the example. Think of words you might hear to describe the people in the picture.

Listening for names and descriptions of people

3 002 Listen to a man and a girl talking about a picture. Point to the people they talk about. Then listen again and write the names.

Fred ________ ________

________ ________ ________

TIP! Say what the people are doing, what they are wearing or what they look like.

Describing people

4 Test your partner! Cover your picture and describe the people.

Part 1

– 5 questions –

003 **Listen and draw lines. There is one example.**

Mary Sam Sally Jim

Charlie Lily Clare

Vocabulary: spelling

1 004 Listen and write the words. Then say the word and spell it out loud.

0 swimsuit

1 ______ 4 ______ 7 ______

2 ______ 5 ______ 8 ______

3 ______ 6 ______

Vocabulary: numbers

2 005 Listen and point. Say the numbers. Then play *Bingo!*

35 72 63 44 13 89 96 52 28 67 38 41

TIP! Make sure that you write answers that make sense in Part 2.

Listening: listening for names, words and numbers

3 006 Look at the sentences. Then listen and write the answers.

Visiting hospital

0	The family are visiting …	Grandpa.
1	Fred wants to show photos of the …	______ ride.
2	Grandpa hurt his …	______.
3	Grandpa is in room number …	______.
4	Fred wants to get some …	______ for Grandpa.
5	Dinner time at the hospital is at …	______.

Part 2

– 5 questions –

Listen and write. There is one example.

Homework

	Who is the homework for?	Mr Best
1	Must write about:	A ______
2	Name of story:	My ______
3	Write homework in:	______ book
4	Number of words:	______
5	Day to give homework to teacher:	______

Vocabulary: groups of words

TIP! In Part 3, look at pictures A–H and think what words the pictures show before you listen.

1 What words do you know? Complete the word webs.

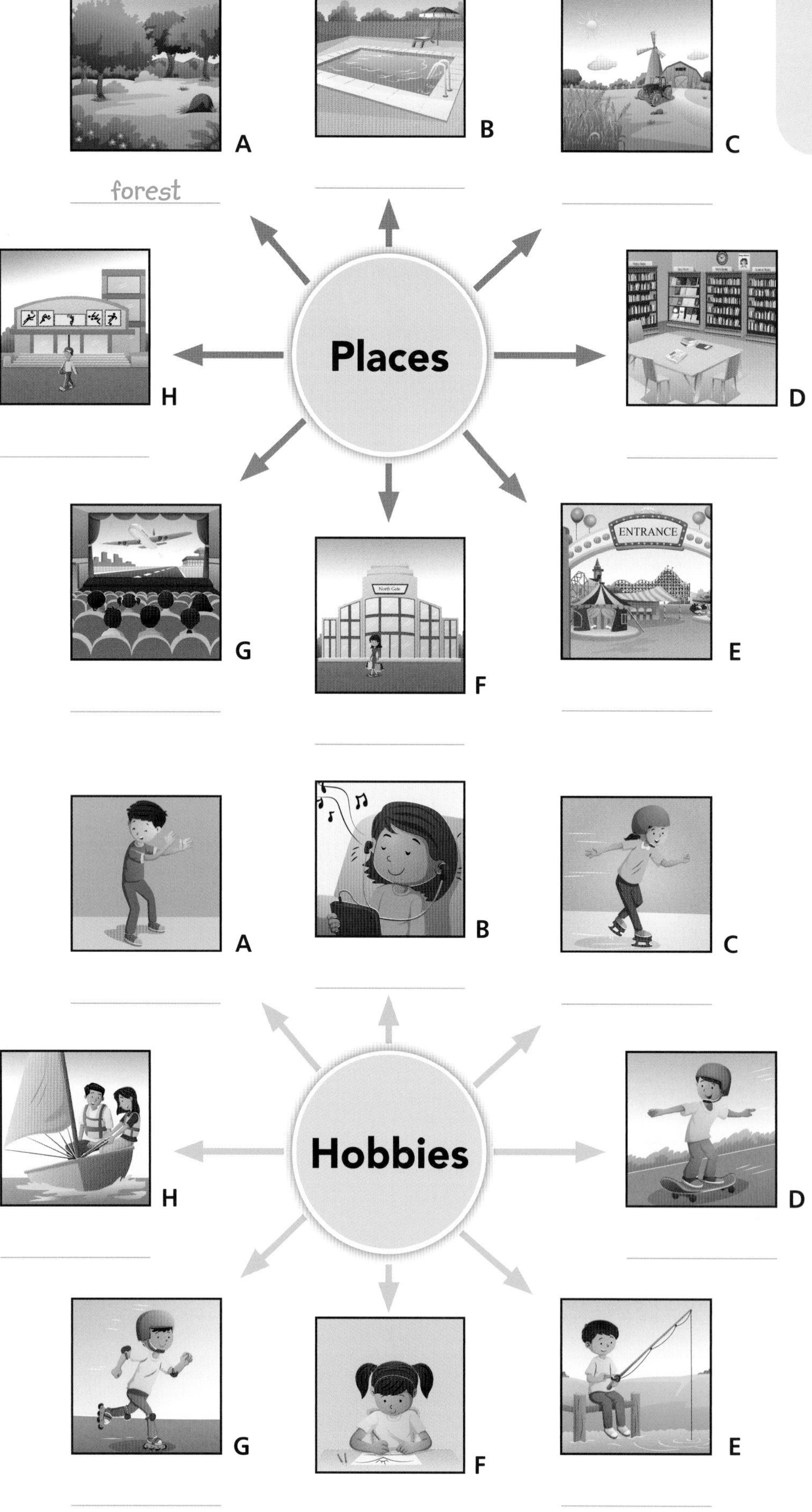

TIP! Listen to all of the question before you write your tick.

Get ready!

2 008 **Mr Snow is talking to Sarah about his family. What are the people in his family doing now? Listen and tick (✔).**

0 his daughter  — A  ☐ B  ☐ C ☑

1 his son  — A  ☐ B  ☐ C ☐

2 his brother  — A  ☐ B  ☐ C ☐

3 his parents  — A  ☐ B  ☐ C ☐

Part 3

– 5 questions –

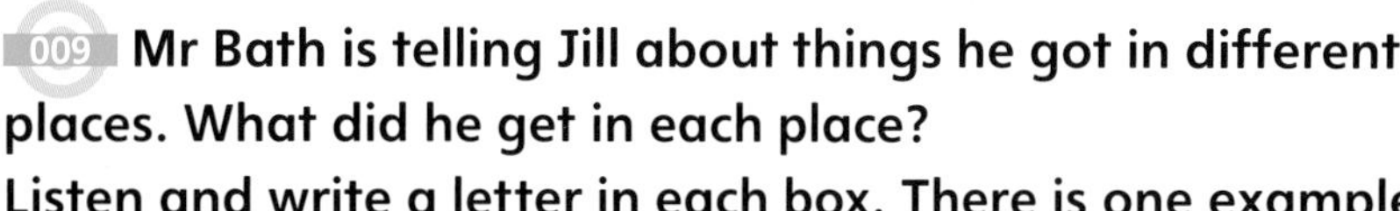

009 Mr Bath is telling Jill about things he got in different places. What did he get in each place?
Listen and write a letter in each box. There is one example.

	the village	B
	the station	
	the bus stop	
	the car park	
	the funfair	
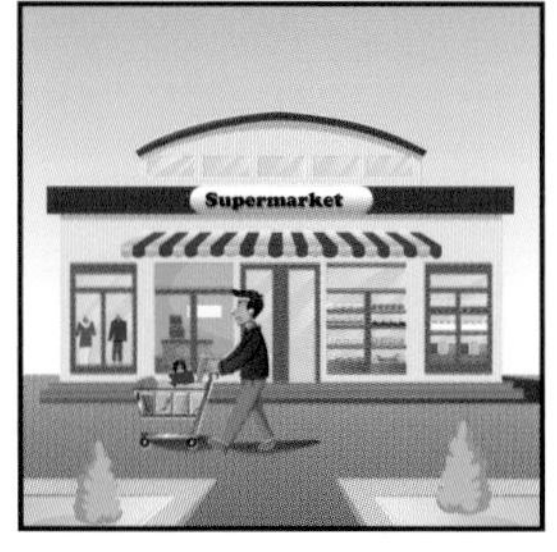	the supermarket	

A

B

C

D

E

F

G

H

Pre-Listening: describing a picture

1 Look and say what you can see.

Listening for specific information

2 010 Look at the pictures and describe them. Then listen and tick (✓) the box.

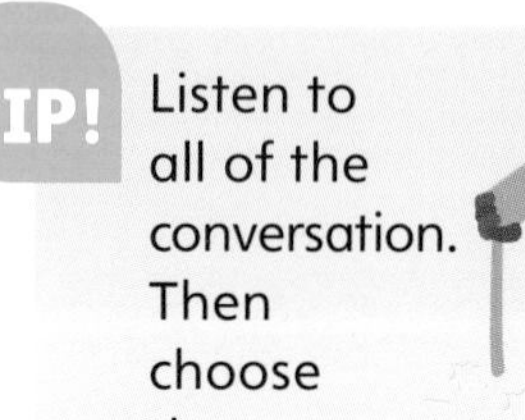

Listen to all of the conversation. Then choose the answer.

0 What does Clare want to eat?

 A ☐
 B ✓
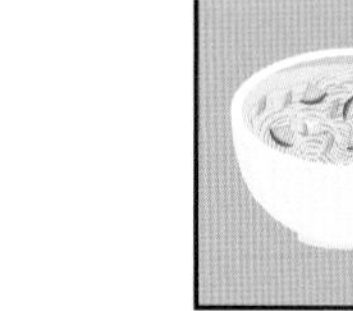 C ☐

1 Which T-shirt is Nick looking for?

 A ☐
 B ☐
 C ☐

2 What sport does Lily want to do at the sports centre?

 A ☐
 B ☐
 C ☐

3 What is Kate doing?

 A ☐
 B ☐
 C ☐

Part 4

– 5 questions –

011 **Listen and tick (✓) the box. There is one example.**

Which film does Vicky want to watch?

A ☑ B ☐ C ☐

1 Who is Daisy's father?

A ☐ B ☐ C ☐

2 Where is Fred's brother now?

A ☐ B ☐ C ☐

3 What is Aunt Julia making?

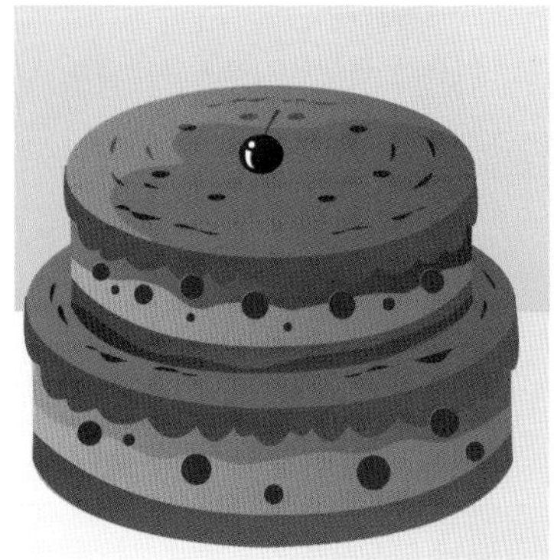

A ☐

B ☐

C ☐

4 Where is the kitten now?

A ☐

B ☐

C ☐

5 What is Dan doing?

A ☐

B ☐

C ☐

Pre-Listening: listening carefully before you answer

1 012 Look at the posters (A–D) and say what you can see. Then listen and write a number in the box. Which poster are the people talking about?

TIP! Look at the pictures before you listen. This helps you choose the correct answer.

A 0

B

C

D

Listening for specific information

2 013 Listen and colour and write. Colour four pictures and write one word.

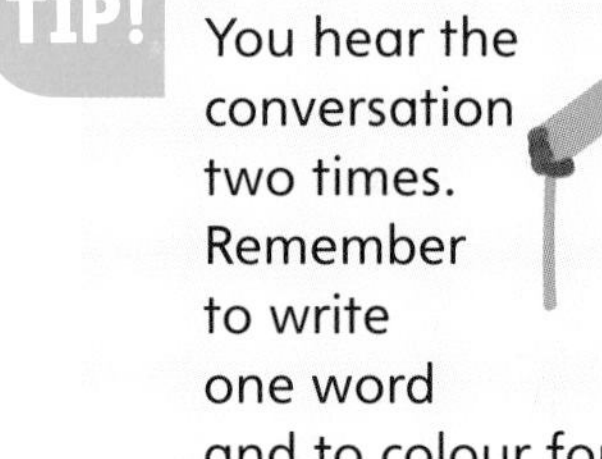

TIP! You hear the conversation two times. Remember to write one word and to colour four things in the picture.

Part 5

– 5 questions –

014 **Listen and colour and write. There is one example.**

Vocabulary: nouns

1 Put a circle around the word that is wrong.

0 Things you wear:	coat	(roof)	helmet	scarf
1 Places:	cinema	market	DVD	café
2 Food and drinks:	milkshake	bat	pasta	sandwich
3 People:	field	pop star	driver	farmer
4 Things in the home:	lamp	blanket	towel	sky

2 Look at the picture and write the words from Exercise 1 on the lines.

0 café
1 ______
2 ______
3 ______
4 ______
5 ______

TIP! In Part 1, the answers are nouns like *kitten* or *swimsuit*. Learn the nouns on the Movers word list.

Grammar: verbs

3 Read the sentences. Then complete the sentences with words from the box.

be buy cook drive ~~feed~~ go ~~grow~~ is like moves put takes

0 Farmers grow food in fields and some also feed their animals there.
1 Some people ______ upstairs and downstairs in a lift. It sometimes ______ slowly.
2 A driver sometimes ______ you to school. They can ______ a car, bus or train.
3 Some people ______ a blanket on their bed when it ______ cold.
4 You can ______ fruit and vegetables in a market. Many people ______ shopping there.
5 You must ______ careful when you ______ pasta because you use hot water.

TIP! In Part 1, the sentences have Starters and Movers verbs in them. Practice copying words carefully.

Part 1

– 5 questions –

Look and read. Choose the correct words and write them on the lines. There is one example.

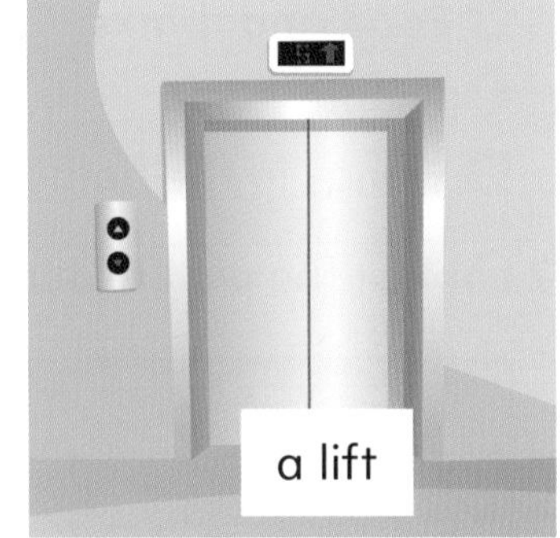

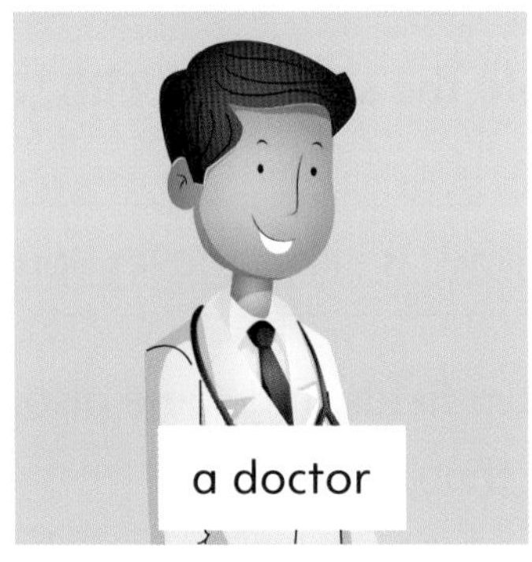

Example

This person works in a hospital and helps people who are ill. a doctor

Questions

1 You can sit and read books in this place. ______

2 This takes people up or down to different floors in a building. ______

3 Go and see this person if your teeth hurt. ______

4 You can buy all kinds of food here. ______

5 This is part of a building that is under the ground. ______

Responses to questions

TIP! In Part 2, look at the questions and answers. Do they match and make sense?

1 Read the sentences. Then write the correct answer from the phrases in the box.

I love them. It's opposite the bus station. I've got some juice. Look, there are some in this comic. ~~So do I!~~ That's a great idea! Yes, I went with my aunt.

0 I love playing tennis. *So do I!*
1 Let's go to the park. ______
2 Did you go to the cinema? ______
3 Where is the new bookshop? ______
4 Shall I get some drinks? ______
5 Do you like noodles? ______
6 I really like stories about aliens. ______

Exam strategy: finding incorrect answers

2 Read the questions. Choose the correct answers. Say why the other answers are wrong.

0 What did you do at the weekend? — I played / ~~playing~~ / ~~play~~ football.

1 Who is your favourite pop star? — He plays the guitar. / Daisy Watson. / Their songs are great.

2 What's the matter, Mary? — She's got a cough. / He's sick today. / My foot hurts.

3 Where is your bag? — It's blue and white / in my bedroom / got my books in it.

4 When do you go swimming? — On Thursdays. / At the pool. / With my sister.

Your turn!

3 Read the conversations. Write a word in the gaps.

0 What did you do on Friday?
- a I *went* to the sports centre.
- b I *played / bought* computer games.
- c I *watched / saw* a film on television.

1 How about buying a DVD for your brother?
- a What a nice ______!
- b He ______ love that.
- c Yes, he ______ watching films.

2 Which is your favourite story?
- a The story ______ pirates is good.
- b I like the pirate story ______.
- c Pirate stories ______ my favourite.

3 Let's go to the park this afternoon.
- a OK, we ______ play football.
- b ______ I bring my football?
- c Do you ______ to play football?

Part 2

– 6 questions –

Read the text and choose the best answer.

Example

Jack: What did you do yesterday, Vicky?

Vicky:

A I'm riding a horse.

B I'm going riding.

(C) I had a riding lesson.

Questions

1 Jack: Did you wear a helmet?

Vicky:

A No, it isn't.

B So do I.

C Yes, I had to.

2 Jack: Where did you ride?

Vicky:
A After school.
B Around the field.
C At the weekend.

3 Jack: Which horse did you ride?

Vicky:
A It's called Mr Jim.
B You would like it.
C They were all grey.

4 Jack: Who helped you?

Vicky:
A Dad and my teacher.
B Shall I help you?
C We could do it.

5 Jack: Was it easy to ride a horse?

Vicky:
A No, I can't.
B No, you weren't.
C No, it wasn't.

6 Jack: I'd love to ride a horse, too.

Vicky:
A I went riding, too.
B Well, come with me.
C It's where I go.

Vocabulary: different kinds of words

1 Look at the words and write them in the correct group.

~~afraid~~ ~~blanket~~ bought carried coats cold dangerous drive field forest frightened hospital ~~laughed~~ ride strongest travel warm website

Things	Actions	Adjectives
blanket	*laughed*	*afraid*

TIP! When you learn a new word, learn what kind of word it is and what words go before and after it.

Understanding the story first

2 Read the first two sentences of the story. What is it about? What do you think happens next?

Sally and Peter ride their bikes most weekends. Last Saturday it was very cold.

Now read all of the story. Were you right?

Sally and Peter ride their **bikes** most weekends. Last Saturday it was very **cold**. The children asked, 'Mum, can we go to the forest near the **lake** on our bikes?' Mum said, 'No, there is lots of ice on the roads — it's dangerous.' Dad said, 'Let's look on the internet and see what you can **do** today.' The family **looked** at the town website to find out something different to do. Peter said, 'Look! There's a new place on Island Road where we can go ice skating.' 'Let's go there!' said Sally. 'OK, get your coats, hats and **scarves**,' said Mum. 'You need to **wear** warm clothes for skating.' 'OK, Mum,' said the children. 'Shall we wear the sweaters Grandma and Grandpa bought us?' 'Yes, do that,' said Mum. 'And I can drive you to see them on the way home. They always love seeing you,' added Dad.

TIP! When you read a story, think what can happen next.

Now answer questions 1–5.

0 Where did Sally and Peter want to go? to the forest
1 Why did their mum say they couldn't go out on their bikes? ____________
2 Where did they look for ideas for something to do? ____________
3 What do they choose to do? ____________
4 What clothes did the children's mum say they should wear? ____________
5 Who is Dad going to take the children to see? ____________

Reading

3 Read the story again. Then write words from Exercise 2 below the pictures.

1 ____________

2 ____________

3 ____________

4 ____________

5 ____________

6 ____________

7 ____________

8 ____________

9 ____________

4 Put the words in order to make possible names for the story. Then choose the best name for the story. Tick (✔) one box.

1 new / rides / Grandpa / bike / his ____________ ☐

2 in / town / Ice / the / skating ____________ ☐

3 the / lake / Ice / on ____________ ☐

Part 3

– 6 questions –

Read the story. Choose a word from the box. Write the correct word next to numbers 1–5. There is one example.

Peter loved going for long ___walks___ with his father. Last week, they went to a small lake.

'Can we swim here?' Peter asked.

'Sorry, Peter. The water's too **(1)** ______________,' his father said.

There was a loud noise, which came from the **(2)** ______________ opposite the lake. 'What's that, Dad?' Peter asked.

'Is it a waterfall, Peter? It's very noisy,' Peter's father said.

'Yes, Dad! I think it is. Come on! Let's go and find it.' And they did!

Peter and his father **(3)** ______________ on to the rocks, took off their boots and socks and put their feet into the water. 'We can swim in this pool,' Peter's father said. 'The water's great! And well done! You are the one who found this brilliant place. Let's **(4)** ______________ Mum a quick message.'

Peter smiled. 'OK. Let's have our **(5)** ______________ here, too, Dad,' he said. 'Where are the sandwiches?'

Example

walks

text

thirsty

forest

headache

picnic

cold

climbed

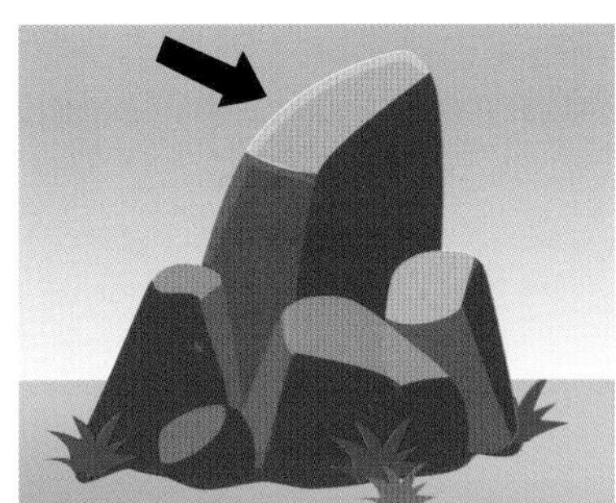
top

(6) Now choose the best name for the story.

Tick one box.

Dad's funny message ☐

An exciting new place ☐

Peter swims in the lake ☐

Identifying the correct word

1 Read and choose the correct word to complete the sentences. What are the animals?

0 Some blue whales are longer (**than**) / **after** / **into** three buses!

1 They have strong legs **but** / **because** / **then** they can't run.

2 They are smaller **then** / **that** / **than** most whales and have small teeth.

3 There **is** / **are** / **was** 350 kinds of these birds in the world.

4 Some of these animals can **jumps** / **jump** / **jumping** between trees.

5 This animal **live** / **lives** / **living** in the jungle and can run and swim. It is orange and black.

Describing similarities and differences

2 Read the text and think what kind of word goes in the gaps. Then choose a word from the box. There are two extra words.

TIP! In Part 4, look at the words before and after the gaps to help you decide what the missing words are.

Lions come from Africa and are the second **(0)** *biggest* cat in the world. They are the only cats **(1)** ______ live in groups. They live in groups of **(2)** ______ than ten lions, and sometimes there are 40 of them! Lions eat other animals and they often catch **(3)** ______ at night. They eat young elephants, crocodiles and sometimes hippos. Lions like **(4)** ______ and sleep for 16–20 hours a day on the ground or in a tree. Mother lions have two or three baby lions, called 'cubs', and the other mother lions **(5)** ______ to look after them.

~~biggest~~ help more sleeps sleeping that them then

Part 4

– 5 questions –

Read the text. Choose the right words and write them on the lines.

Bats

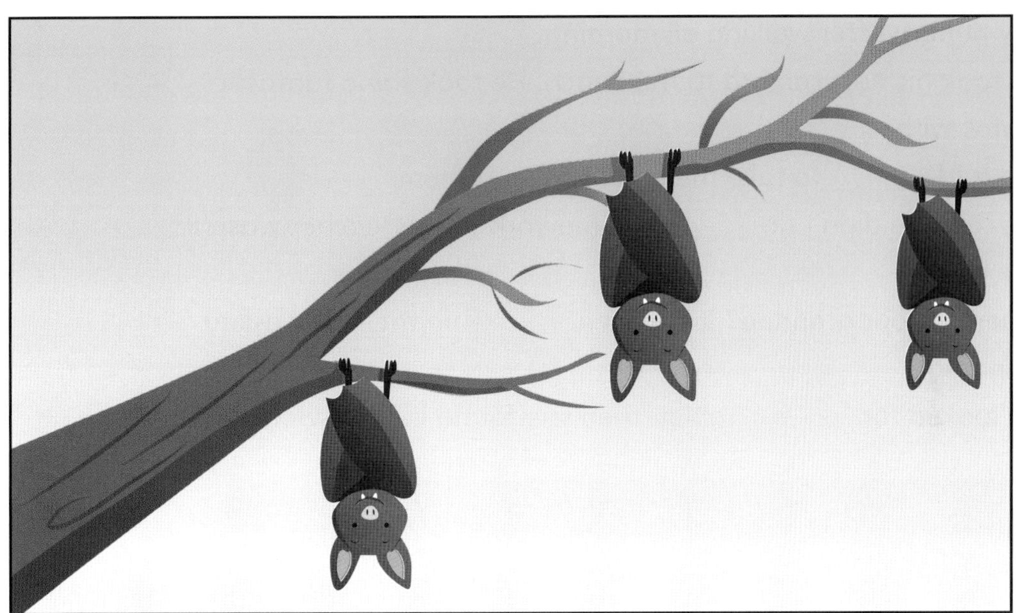

Example Bats are small animals that live in different countries of the world. There

1 are hundreds of different kinds but ______________ kind of bat can fly. Many bats live in trees or roofs, but some live inside mountains. Most bats sleep in the day and

2 look for their food ______________ night. Some bats eat fruit, but

3 ______________ eat spiders and flies. Some bigger bats eat mice.

4 When bats ______________ flying, they have to listen very carefully with their ears

5 because they don't see very ______________ with their eyes.

Example	These	There	Them
1	both	every	this
2	into	near	at
3	another	everyone	lots
4	are	have	do
5	well	better	worse

Grammar: nouns, pronouns and possessive adjectives

1 Read the sentences and complete them with the words from the box.

her	him	~~It~~	it	their	them	They

0 Then the cow started to run after them. 'Look out! It is very fast!' said Daisy.
1 The family sat down by the river and had a picnic. ______ were very hungry after walking all morning.
2 Jim took his new camera to the beach. He took some fantastic photos with ______.
3 Dad told ______ to take their helmets with them.
4 The children didn't do ______ homework so the teacher wasn't very happy.
5 'Where is your grandpa? I can't see ______ in the field,' asked Grandma.
6 Sue looked for ______ tablet, then she found it in the dog's bed.

TIP! In this part, learn to recognise which words are referred to when we use pronouns and possessive adjectives.

Exam strategy: say the same thing in a different way

2 Read the sentences from different stories. Colour the words in them that you can use to complete the second sentences. Then write in the gaps.

0 On Friday the family ate breakfast in the garden.
The family had breakfast in the garden on Friday.
1 Last week, Sam's dad said, 'Let's go to the new shopping centre. I would like to buy a new coffee machine.'
Sam's dad wanted to buy a new ______ at the shopping centre.
2 It snowed a lot on Thursday, so Bill's school was closed.
Bill couldn't go to ______ on Thursday, because it snowed a lot.
3 'I'd like to make meatballs for dinner, but we haven't got any meat!' said Vicky's mum.
Vicky's mother needed to buy ______ to make dinner that day.
4 'I know a very good website where we can buy some new shoes,' said Fred.
Fred knew a ______ where you could buy new shoes.
5 'Thanks, Mum and Dad,' said Matt. 'My birthday party was brilliant.'
Matt thanked his parents for a ______ birthday party.

TIP! In Part 5, the words you use to complete the sentences are always in the story and you copy 1, 2 or 3 words.

Get ready!

3 Look at the pictures. What do you think happens in the story? Read the story and answer the questions.

Zoe's family lived in an apartment in the city centre, but in the school holidays she went to see her grandparents on their farm in the countryside. Last Saturday, Zoe's parents drove her there. Zoe was very happy. 'I'd like to feed the baby goats! When she texted me last week, Grandma told me there are ten of them this year!'

Examples

Where was Zoe's apartment? in the city centre

Where did Zoe go in the school holidays?

her grandparents' farm

Questions

1 How did Zoe's grandma tell her there were lots of baby animals this year? ____________

2 What was Zoe happy about feeding? ____________

They were surprised when they got to the farm and saw there was nothing in the garden where Zoe's grandparents grew carrots and peas. 'Some animals ate all the vegetables!' said Zoe's grandma, 'I can't make vegetable soup for you, like I always do. There were lots of vegetables in our garden last week and we can't find the animals that ate them.' 'Well, I want to know which animals ate all the vegetables!' said Zoe.

3 What wasn't in the garden when Zoe's family got to the farm? ____________

4 What did Grandma always make for Zoe's family? ____________

5 What did Zoe say she wanted to know? ____________

Zoe found an old cage in one of the farm buildings and she put it in the garden. 'I think it's a hungry goat that is eating all the carrots and peas. Goats like vegetables,' thought Zoe, so she asked her grandpa to give her some salad leaves and she put them in the cage. That night Zoe dreamed about a huge goat that was eating all the vegetables and the flowers, too! In the morning, Zoe's grandma said, 'Zoe, come quickly! I know what was eating all our food now.' And she showed Zoe a family of rabbits. 'What naughty rabbits!' said Zoe.

6 What did Zoe put in the cage, so that she could catch the animals that were eating the vegetables? ____________

Part 5

– 7 questions –

Look at the pictures and read the story. Write some words to complete the sentences about the story. You can use 1, 2 or 3 words.

Lily's busy morning

Lily really enjoyed learning and loved school. Last Thursday evening she carefully chose the things she needed for all of her lessons and took her school clothes out of the cupboard and put them on her chair.

On Friday morning, Lily woke up at six o'clock. She went quietly to the bathroom and had a shower. Then she put on her school shirt and skirt and went downstairs to make her breakfast. She liked doing that. She found some bread and grapes and made some hot chocolate to drink.

Examples

On Thursday evening Lily found everything she needed for school.

Lily woke up at six o'clock on Friday morning.

Questions

1 After her ______________, Lily got dressed and went downstairs.

2 For her breakfast, Lily ate some ______________ and drank some hot chocolate.

Lily put her books and pens and pencils in her bag at seven o'clock and then washed her cup and plate. Then she gave the cat its food. Then she read the answers to some homework questions carefully. There were no mistakes! Then she read about her favourite animals, polar bears, on her father's laptop.

At eight o'clock, her parents came downstairs. They were surprised. Lily had her school clothes on.

3 Lily fed the ______________.

4 Lily looked at the ______________ to some questions and read about some polar bears.

5 When Lily's parents saw their daughter in her school clothes, they were ______________.

'There's no school today!' her father said.

Lily's mother quickly had an idea. 'We can go to the library this morning. You can learn lots of new things there!' she said.

Lily smiled. Mum was right.

6 ______________ had a good idea!

7 Lily was happy. She could learn a hundred new things at the ______________.

Vocabulary

1 Put a tick (✔) if you can see or a cross (✘) if you can't see the things in the picture.

clouds	☐	moon	☐	monkeys	☐	tree	☐
ship	☐	jellyfish	☐	parrots	☐	girl	☐
boy	☐	bottle	☐	man	☐	woman	☐
bowl	☐	helicopter	☐	rainbow	☐		

TIP! In Part 6, think of questions about the picture and how to answer them.

Answering questions about a picture

2 Match the questions and answers.

A bottle with a message in it.
She's climbing a tree.
A man and a woman.
~~They are by a waterfall.~~
It's jumping out of the water.
A helicopter and some clouds.
He's taking a photo.

0 Where are the people and animals? *They are by a waterfall.*
1 What can you see in the sky? ____________
2 What is the fish doing? ____________
3 Who is in the boat? ____________
4 What is the man trying to catch? ____________
5 What is the boy doing? ____________
6 What is the girl doing? ____________

Your turn!

3 Look at the picture and the mixed up words. Make sentences about the picture.

TIP! Think carefully about the order of the words. In Part 6 you write two complete sentences about the picture.

Example

garden / day / It's / sunny / the / a / in

It's a sunny day in the garden.

1 man / and / lemonade / woman / drinking / The / are

2 baby / drawing / The / is / the / girl

3 table / a / on / There's / book / the

4 game / children / are / football / a / of / Two / playing

5 swimming / with / in / pool / girls / ball / are / The / playing / a / the

Part 6

– 6 questions –

Look and read and write.

Examples

What are the chickens doing? eating

Who is driving the tractor? the woman

Complete the sentences.

1. Two of the buildings have got a round ________________.

2. The boy is wearing a pair of ________________.

Answer the questions.

3. Where are the rabbits? ________________________________

4. Which animal is crossing the river? ________________________________

Now write two sentences about the picture.

5. ____

6. ____

Describing differences

1 Look at the two pictures. Put a circle around the four differences. Then in pairs write sentences. Take turns to describe the differences.

Picture 1

Picture 2

Picture 1	Picture 2
0 Here the girl has got *blue* skates.	0 Here the girl has got *red* skates.
1 ______	1 ______
2 ______	2 ______
3 ______	3 ______
4 ______	4 ______

TIP! In this part of the test the differences are often colours, size, number, position or activities.

Further practice

2 Look at picture 1. Draw five differences in picture 2 and colour it. In pairs, describe your picture and draw your partner's picture in your notebook.

Find the differences

www.cambridge.org/SageMovers12

Answering support questions

1 **Look at the pictures and answer the questions.**

Mary goes to the funfair

Mary and her dad are at home. Mary is saying, 'Can we go to the funfair, Dad? Mary's father is saying 'Yes, we can go this afternoon.'

Where are Mary and her father?
What ride does Mary want to go on?
How many people are waiting to go on the ride?

Where are they now?
Is Mary enjoying the ride?
What about her father?

Who wants to go on the ride again?
How does Mary's father feel?
What is Mary saying?
What is Mary's father saying?

TIP! Think of questions about the pictures to help you talk about them. In the exam, you don't see the questions.

Telling a coherent story

2 **Look at the pictures and put them in order 1–4.**

The monkeys help Jim

a 

b 

c 

d 

TIP! In the exam, first look at all the pictures quickly to try to understand the story. Then say one or two sentences about each picture.

Part 2

Paul's friends come to help!

Categorising vocabulary

1 Look and say the words. Then write them in the table.

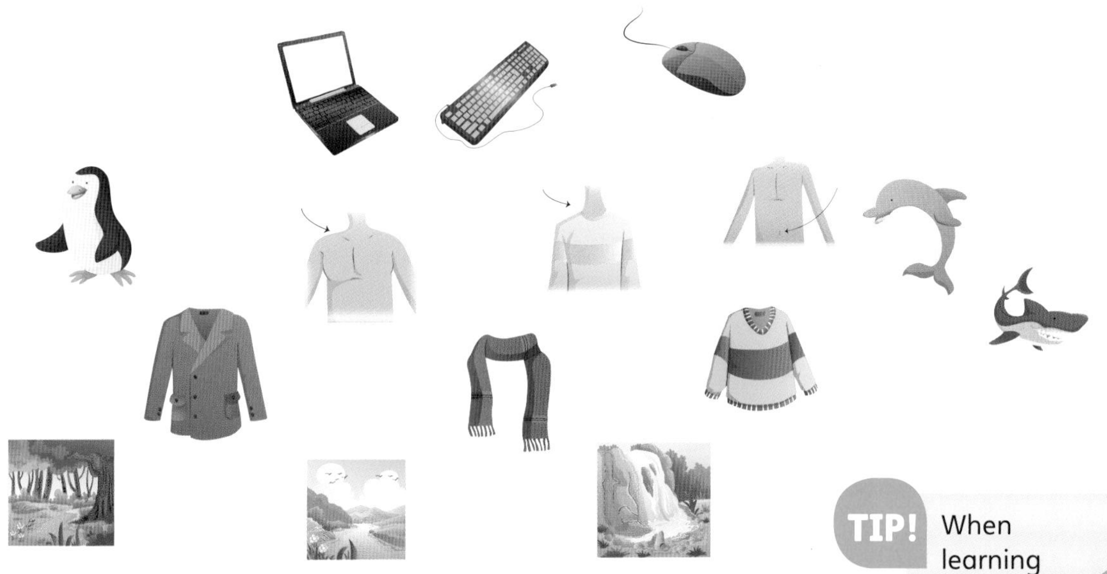

Computers	Parts of the body	Sea animals	Clothes	Places
laptop				

TIP! When learning new words or revising vocabulary put words in groups that are the same.

Describing similarities and differences

2 Look at the pictures and complete the sentences.

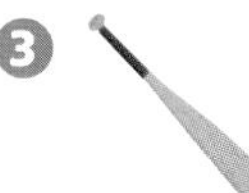

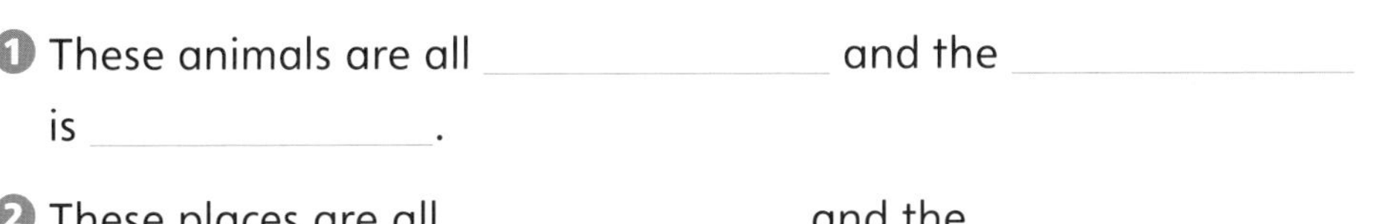

0 The coat, the sweater and the swimsuit are all ___red___ and the scarf is ___blue___.

1 These animals are all ________ and the ________ is ________.

2 These places are all ________ and the ________ is ________.

3 You play ________ with these things and you watch a ________ with this thing.

TIP! You only have to give simple reasons for the different picture.

Odd one out

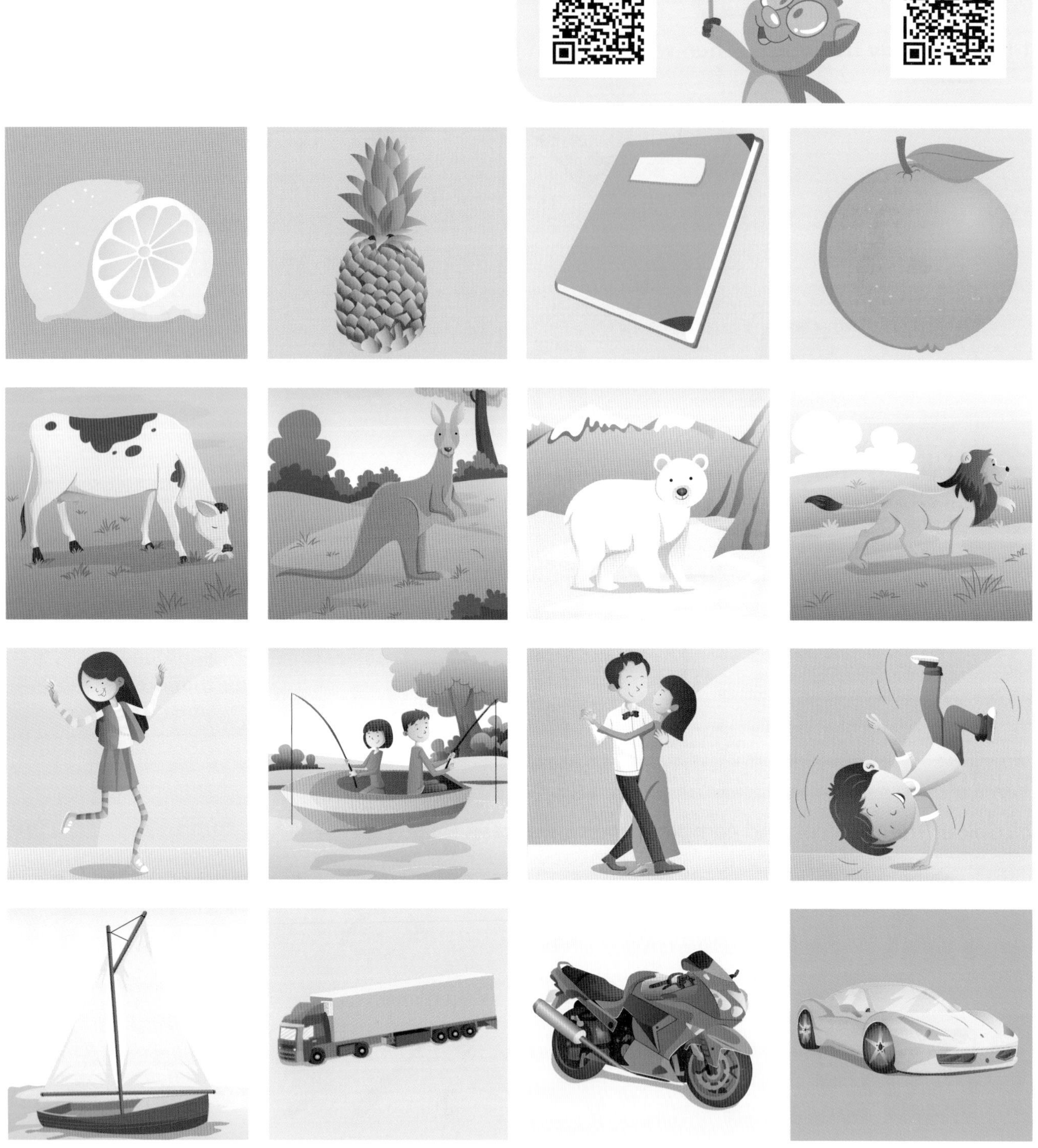

Part 4

Tell me something about your classroom.

Part 1

– 5 questions –

015 **Listen and draw lines. There is one example.**

Lily Fred Vicky Zoe

Jim Paul Julia

Part 2

– 5 questions –

 **Listen and write. There is one example.**

Going to a friend's house

Example

Who going to see ______Mary______ Point

Questions

1 Where friend lives: in ______________ Tree Road

2 Which day to go there: on ______________

3 When to go there: at ______________ o'clock

4 What to do there: ______________

5 How to travel there: by ______________

Part 3

– 5 questions –

017 **Mrs Grace is telling Peter about her birthday presents. What did each person give to Mrs Grace? Listen and write a letter in each box. There is one example.**

her grandson	E
her uncle	
her cousin	
her daughter	
her granddaughter	
her son	

A

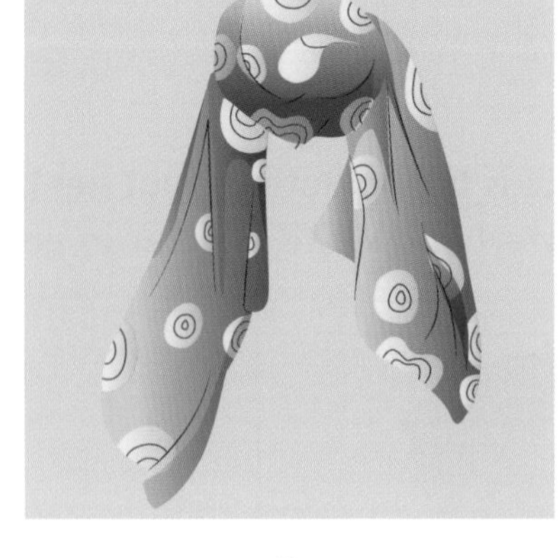

B

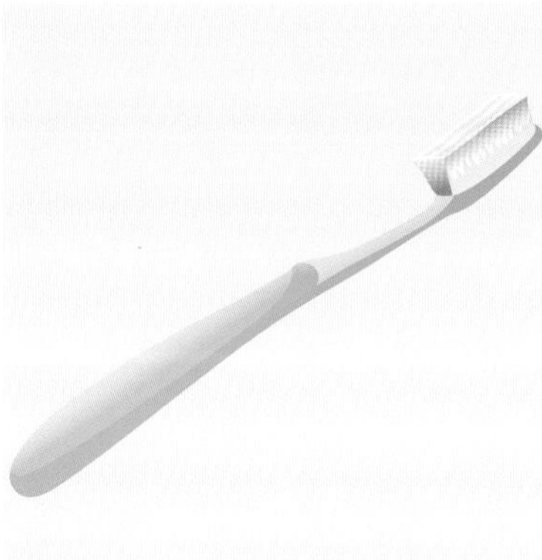

C

D

E

F

G

H

Part 4

– 5 questions –

018 **Listen and tick (✓) the box. There is one example.**

Which sport is Charlie learning to play now?

A ☐

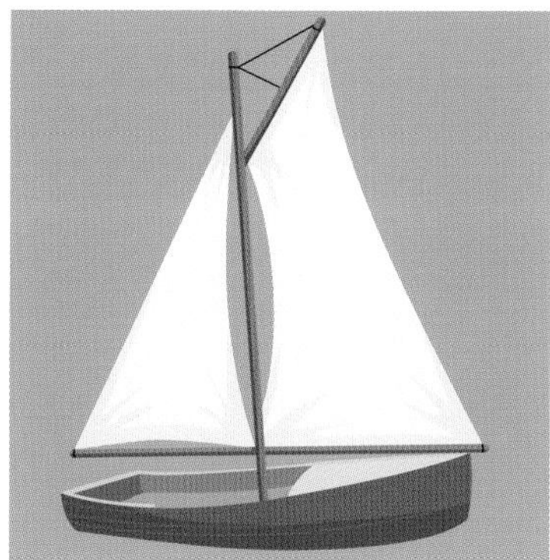

B ☐

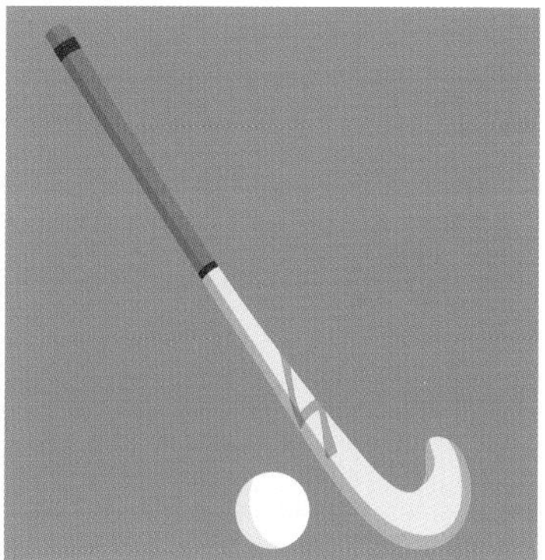

C ✓

1 What does Dad want Jane to do?

A ☐

B ☐

C ☐

2 Where is Jack's red sweater now?

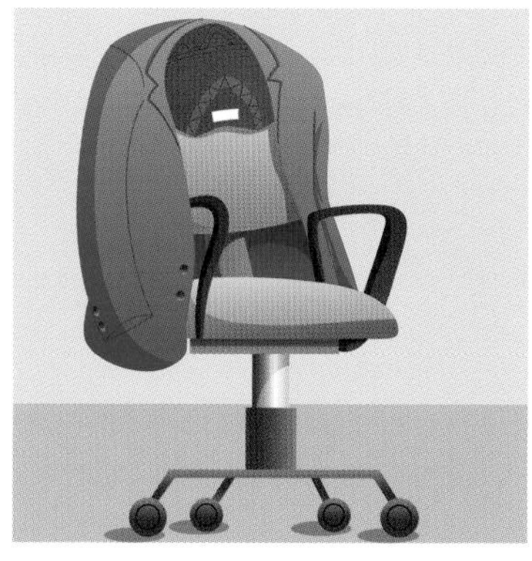

A ☐

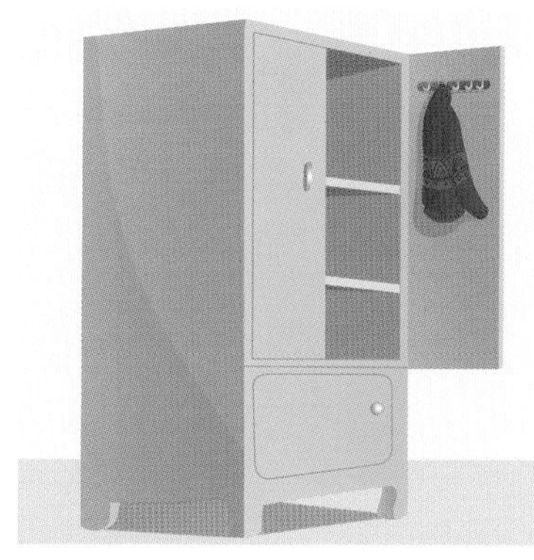

B ☐

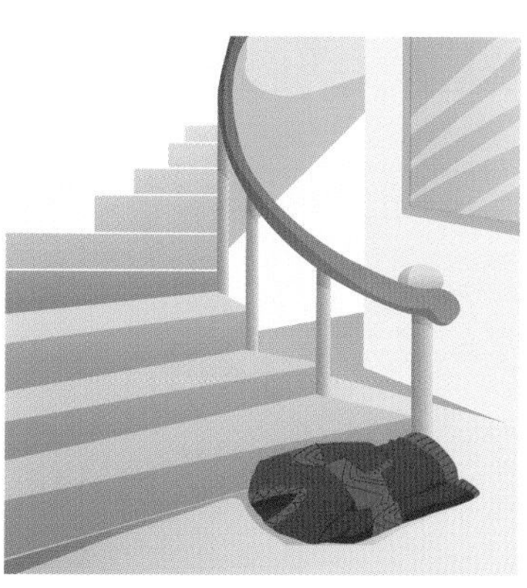

C ☐

3 Which friend is called Clare?

A

B

C

4 Which website is Mum looking at?

A

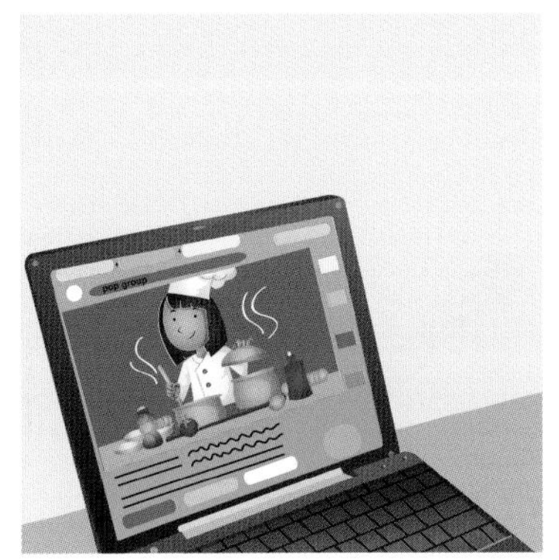

B

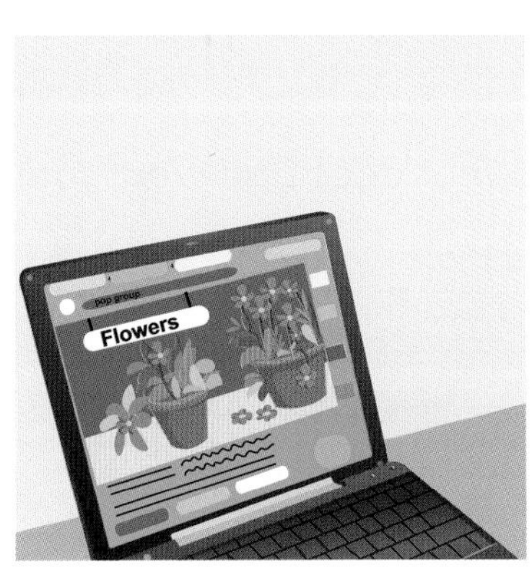

C

5 What is the baby doing now?

A

B

C

Part 5

– 5 questions –

019 **Listen and colour and write. There is one example.**

Part 1

– 5 questions –

Look and read. Choose the correct words and write them on the lines. There is one example.

Example

Onions, beans and peas are examples of these. ___vegetables___

Questions

1 This can fly and some of them can talk. ______

2 People make this from milk. You can put it in sandwiches. ______

3 This has a large shell on its back and moves very slowly. ______

4 Some people put lemon in this drink. ______

5 This lives in the sea and some people are afraid of it. ______

Part 2

– 6 questions –

Read the text and choose the best answer.

Example

Mary: Do you like playing the piano, Dan?

Dan:
(A) Yes, very much.
B Yes, please.
C Yes, I can.

Questions

1 Mary: When do you practise?

Dan:
A Last Tuesday.
B Yes, I have to.
C After school.

2 **Mary:** Where is your piano?

Dan:
A That isn't right.
B In the living room.
C It's on the top.

3 **Mary:** Is it very difficult to play the piano?

Dan:
A Yes, but I enjoy it.
B Yes, it's easy.
C Yes, I'm playing it.

4 **Mary:** What kind of music is your favourite?

Dan:
A I like music.
B I like it best.
C I like everything.

5 **Mary:** How about playing something for me?

Dan:
A OK, come with me.
B I'm fine, thank you.
C Yes, it was brilliant.

6 **Mary:** I want to learn to play the guitar.

Dan:
A You can tell me.
B So do I!
C It's not mine.

Part 3

– 6 questions –

Read the story. Choose a word from the box. Write the correct word next to numbers 1–5. There is one example.

Lucy enjoyed reading stories to her ___little___ brother, Hugo. His favourite was about an old man who **(1)** ______________ a clever monkey in the jungle to make banana cakes! The old man had a long beard and funny moustache. Last Saturday, Hugo said, 'Why can't I have a beard and moustache, Lucy?'

'Because only men can grow those.'

Hugo was **(2)** ______________ when his big sister said that.

On Sunday, Lucy found her paint box. 'I've got a great **(3)** ______________, Hugo,' she said.

Lucy carefully painted a black moustache and a beard on her brother's face.

When she was happy with her work, Hugo looked at his face in the **(4)** ______________ in the bathroom.

'Wow!' he said. 'I love my moustache and beard, but I can never clean my face again.'

'Don't **(5)** ______________ your face now, Hugo,' Lucy said. 'But you must do that before you go to bed. Sorry!'

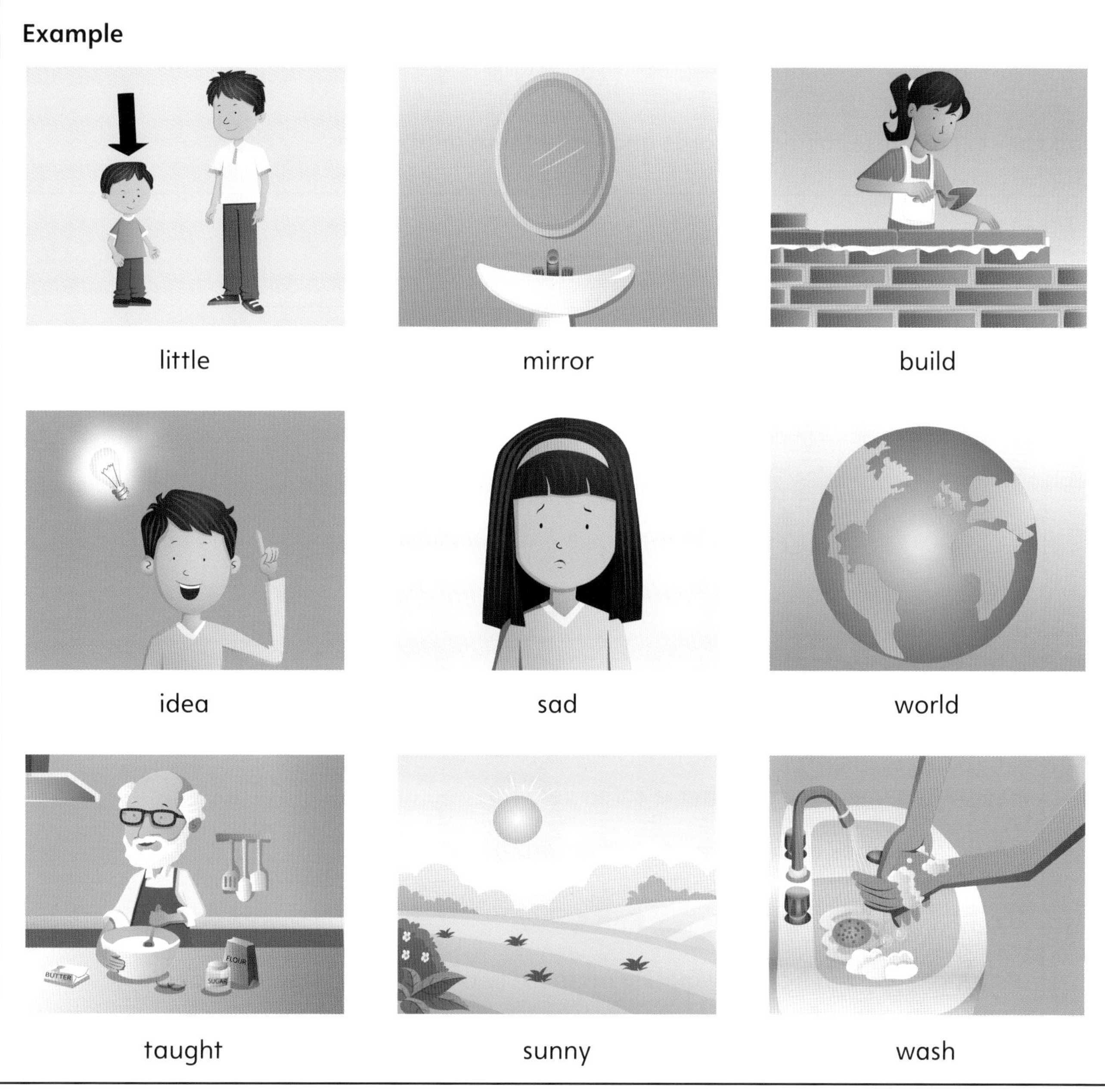

(6) Now choose the best name for the story.

Tick one box

Hugo writes a story ☐

Lucy helps her brother ☐

An old man finds a monkey ☐

Part 4

– 5 questions –

Read the text. Choose the right words and write them on the lines.

Kangaroos

Example Kangaroos sometimes get very hungry because they live ___in___ countries where the weather is often very hot and dry. The grass and small plants

1 that kangaroos eat don't grow well when there isn't ________ rain!

2 Kangaroos have two huge feet and two of ________ legs are long and strong. They can hop very quickly on these two legs. But kangaroos can't move

3 quickly when they walk ________ all four legs. Kangaroos have strong

4 tails, which help them to ________. Did you know that kangaroos can

5 swim too? ________ are four kinds of kangaroo and most live in Australia.

Example	in	by	with
1	many	any	lots
2	they	them	their
3	up	on	off
4	jump	jumps	jumping
5	Those	Another	There

Part 5

– 7 questions –

Look at the pictures and read the story. Write some words to complete the sentences about the story. You can use 1, 2 or 3 words.

Who takes the best photos?

Nick and his older cousin, Alice, both enjoyed taking photos of different people. Nick took his with his camera. Alice took hers with her phone.

Last Monday, they went to the new shopping centre with Alice's parents to buy some new clothes. In their favourite shop they saw May Night, a famous pop star! It was very exciting to see her and Nick and Alice wanted to take some photos of her.

Examples

Alice was ___older___ than her cousin, Nick.

One of their hobbies was taking photos ___of different people___.

Questions

1 Last Monday, Alice's parents took Alice and Nick to the new ____________.

2 The children saw a ____________ called May Night in a clothes shop.

May laughed and said, 'OK!' when they asked her to stand and smile in different parts of the store.

When they got back home, Nick and Alice looked at their photos on Alice's laptop.

'Mine are fantastic!' said Alice.

'Yes, but mine are better than yours!' said Nick.

3 Alice and Nick took photos of May in ______________ of the shop.

4 The children looked at the pictures on ______________ when they got home.

5 Nick thought his photos were ______________ Alice's!

Alice sent all their photos to a pop music comic that they both read every week. Nick was really happy when he saw three of his photos and three of Alice's photos in the comic! He sent a text to Alice which said, 'I showed our photos to all of my friends in school this morning. I think we BOTH take fantastic photos!'

'Me too!' Alice said. 'Hooray! Well done, Nick, and well done me!'

6 Nick saw the photos of May in the ____________.

7 Nick was really happy and texted ____________ to say all the photos were fantastic.

Part 6

– 6 questions –

Look and read and write.

Examples

How many islands are there? _two_

What's the weather like? _sunny and windy_

Complete the sentences.

1 There is some ______________ in an old box under the sea.

2 The dolphins are grey, pink and ______________.

Answer the questions.

3 Where are the three shells? ______________

4 Who is jumping into the sea? ______________

Now write two sentences about the picture.

5 ______________

6 ______________

Find the differences

Learning about trees!

Odd one out

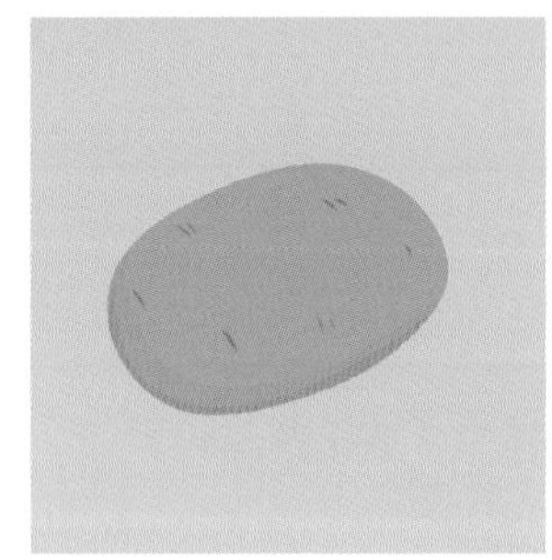

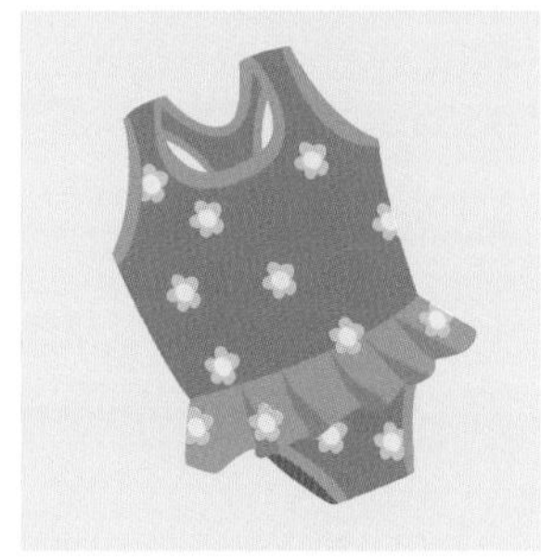

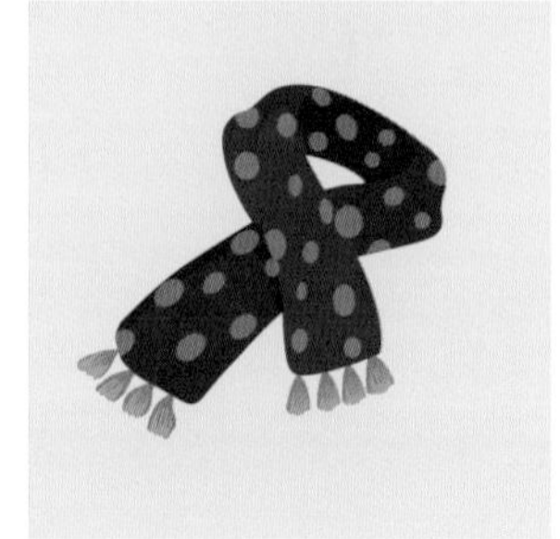

FUN Skills

Home Booklet 4

David Valente

Reading

Read and choose the correct words and write them on the lines.

parrot

balcony

~~jungle~~

city centre

roller skates

milkshake

village

shopping centre

This is a rainforest with many trees, birds and monkeys. **Example** *jungle*

You can see this red, orange, yellow and blue bird in the rainforest. **1** ____________

You can sit or stand here. It is a platform outside a house or flat. **2** ____________

This is a cold, sweet drink with chocolate or fruit that you have in a café. **3** ____________

You can find many buildings, bus stations, car parks, cinemas and a big square here. **4** ____________

This is a small town, often in the countryside. **5** ____________

Fun boost

Find a photo or draw a picture of your favourite place in your village, town or city.

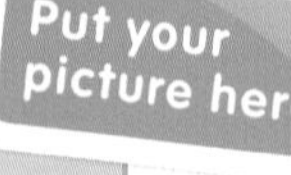

Where is it?

What can you do there?

Why do you like it?

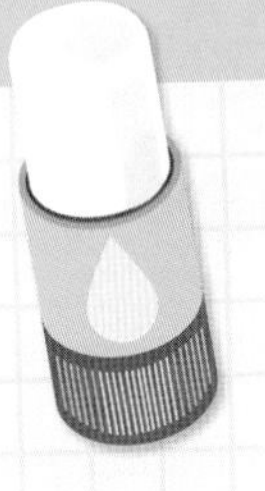

Answer the three questions.

Reading

Read the text and choose the best answer.

Example

Fred: How was your weekend?

Jim: (A:) It was brilliant. I saw someone famous at the shopping centre!

B: I'll ask my aunt and uncle.

C: My bedroom is very cold.

1

Jim: Where did you go on Saturday afternoon, Fred?

Fred: **A:** At three o'clock.

B: I'm staying home all afternoon.

C: I went to the swimming pool.

2

Fred: Did you go sailing with your family on Sunday morning, Jim?

Jim: **A:** I really love the sea.

B: We had a great time at the beach!

C: No, I didn't. I was sick.

3

Jim: What did you eat at the funfair on Friday evening?

Fred: **A:** My favourite food is meatballs and chips.

B: I had noodles and fish and a banana milkshake.

C: My dad can cook a cheese and tomato pizza.

4

Fred: What did you see from the top of the mountain on Saturday?

Jim: **A:** I saw the big waterfall in the forest.

B: I was really brave because it was dangerous.

C: I put on my big boots, a jacket and a helmet.

5

Jim: How much homework did you do at the weekend?

Fred: **A:** I asked the teacher.

B: I didn't do any. I'm really naughty!

C: I can play an exciting computer game.

Fun boost

Choose three of the Fun Skills characters. Tell your family EXCITING things about them. What did they do last weekend?

Reading

Read and choose the correct words and write them on the lines.

Sasha's blog

Don't feed the animals!

On Thursday, I went on a school trip to the zoo with my friends and Mrs Petrov, my English *teacher* . It was exciting to walk around and see all the different animals. We saw dolphins swimming in the pool and kangaroos jumping up and down on the grass.

The giant **1** _______ looked thirsty and hot under the tree because it was a really sunny day with a **2** _______ of about 30°. I **3** _______ my water bottle to give them a drink, but Mrs Petrov said, 'No, don't! It's too dangerous. They could bite your hand!'

Then we went to see the birds. They were many different colours. My favourite ones were the **4** _______ . One was called Peter. He came and sat on my shoulder and asked, 'Sasha, how are you today?' It was VERY funny. My friends and I **5** _______ a lot. We had a brilliant day!

opened

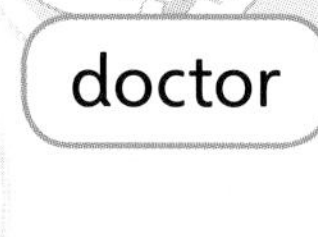

Fun boost

Draw a comic about a trip to the bottom of the sea. Tell the story to your family.

1 What did you take?
2 How did you get there?
3 Who did you go with?
4 What fun things did you do?

Reading

Read and choose the correct words. Write them in the story.

All about sharks

Sharks are big fish that live *in* seas, rivers and lakes around the world. Some sharks live **1** _______ the beach and some live in the open sea. There are more than 500 shark families in the world. Some are smaller **2** _______ a person's hand, but the great white shark is the **3** _______ – more than six metres long!

Many sharks have long noses with very big mouths and heads. Most sharks **4** _______ small fish and have hundreds of teeth. Many people are afraid **5** _______ sharks, but sharks like to eat other fish, not people!

Example

	(**A** in)	**B** on	**C** at
1	**A** down	**B** near	**C** inside
2	**A** because	**B** when	**C** than
3	**A** biggest	**B** big	**C** bigger
4	**A** ate	**B** eaten	**C** eat
5	**A** off	**B** of	**C** out of

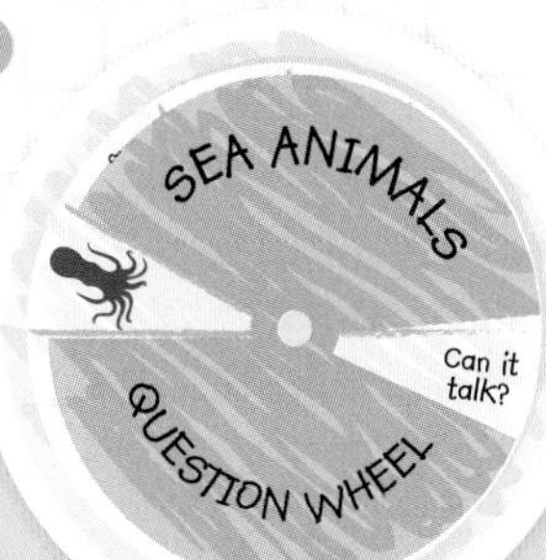

Fun boost

Make a Sea Animals Question Wheel. Ask and answer questions with your family.

1. Draw a circle and make 12 sections. Draw six animals – dolphin, shark, whale, crocodile, jellyfish, octopus – and write six questions: *What does it eat? Where does it live? What does it look like? Does it play? Can it talk? Do you like it?*
2. Draw another circle. Cut out two windows the same size as the sections and add the title: SEA ANIMALS QUESTION WHEEL.
3. Put the two circles together with a paper fastener. Turn the top wheel to play the game.

Reading

Look at the pictures and read the story. Draw and colour the six missing things.

Our island holiday

Last year, I went on a fantastic holiday to a beautiful island with my family. One day, Mum said my sister Eva and I could go sailing. Mum's boat was near ours, but Eva and I were excited to have a boat just for us.

The sun was in the sky and there were birds near our boat. It was great fun! We had some yummy sandwiches for lunch. Eva had an egg and tomato sandwich and I had a cheese sandwich.

When I opened my lunch bag, the boat moved quickly, my sandwich fell in the water and a duck ate it!! 'OH NO!' I said, 'Eva, I'm SO hungry!'

Eva gave me one of her sandwiches because she is the best sister in the world! I was really happy and the duck was, too!

Later that day, when we were at the beach, I bought two big chocolate ice creams, one for Eva and one for me. YUM!

Fun boost

Draw and colour three favourite things in your YUMMY holiday sandwich.

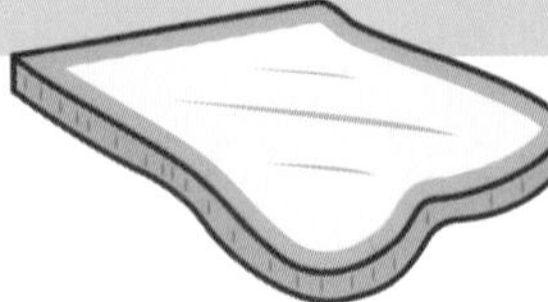

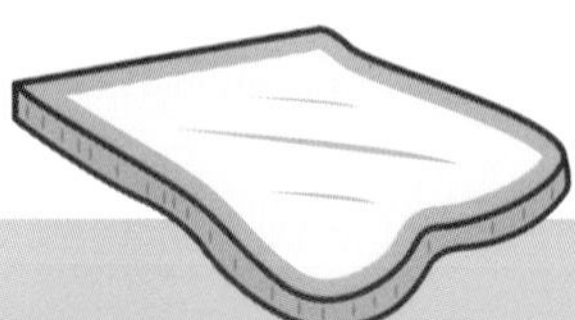

Reading

Read the story. Draw what the children bought.

My birthday!

It was my tenth birthday last week. My friends and I went to a huge shopping centre with my parents. Then we went to a café and ate purple and green cupcakes! We had a great time because we all bought something we really like. Vicky bought a new skateboard, Dan bought a new book from the big bookshop and Eva bought a tennis racket because she plays every week. Tom got some new paints and Peter got a fantastic red guitar. Zoe bought a pair of roller skates. She loves them. The best thing was that my parents bought me some presents for my birthday! I got some orange ice skates and my favourite superhero comic books. What a GREAT day!

Fun boost

Choose three friends or family members. Today is their birthday! Write their names on each present!

Listening

02 **Listen and draw lines. There is one extra person.**

Emma Jack Lily Paul

Charlie Clare Peter

Fun boost

Make a Mix-and-Match flip book.

1 Fold two sheets of A4 paper in half vertically.

2 Cut into three equal sections horizontally.

3 On each page, draw three foods, one in each section.

4 Mix and match the strips. Ask your family.

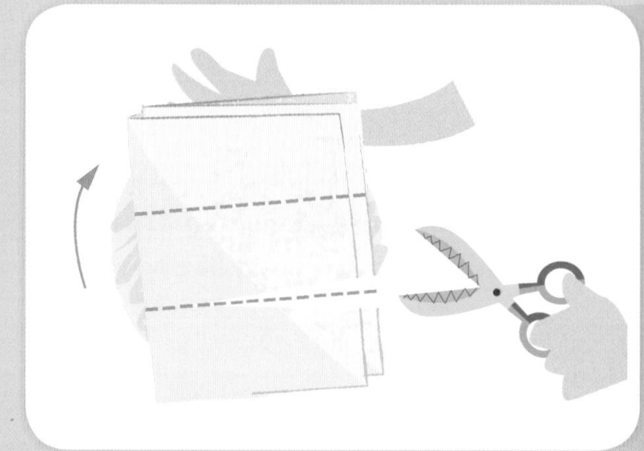

Do you like ________ with ________ and ________ ?

Listening

03 Listen and number. Then complete the sentences.

At the children's hospital

1 Ben has got a ____________ and is thirsty.
2 Paul has got a cough and is very ____________ .
3 Vicky has got an ____________ .
4 Peter is weak and has got a ____________ .
5 Zoe has got a very ____________ toothache.

Fun boost

Choose an illness from the pictures. Mime and ask your family to say the illness.

a cold
an earache
a cough
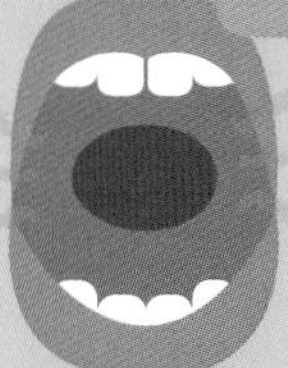
tired
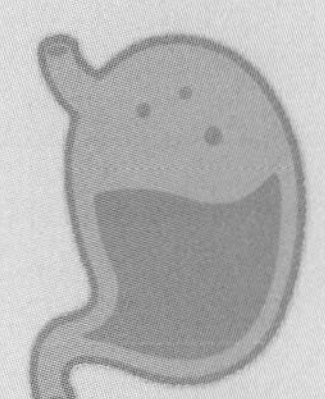
a stomach-ache
a toothache
a temperature

1 Circle the different word.

1 ocean stream moon river
2 land island desert sea
3 woods forest jungle air
4 cave ocean desert hill
5 fire stone hill rock
6 tree forest stream woods
7 waterfall stream land river
8 mountain ocean sea beach

2 Unscramble the words and complete the puzzle.

1 dtrees
2 dlna
3 vcea
4 llhi
5 ria
6 odosw
7 teson
8 mertas
9 rife
10 necoa
11 streof

What's the secret word?

____

1 D E S E R T
2
3
4
5
6
7
8
9
10
11

Sounds and spelling

3 5.04 Listen and repeat. ~~Cross out~~ the *e* if it's silent.

cave June children motorcycle desert zone

4 5.05 Listen and complete the table.

Silent *e*	You say/hear the *e*
stone	environment

DIVERSICUS

1 Read and correct.

1 Mr. and Mrs. Friendly know everything about the trip.

Mr. and Mrs. Friendly don't know anything about the trip.

2 They had to look for a store that sold belts.

______

3 Su-Lin spent an hour writing letters. ______

4 A bear appeared behind a tree. ______

5 They saw lots of amazing websites. ______

2 Complete the text with the simple past form of the verbs.

Jim's Diary

Last week, we [1] went (go) on a school trip to the beach. We [2] ______ (leave) after school on Friday, but we didn't get to the beach until eight o'clock. It [3] ______ (take) five and a half hours because we had to stop on the way. I forgot to take my pajamas, and we had to buy some. Then Su-Lin [4] ______ (find) a post office. She [5] ______ (buy) some stamps and then [6] ______ (begin) to write her postcards. She [7] ______ (spend) an hour writing them!

When we [8] ______ (get) to the beach and began to put up the tents, it was dark. We [9] ______ (put) them up OK, but then Jenny heard a noise. She went outside and saw a kangaroo. She [10] ______ (run) away from it, but she ran into Pablo and together they [11] ______ (fall) and broke the tent. Jenny and Pablo [12] ______ (cut) their knees and elbows, so the next day they both stayed at the beach, and I took care of them.

3 Review the story.

I think the story is **great** / **good** / **OK** / **not very good**.

My favorite character is ______.

My favorite part is when ______.

1 Read and answer.

Oliver loved reading books about brave people who sailed across oceans to find new islands or who stayed for months in dry, hot deserts to study them. One day he read about the first woman who drove across the African desert.

Oliver decided to go on an adventure, too. He went out into the yard and started to think. What did he need for his adventure? Everyone who went on an adventure took food, a backpack, and a map, of course!

He began drawing a map of his yard because he didn't want to get lost. Before he left the house, he told his little sister Zoe about his trip, and she was very excited about it. Oliver decided to let his sister go with him on the adventure. It took them almost five minutes to study the yard. They drew some plants and flowers, but then their mom called them. It was time for lunch. They forgot about the yard and their adventure until the afternoon.

1 What did Oliver love reading? He loved reading books about brave people.
2 What did he decide to do? ______
3 What did he begin drawing? ______
4 What did Oliver and Zoe draw? ______
5 Why did their mom call them? ______

______

2 Look at the code. Write the message.

a	b	c	d	e	f	g	h	i	j	k	l	m
+	÷	∞	▼	±	>	≠	/	√	✖	↓	Δ	♈

n	o	p	q	r	s	t	u	v	w	x	y	z
ч	φ	Ω	Σ	♦	▲	◗	●	○	✚	■	★	□

>♦+ч↓ +ч▼ /+♦♦★ Δ±>◗ + ♈φч◗/ +≠φ. ◗/±★
◗♦+○±Δ±▼ ◗/♦φ●≠/ ◗/± ▼±▲±♦◗, ÷●◗ √◗ ✚+▲
▼√>>√∞●Δ◗. ✚/±ч ◗/±★ >φ●ч▼ + ▲◗♦±+♈,
√◗ ✚+▲ ▼♦★. ◗/±★ /+▼ ◗φ ∞φ♈± ÷+∞↓.

Frank / _ _ _ / _ _ _ _ _ / _ _ _ _ / _ / _ _ _ _ _ / _ _ _ . / _ _ _ _ /
_ _ _ _ _ _ _ _ / _ _ _ _ _ _ _ / _ _ _ / _ _ _ _ _ _ , / _ _ _ / _ _ /
_ _ _ / _ _ _ _ _ _ _ _ _ . / _ _ _ _ / _ _ _ _ / _ _ _ _ _ / _ / _ _ _ _ _ _ ,
/ _ _ / _ _ _ / _ _ _ . / _ _ _ _ / _ _ _ / _ _ / _ _ _ _ / _ _ _ _ .

1 Look at the pictures. Complete the crossword.

Across (→)

3 4 5 7 9

Down (↓)

1 2 6 8

1 TURTLE

2 Look and read. Choose the correct words and write them on the lines. There is one example.

an octopus · a penguin · a camel · insects · eagles

a kangaroo · a turtle · dinosaurs

a bear · a butterfly · a swan

This wild animal might live in a cave. It may be very dangerous. a bear

1 This big bird is white or black, with a very long neck. It lives close to streams or rivers. ________

2 This animal lives in the ocean. It has eight "arms and legs." ________

3 These animals are extinct. They lived long ago, and we can find out about them in museums. ________

4 These small creatures have six legs, and most have wings. A beetle is one of these. ________

5 This green and brown animal is very slow. It has a shell on its back. ________

6 This beautiful insect may have a lot of different colors. It has four wings. ________

7 These very large strong birds live in tall trees or at the tops of mountains. ________

1 Circle the correct words.

1 I like ice skating, but if you don't wear the right clothes, it's (too) / **enough** cold.

2 My sister had a birthday party yesterday, and I couldn't study because there was too **much** / **many** noise.

3 Pets shouldn't go close to the road. It's **too** / **enough** dangerous.

4 I love going to soccer games, but sometimes there are too **much** / **many** people.

5 Last night I went to bed early, and I didn't see the end of the TV show because I was **too** / **enough** tired.

6 My mom doesn't want me to walk through the park when it's dark because she says it isn't safe **too** / **enough**.

7 My dog doesn't enjoy going for long walks. He's **too** / **enough** lazy.

8 My dad didn't let me get into the car with my soccer cleats on. He said they weren't clean **too** / **enough**.

2 Read the text. Choose the correct words and write them on the lines.

All of the deserts in Australia are huge. The desert is one of the [1] driest environments in the world. There isn't enough water, and [2] ________ creatures can't live there because it's [3] ________ hot. There's a lot of sun on the sand, rocks, and stones during the day, and this [4] ________ the temperature go up.

People took camels to Australia 200 years [5] ________ because they can live in this environment. They [6] ________ live without water for several days. Camels are called "ships of the desert."

When people [7] ________ in the desert, they have to be very careful. They should take [8] ________ water with them because it might be a long way to the next town.

1	dry	driest	drier	5	after	ago	last
2	much	most	lot	6	can	can't	don't
3	too	enough	more	7	travels	travel	traveled
4	makes	making	made	8	too	enough	little

1 Are these animals *extinct* or *endangered*?

1 Pandas are endangered.

2 Dinosaurs are ______.

3 Gorillas are ______.

4 Elephants are ______.

5 Dodos are ______.

6 Polar bears are ______.

2 Read the problems that animals have because of humans. Match the problems to the animals.

1 Many animals are endangered because hunters kill them for their beautiful fur, shell, or skin. [a] [b] [ ]

2 Some animals eat plastic in the ocean because they think it is food. Others die because they swim into something made of plastic and can't escape. [ ] [ ]

3 When we build roads or cities, we change the place where animals live. This often means that the animals can't live there any more. [ ]

a

b

c

d

e

3 Read about the Tasmanian tiger and answer the questions.

1 What did the Tasmanian tiger look like?

2 How did it move?

3 Why are Tasmanian tigers (probably) extinct?

4 Sometimes people say "I saw a Tasmanian tiger in the Australian desert!" Do you think this is possible? Why? / Why not?

4 Look at the information about kangaroos and platypuses in the Venn diagram. Talk to a friend about how they are similar and how they are different.

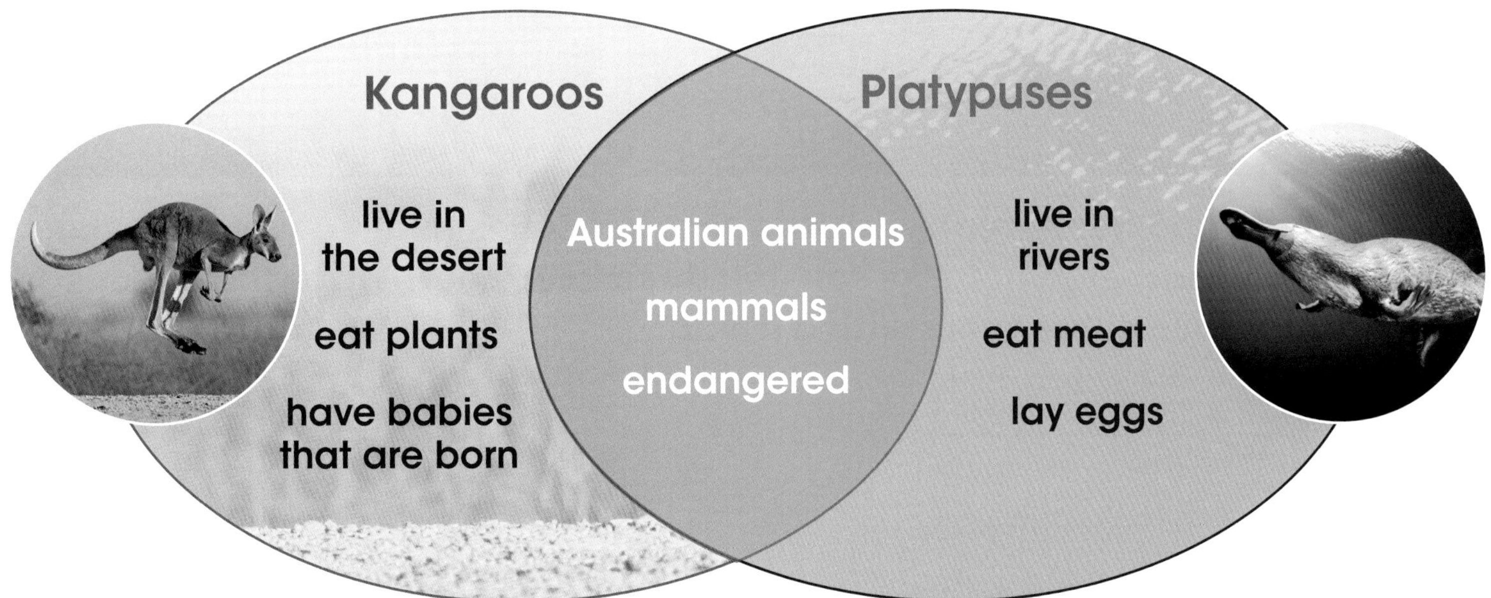

1 Order the events from the poem 1–6.

a [ ] The family visits the Jenolan Caves.
b [ ] Amy's dad loses his glasses.
c [1] Amy and her parents go to Australia.
d [ ] Amy says "Let's go somewhere cold."
e [ ] Amy finds her dad's glasses.
f [ ] They say it's too hot for them.

2 Complete the next verse of the poem with the words in the box.

car ~~caves~~ dad day far long sky way

When we left the nice [1] caves at the end of the [2] ________,
The light from the [3] ________ showed us the [4] ________.
"Were we down there so [5] ________?" my mom said near the [6] ________.
"Hours," my [7] ________ said. "We all walked so [8] ________."

3 Amy and her parents visit the Jenolan Caves to get away from the hot weather. What else can you do to keep cool? Write three ideas and then share them with a friend.

You can go swimming.

____

____

____

4 **Amy is asking her dad some questions about his first trip to Australia. What does Amy's dad say? Read the conversation and choose the best answer. Write a letter (A–H) for each answer. You do not need to use all the letters. There is one example.**

Example

 **Amy:** Did you go to Australia when you were young, Dad?

 **Dad:** H

Questions

1 **Amy:** How long were you there?

 **Dad:** ______

2 **Amy:** Really? And who did you go with?

 **Dad:** ______

3 **Amy:** Where did you stay?

 **Dad:** ______

4 **Amy:** That's great. And what did you do there?

 **Dad:** ______

5 **Amy:** Did you enjoy it?

 **Dad:** ______

A Oh, for about five weeks.

B What? Tom didn't go!

C Yes, I did. Tom loved it, too.

D My friend Tom – we had a great time!

E You're welcome! Please stay with us.

F Lots of things – one was camel riding!

G Tom's uncle lives in a large house in Sydney. We stayed with him for a few weeks.

H Yes, I did! I was only 21 when I went there. **(example)**

1 5.06 **Listen and write. There is one example.**

The World of Animals Museum

	A class visit from:	___Castle___ School
1	Date of visit:	May ______ rd
2	Student's name:	______ Swan
3	Favorite thing:	______
4	Café:	had ______ to drink
5	Bought a book about:	______

1 Read the instructions. Play the game.

INSTRUCTIONS

Choose four pictures. Write the words in your notebook. You need to collect these.

Roll the dice and move.

Collect your four words. Check (✓) them in your notebook.

On green spaces, say the word.

On ? spaces, answer the question on the card.

On orange spaces, say and spell the past tense of the verb.

Review Units 1–2

Do you have a birthday on January 1st?

1 Ask people in your class and write their names.

Find someone who:

- ______ has a birthday on January 1st.
- ______ went skiing in February.
- ______ has a birthday in May.
- ______ went camping in July.
- ______ swam in the ocean in August.
- ______ went for a walk in the woods in October.

2 What did you find out about the class?

Someone has a birthday on January 1st.

3 Read the email. How many questions does Katy ask? ______

Hello!

Hi William!

How are you? Thank you so much for your email. I just got home from school. We had an amazing week. It was science week at school, and we found out lots of interesting information about the environment and other things.

Last Monday, we went to the science museum. We heard about wild animals like turtles and eagles. We then explored the insect section, which was the best! We saw a lot of butterflies and beetles, but we didn't have enough time to see them all. There were too many! We might go again in January when you come and visit, if you want.

Then two days ago, on September 8th, we went to some woods near the stream. Do you remember we walked there last June? We slept overnight in a tent. It was my first time camping, and I forgot to bring my flashlight! We explored some caves and found out how to make a fire with wood and stones. I couldn't do it, but someone else in my class could.

Did you go on a school trip yet this year? Please write soon and tell me about it!

Love

Katy

4 Read Katy's email again. Answer the questions.

1 Why did Katy have an amazing week? Because it's been science week at school.
2 What did Katy find out? ______
3 Which section did Katy enjoy the most? ______
4 Did Katy see everything she wanted to see in the museum? ______
5 When might Katy go again? ______
6 Where did Katy go on September 8th? ______
7 Did William go there before? ______
8 What did she forget to take? ______

5 Plan a reply to Katy's email. Think about your last school trip.

- Where did you go? Look at the pictures and check (✓).

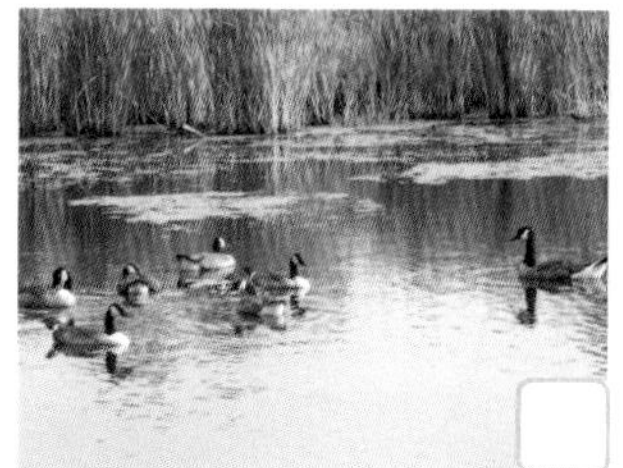

- What date did you go? ______
- What did you see? ______
- What did you learn about? ______
- What did you like the best? ______

6 Write your email. Use your notes from Activity 5.

CHECK!
Did you answer all the questions in Activity 5?
Did you use the format of an email?
Did you use the correct vocabulary and grammar?
Is your spelling correct?

Let's celebrate!

DIVERSICUS

My unit goals

- I want to ______________________
- To do this, I will ______________________
- I will say and write ____ new words.

My mission diary

How was it? Draw a face.

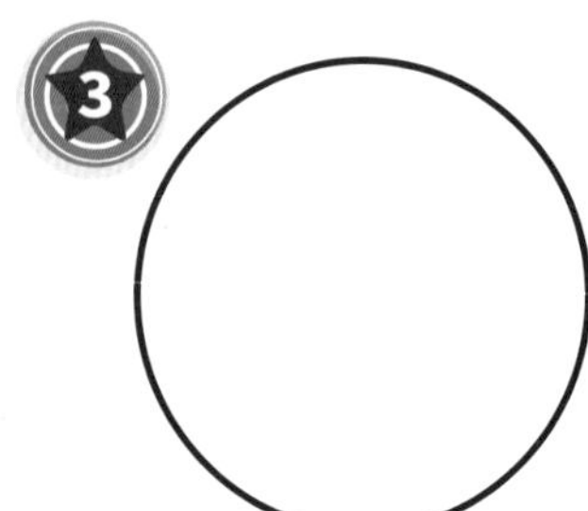

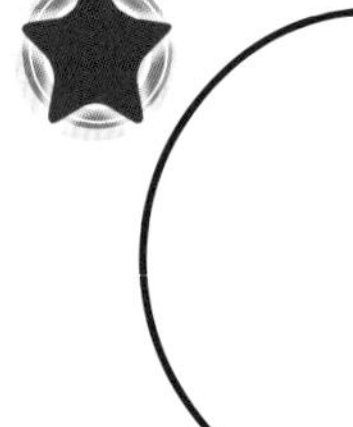

My favorite stage:

____

I can talk about games and competitions. ☐

I can talk about experiences using the present perfect. ☐

I can talk about festivals and music. ☐

I can understand information to match pictures. ☐

I completed Level 4 Unit 3. ☑

Go to page 134 and add to your word stack!

1 Read and complete the sentences.

1 People drive fast in speed cars to win a ___race___ .
2 ______________ is a board game with a king and queen.
3 ______________ is a popular ball game on the beach.
4 A ______________ is someone who wins.
5 A ______________ is a group of players who play together.
6 A ______________ is a competition with questions.
7 He won first ______________ in the painting competition.
8 Can I help you with that crossword ______________ ? I love them!
9 I didn't enjoy that soccer ______________ . The teams didn't play well.

2 Read and match. Then check your answers and spelling in Activity 1.

1 Which team won the volleyball game?
2 How did she finish the puzzle so quickly?
3 Did he win a prize for chess?
4 Why was he unhappy about the race?
5 Who was the winner of the quiz?

a No, it was for drawing.
b The yellow team did.
c Because he didn't win it.
d Sophia – she knows a lot!
e Her dad helped her.

Sounds and spelling

3 5.07 Listen and repeat. Write the words in the correct box.

b		v	
October	______	______	______
______	______	______	______
______	______	______	______

1 Choose words from the box to complete the sentences. You do not need to use all the words.

castle	chess	costume	~~excellent~~	ice creams	Ivan	Jenny	Jim	king	lucky	plane	queen	sofa	volleyball	weekend

1 Su-Lin says "Excellent! Good job!" to Jenny and Pablo.
2 Su-Lin and Jim are playing ________.
3 Su-Lin can take Jim's ________ now, so he's lost the game.
4 ________'s gone to get the volleyball.
5 How many ________ did Ivan buy?
6 There were four people on the ________ that Ivan lifted.
7 Su-Lin's seen a picture of Ivan with the ________.
8 Next ________, it's Rio Carnival.
9 Ivan's going to wear a king ________.
10 ________ lifts a castle, but it's from the game.

2 Read and correct.

1 Jenny and Pablo have won the ~~tennis~~ game. volleyball
2 When someone can take your queen, you lose a game of chess. ________
3 The ball was above the ice-cream cart. ________
4 Ivan's bought four ice-creams cones. ________
5 Ivan's ice-cream cone is the smallest one. ________
6 Rio Carnival's the biggest birthday party in the world. ________
7 Ivan says he's going to be the king of the carnival. ________
8 Ivan thinks everyone can lift a castle. ________

3 Review the story.

I think the story is **great** / **good** / **OK** / **not very good**.
My favorite character is ________.
My favorite part is when ________________.

1 Read the information. Complete the diagram with names A–D and positive (+) or negative (–) sentences in the present perfect.

Four children are sitting at a table. There are three girls and one boy, called Harry. The boy's sitting opposite Katy. They're talking about the start of this school year. What have they done?

Betty's sitting between Harry and Katy. Betty's won three volleyball games.

Harry hasn't eaten pizza, but he's cooked pasta for his parents.

The child opposite Holly hasn't lost a game of chess.

A girl next to Katy hasn't drunk coffee, but she's seen two eagles.

The girl who's made two new friends hasn't been to the theater.

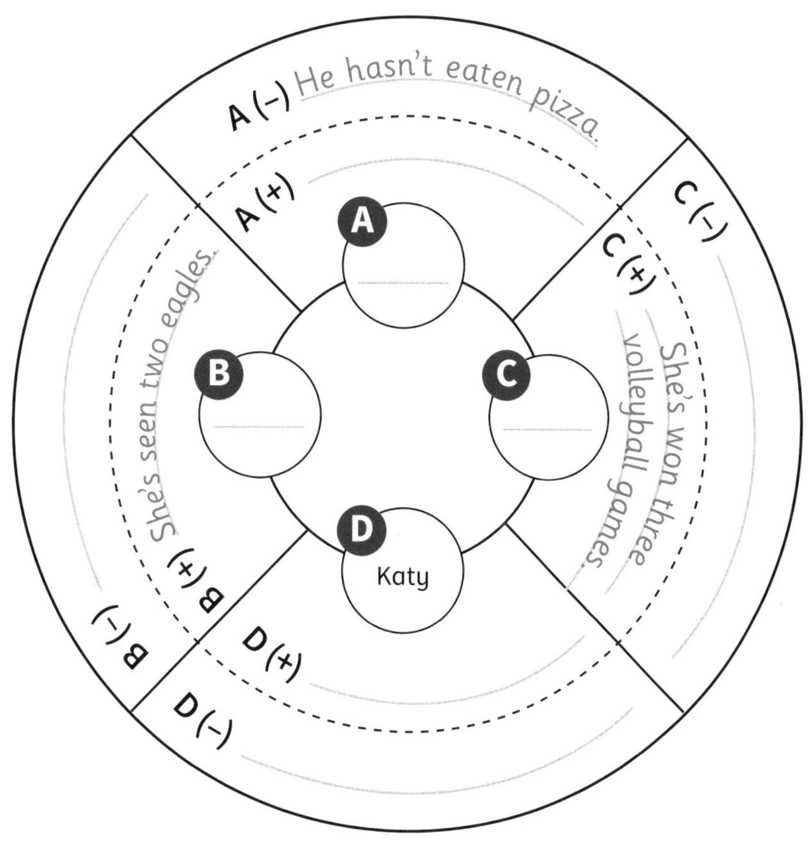

2 Ask and answer with a partner.

~~be~~ camel chess ~~competition~~ crossword puzzle desert
do highway play prize race run see travel walk win

Have you ever been in a competition?

Yes, I have. No, I haven't.

1 Write the words in the correct picture.

badminton ~~chess~~ ~~concert~~ ~~drum~~ golf guitar game musician
piano ~~prize~~ race rock music stage violin volleyball winner

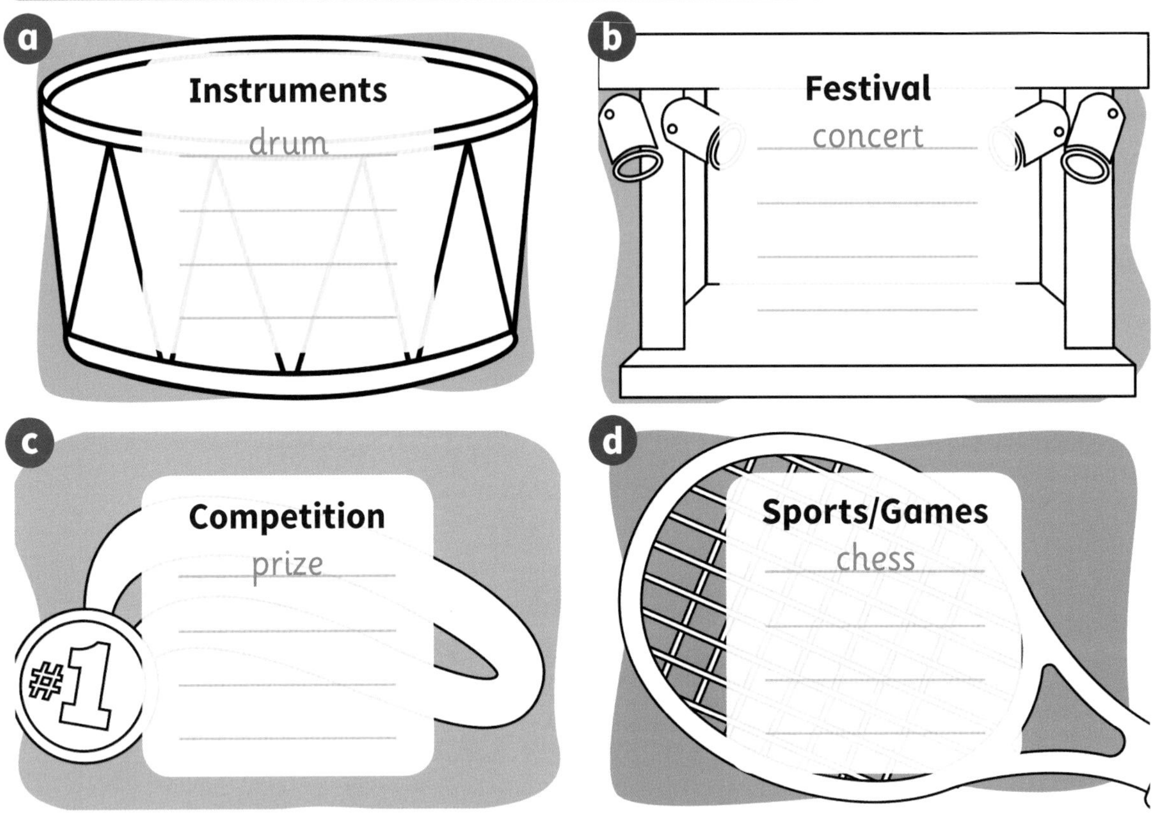

2 Read and circle the correct words.

Last weekend, my parents took me to a music [1]**festival** / **traffic** in a field near our town. It was great. There was a small [2]**drum** / **stage** outside, where the rock musicians played. The [3]**musician** / **waiter** who played the drums was amazing. He played really [4]**better** / **well**, and the singer sang [5]**noisy** / **loudly** because it was rock music. Dad didn't like the [6]**songs** / **streams** much. He thought they were too noisy, and that the musicians didn't know how to play their [7]**instruments** / **stones**, but Mom loved the [8]**concert** / **game**. She danced all evening, and so did I!

3 Write about a festival in your country.

- Where is it?
- When is it?
- What can you see and do?

1 Put the words in order. Write the sentences.

1 (the email) (I haven't) (yet.) (sent him)
I haven't sent him the email yet.

2 (just) (Frank's grandma.) (visited) (We've)

3 (homework for tomorrow.) (already) (I've) (done all my)

4 (washed) (She's) (her hair.) (just)

5 (you been) (yet?) (Have) (to the dentist)

6 (yet.) (He hasn't) (breakfast) (finished)

7 (already) (They've) (for lunch.) (bought the food)

8 (the picture) (taken) (yet?) (Has she)

2 Read the postcard and write the missing words.

I've [1] just bought this postcard to tell you about my vacation in Brazil! I've already done a lot of amazing things. I've [2] ______ volleyball on the beach, and I've [3] ______ pineapple juice with coconut milk. Yesterday evening, we went to the biggest festival that I've ever seen and it was fantastic. There [4] ______ a lot of dancers and musicians. The dancers wore necklaces and colorful [5] ______ with feathers. The musicians played different [6] ______ on their instruments.

1 Answer the questions about the history of the guitar.

1 Where can you see the oldest instrument?

____

2 What did the traveling singers play hundreds of years ago?

____

3 When and where did people use guitars with six strings for the first time?

____

4 Who designed the classical guitar?

____

5 What's different about the sound of an electric guitar?

____

2 Match the descriptions to the pictures. Write the numbers.

1 This instrument always had more strings than a guitar.

2 You need electricity to play this guitar.

3 This is the design of today's classical guitars.

4 It is possible that Queen Hatshepsut listened to this instrument.

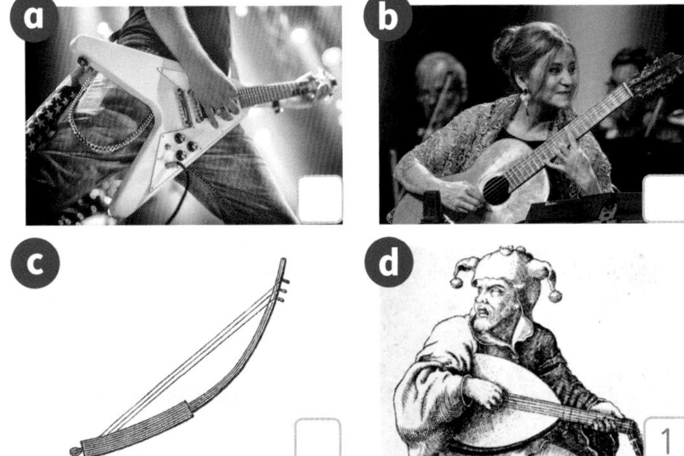

3 What is your favorite musical instrument? Look for a picture of the first instrument and a picture of it today.

My favorite instrument is _______________.

People played it for the first time in _______________.

4 Answer the questions about Carnival in Brazil.

1 When do they celebrate Carnival?

2 How do they celebrate it?

3 What is the name of the music you can hear everywhere?

4 Why do you think this music is so popular?

5 Write about how you celebrate Carnival in your country.

- Do you celebrate at home or at school?
- Do you wear a costume?
- Is there a party or a parade?

6 How did you make your musical instrument? Write about it and draw a picture.

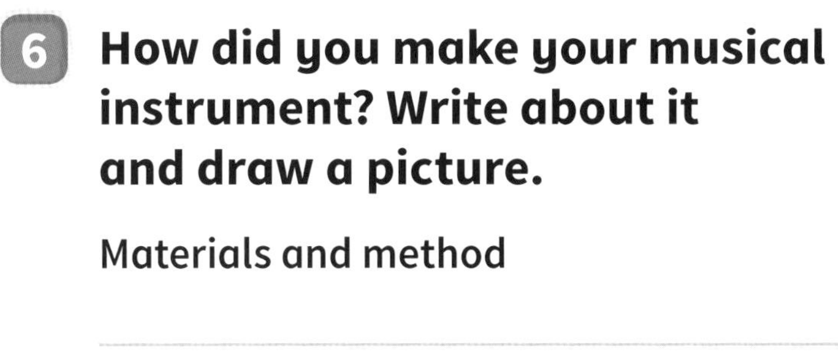

Materials and method

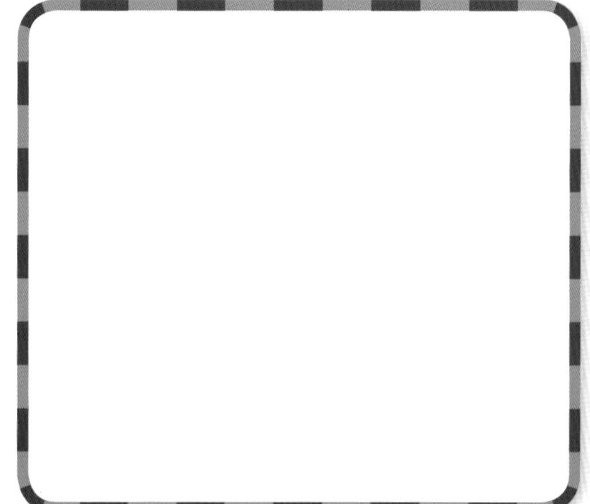

1 Order the events from Rebeca's story.

a

☐ She met the girls' soccer team.

b

☐ They won an important competition.

c

☐ The coach chose her for the girls' team.

d

1 She played soccer with the boys in school.

e

☐ She wants to travel to different countries.

f

☐ She practiced with her dad and brother.

2 Answer the questions about Rebeca.

1 Where is she from? ______________________

2 What does her mom think about soccer? ______________________

3 What did the boys think at first about playing with her? ______________________

____

4 How long did she practice with her dad and brother? ______________________

____

5 Why does she want to learn to speak English? ______________________

____

3 What do you want to be really good at? How are you going to work hard at it?

____

____

4 5.08 Listen and write. There is one example.

Last year's WINNERS

Soccer Festival

1	When?	from ______ to July 30th
2	Where / last game?	______ Stadium
3	How many teams?	______
4	Who is the festival for?	______ under 17
5	The last day to enter:	______ 30th by midnight

1 5.09 **Where did Michael get each of these things? Listen and write a letter in each box. There is one example.**

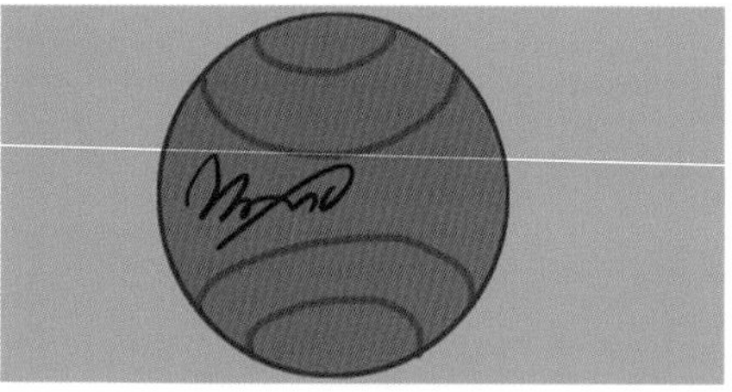

D Volleyball

☐ Book

☐ Guitar

☐ Turtle

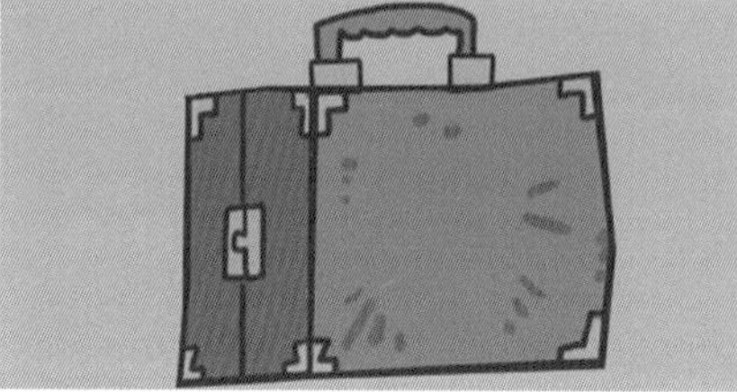

☐ Suitcase

☐ Ticket

A 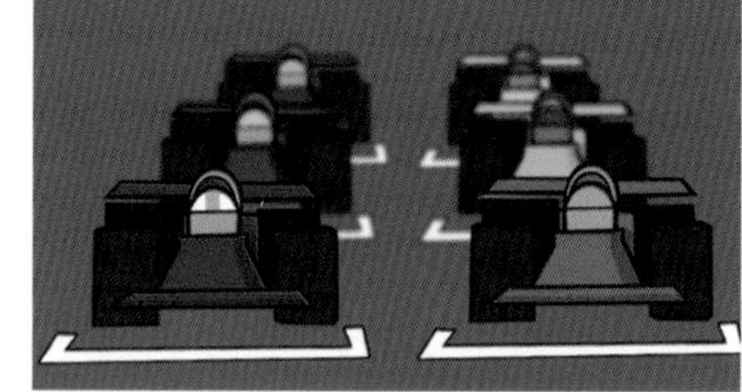

B 

C 

D 

E 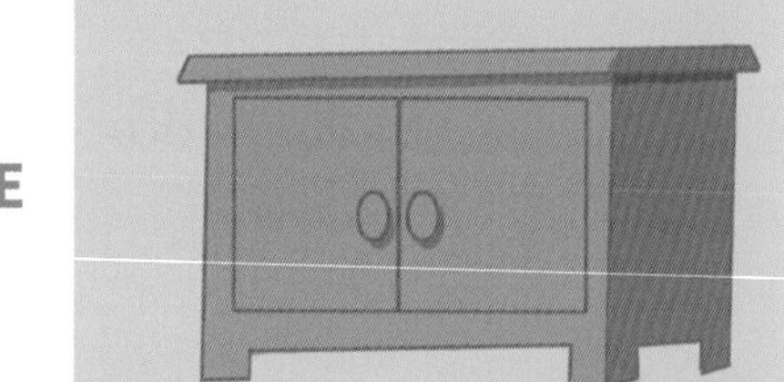

F 

G 

H 

1 Read the instructions. Play the game.

FINISH	[picture]	?	You've stopped to go to a pop concert. Move back 5 spaces.	?	have
put	?	[picture]	be	[picture]	?
?	do	[picture]	You went to bed late before the game. Move back 3 spaces.	?	You've just taken your friend's queen at chess. Take another turn.
You're trying hard to win the game. Move forward 4 spaces.	[picture]	?	see	[picture]	?
go	?	You haven't finished the crossword puzzle. Miss a turn.	[picture]	lose	[picture]
START	[picture]	win	?	You've won your race. Move forward 2 spaces.	[picture]

INSTRUCTIONS

Roll the dice and move across the board.

On **green** spaces, say the word.

On **?** spaces, answer the question on the card.

On **purple** spaces, say and spell the past participle of the verb.

4 Time of our lives

My unit goals

- I want to ______________________________
- To do this, I will ______________________________
- I will say and write ____ new words.

My mission diary

How was it? Draw a face.

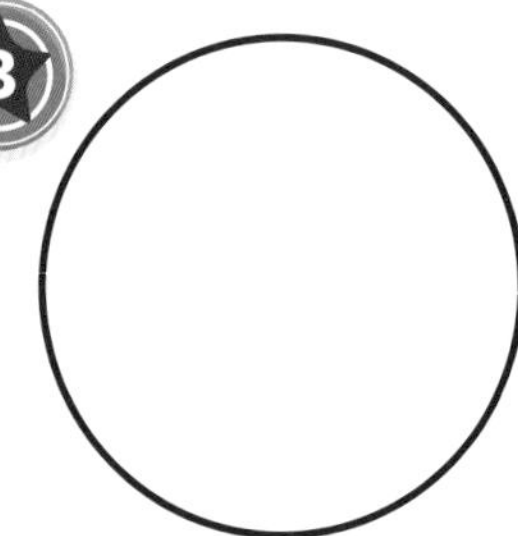

My favorite stage:

- I can talk about what was happening in the past. ☐
- I can tell the time. ☐
- I can ask and answer questions with *How long*, *for*, and *since*. ☐
- I can listen for information to choose the correct answer. ☐
- I completed Level 4 Unit 4. ☑

Go to page 134 and add to your word stack!

1 Match. Write the verbs.

1 m make ed
m meet arch

2 fe ______ fer
fe ______ ~~ake~~

3 se ______ alk
se ______ pair

4 pre ______ ad
pre ______ ~~eet~~

5 t ______ nd
t ______ pare

6 re ______ ry
re ______ el

2 Complete the sentences with the words in the box.

clean	took care of	make sure	make	~~picked up~~	repair

1 Mom's just picked up Grandma from the station.
2 Last weekend, my older cousin ______ me.
3 My dad's going to ______ my bike.
4 Who's going to ______ lunch today? I'm really hungry!
5 Michael, when are you going to ______ your bedroom?
6 Please ______ you write your names at the top of the test.

Sounds and spelling

3 5.10 Listen and repeat. Circle the *ee* sound.

m(ee)t messy lucky wheel

4 Read and write the missing words.

1 Is it safe to climb that _ _ _ _ in your yard?
2 I write in my _ _ _ _ _ every day.
3 Be quiet, please! You're very _ _ _ _ _ today!

DIVERSICUS

1 Read and answer.

1 What did the Friendly family hit on the jungle path? They hit a hole.

2 How was Mr. Friendly driving? ______

3 When did the bus arrive? ______

4 What was Mrs. Friendly doing on the bus? ______

5 Who's going to help Mr. Friendly in the jungle? ______

6 What are Jim and Jenny going to do now? ______

2 Complete the text with the words in the box.

driving	jungle	make	dirt road	pleased	was	while	~~worried~~

Su-Lin's Diary

Yesterday, everyone was [1] worried because the Friendly family got to Diversicus late. It was time to [2] ______ lunch, but they were having an adventure in the [3] ______! While Jim and Jenny were having this adventure, we had to study for a test. I didn't mind because I like studying, but Pablo wasn't very [4] ______.

This is what happened. They were driving along a [5] ______ in the jungle when they had a problem. Mr. Friendly wasn't going fast – he was [6] ______ carefully – but he hit a hole and a tire blew. They had to change the tire. A bus came [7] ______ they were repairing the tire, so they got on. On the bus, everyone [8] ______ singing, and they were having a great time. When they got here, Mr. Friendly went back to the jungle with Marc to get their car. Jim and Jenny's mom said they had to study for the test. We're all going to do it tomorrow. No problem – I'm ready!

3 Review the story.

I think the story is **great** / **good** / **OK** / **not very good**.

My favorite character is ______.

My favorite part is when ______.

1 Read and match.

1	I was cleaning my room when	a	Grandma phoned her.
2	While they were playing	b	when the train left.
3	I was taking care of my little brother	c	we saw our math teacher.
4	He was making lunch when	d	mom when Dad called me.
5	While Mom was repairing my bike,	e	he cut his finger.
6	While we were walking to school,	f	when he fell.
7	I was getting a book for my	g	I found my mom's bracelet.
8	They were running into the station	h	volleyball, it started to rain.

2 Look at the three pictures. Answer the questions about the first picture.

Think of a name for the older boy. ....

Think of a name for the younger boy. ....

Where were they? ....

Who were they with? ....

What were they doing? ....

Now write 20 or more words about the story.

....

....

....

....

1 Read and match. Write the numbers.

1 Yesterday, Richard woke up at five after nine.

2 He took a shower at twenty after nine.

3 He ate cereal for breakfast at a quarter to ten.

4 He was going to work on the bus when he met George at ten after ten.

5 He sent Holly a message at twenty to one.

6 Holly and Richard had lunch together at five to one.

7 Richard finished work at twenty-five after six.

8 At home, he made dinner at a quarter to eight.

a ☐

b  ☐

c  ☐

d  ☐

e 1

f  ☐

g  ☐

h  ☐

2 Look at the clocks and write the times.

1 It's twenty-five after two.

2  ______________

3  ______________

4  ______________

3 Write five times. Work with a friend. Say what you do at those times.

You wrote twenty to eight. What do you do at that time?

I have breakfast at twenty to eight.

1 Complete the sentences with *for* or *since*.

1 She's lived here ___for___ six months.
2 I haven't been to school ______ June 21st.
3 We've studied English ______ four years.
4 I've known my teacher ______ September.
5 She hasn't seen me ______ Monday.
6 I've had this book ______ four months.
7 They've stayed in that hotel ______ two days.
8 Mrs. Black has taught this class ______ January 15th.
9 He's been in that classroom ______ twenty-five after three.

2 Complete the interview with the questions in the box.

~~Are you married?~~ Have you ever been to New York? Have you played at many festivals? How long have you had that guitar? How long have you lived in London? How long have you played the guitar? Have you studied the guitar? How long have you been married?

Interview with BRUNO JUPITER

Yesterday, I spoke to Bruno Jupiter about his life as a musician. First, a personal question, Bruno.

1 Are you married?
Yes, I am. My wife's name is Sarah.

2 ______
I've been married for five years.

3 ______
No, I haven't. I've never studied the guitar with a teacher. I taught myself.

4 ______
I've played it since I was a boy.

5 ______
This is my favorite guitar. I've had it since I was 18.

6 ______
Yes, lots – in many different countries!

7 ______
Yes, I have. I've stayed in New York twice.

8 ______
I've lived in London for three years.

1 Label the map with the words in the box.

a line of latitude ~~a line of longitude~~ the equator the Greenwich Meridian

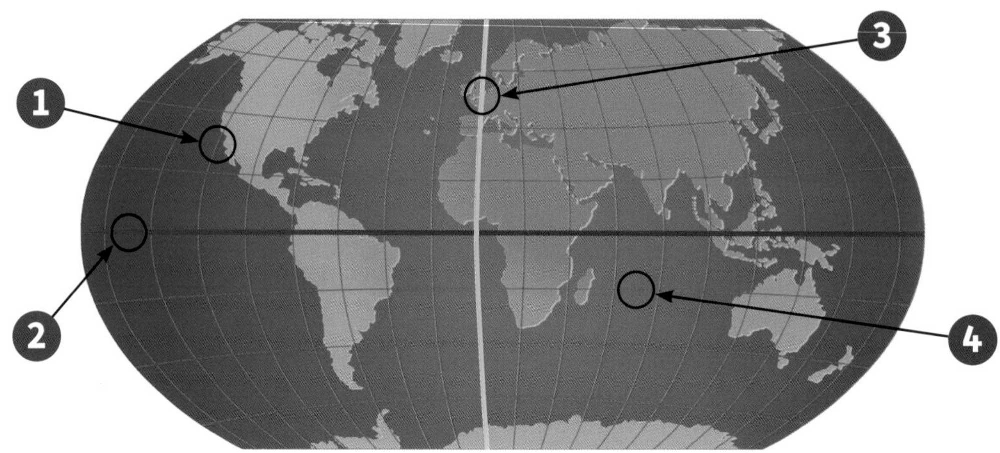

1 a line of longitude
2 ______
3 ______
4 ______

2 Match to make sentences.

1	Lines of longitude	a	in different time zones.
2	Lines of latitude	b	go around Earth.
3	The Greenwich Meridian	c	go up and down Earth.
4	Some larger countries	d	passes through London.
5	Different countries are	e	have three or more time zones.

3 Imagine that it is 8:00 in the morning. Answer the questions.

1 You're at home. What are you doing? ______
2 What time is it now in London? ______
3 What do you think children are doing there? ______

4 Find out which countries the Greenwich Meridian passes through. Use the Internet to help you.

______

______

5 How do you celebrate New Year's Eve in your country?

Do you eat any special food? What is it?

____

Are there any special traditions, like putting an onion on your door?

____

6 Complete the fact file about Colombia. Use the Internet to help you.

Name: Colombia

Continent: ____________________

Capital city: ____________________

Language: ____________________

Time zone: ____________________

Size: ____________________ square kilometers

Number of inhabitants: ____________________

Borders with:

Peru, ____________________

Oceans/Seas:

____

Mountains:

____

1 Look at the story and the pictures to complete the sentences.

1 We know Mother Mountain lives in the forest because she wears ______________________ ______________________.

2 Mother Mountain takes care of the forest, so the animals know ______________________ ______________________.

3 We think the bear seemed to be saying "Thank you, Mother Mountain" because ______________________ ______________________.

4 The men promised never to cut down trees or hurt animals because ______________________ ______________________.

2 Work with a friend. Complete the paragraph about another Mother Mountain legend. Use the picture to help you.

A few minutes later, a woman came to a river in the forest. She had a big bag of trash. She lifted up the bag and threw it into the river. ______________________
____
____
____

3 5.11 **Listen, color, and write. There is one example.**

1 5.12 Listen and check (✓) the box. There is one example.

What was Katy's first job?

 A ☐

 B ☐

 C ☑

1 What doesn't she like about her job now?

 A ☐

 B ☐

 C ☐

2 What is the easiest thing about this job?

 A ☐

 B ☐

 C ☐

3 Which game are they going to play?

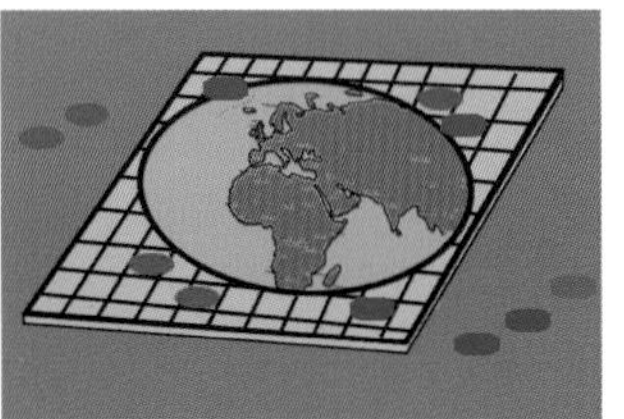 A ☐

 B ☐

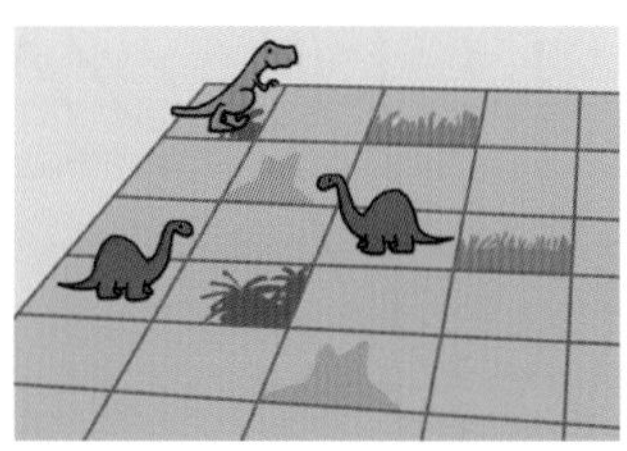 C ☐

4 What is Katy going to do in August?

 A ☐

 B ☐

 C ☐

5 How is she going to travel there?

 A ☐

 B ☐

 C ☐

1 Read the instructions. Play the game.

FINISH

START

INSTRUCTIONS

Roll the dice and move across the board.

On green spaces, say the word.

On orange spaces, say what the people were doing.

On purple spaces, say the time.

On ? spaces, answer the question on the card.

Go up the ladder. Go down the rope.

Review • • • • Units 3–4

1 Work with a partner. Student A chooses a person. Student B asks questions to find out who it is.

Ben

Sophia

Holly

Harry

Emma

Frank

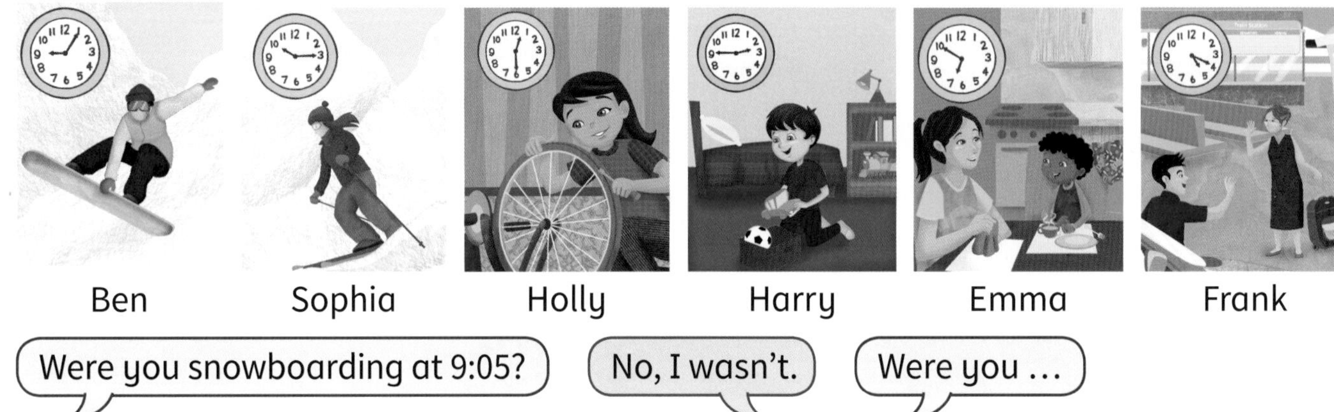

Were you snowboarding at 9:05?

No, I wasn't.

Were you …

2 Read the interview. Then cover the text and try to remember all the things Sara has done.

Amy: Hi Sara. I need to write a report about an adventurous person. Could I ask you some questions? You're the most adventurous person I know.

Sara: Really? You think I'm adventurous? Yes, please go ahead!

Amy: Have you ever played volleyball at the beach?

Sara: Yes! I was on the school beach volleyball team. We won first prize in the city competition.

Amy: Have you ever camped in the woods?

Sara: Yes, I've camped in the woods lots of times. I love sleeping under the stars.

Amy: Have you ever slept overnight in a cave?

Sara: No, I haven't. I'm too scared of bears, but I've explored inside a cave. It was very dark. I needed my flashlight.

Amy: Have you ever climbed a mountain?

Sara: Yes, I have. I climbed Mt. Fuji in Japan. I watched the sunrise from on top of the mountain. It was amazing.

Amy: Thanks for answering my questions, Sara. You sure have done a lot of adventurous things!

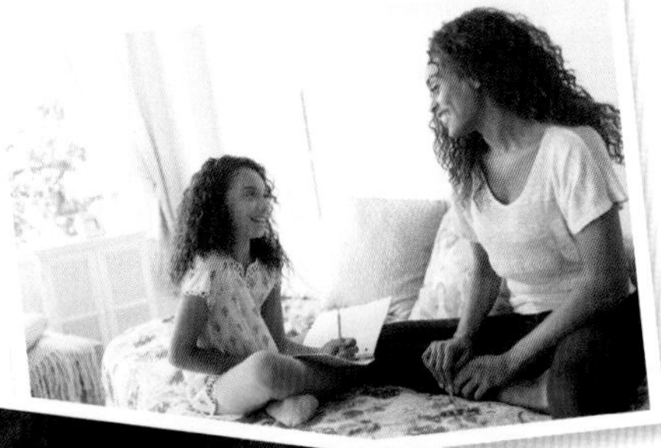

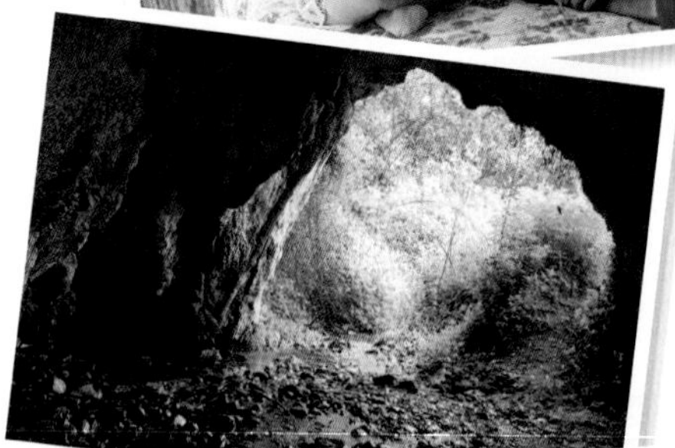

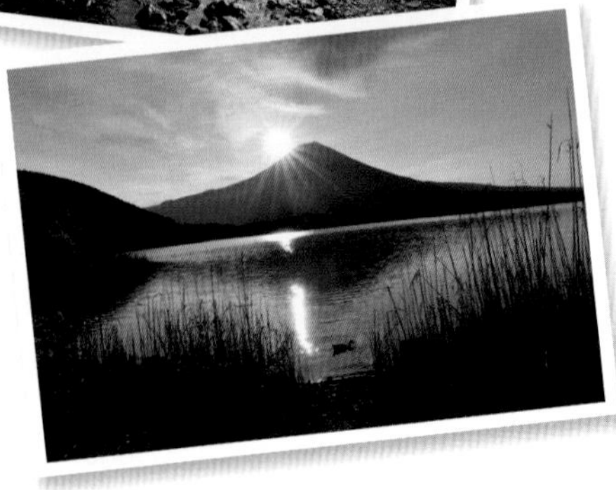

3 Read Amy's interview again. Correct the sentences

1 Sara has won first prize in a chess competition.

____

2 Sara has camped in the wood a few times.

____

3 Sara has slept overnight in a cave.

____

4 Sara has climbed Mt. Everest in Nepal.

____

4 Plan your own interview for an adventurous person. Think of four questions and then ask and answer.

1 ______________________________?

______________________________.

2 ______________________________?

______________________________.

3 ______________________________?

______________________________.

4 ______________________________?

______________________________.

CHECK!
Have you started your questions with *Have you ever …* ?
Have you used the format of an interview?
Have you used the correct vocabulary and grammar?
Is your spelling correct?

Let it snow!

My unit goals

- I want to ______________________
- To do this, I will ______________________
- I will say and write ____ new words.

My mission diary

How was it? Draw a face.

My favorite stage:

DIVERSICUS

- I can name the seasons and different types of weather. ☐
- I can make offers to help people. ☐
- I can talk about why something happens. ☐
- I can ask and answer questions to find out information. ☐
- I completed Level 4 Unit 5. ☑

Go to page 134 and add to your word stack!

1 Read the sentences. Complete the crossword.

Across (→)

2 When clouds are very low and you can't see much, there's …
4 This is the hottest season.
5 This is the coldest season.
6 When water is at a temperature of 0°C, it changes into …
7 There was a lot of fog. It was very …

Down (↓)

1 When there's a … with a lot of wind and rain, the sea is very dangerous.
3 This is the opposite of cool.
4 This the season after winter.
7 This is the season before winter.

1 S T O R M

2 In each group, join three words from a word family with a line.

1

spring	get	bring
send	early	repair
~~fall~~	~~winter~~	~~summer~~

2

festival	Thursday	Wednesday
January	Monday	concert
Friday	song	Saturday

3

quarter	warm	fog
foggy	late	ice
sunny	beetle	storm

4

February	December	March
bottle	can	April
May	might	bowl

Sounds and spelling

3 5.13 Listen and repeat. Underline the stressed syllable in each word.

summer winter November winner calendar passenger doctor

4 Think of other words that end with these letters and follow the same stress patterns.

DIVERSICUS

1 Read and write *yes* or *no*.

1 Rose has given the children a group project to do. no
2 Jenny and Pablo have chosen the easiest ones. ______
3 They have wi-fi. ______
4 There's an excellent bookstore in the museum. ______
5 Su-Lin will find out about the environment. ______
6 Ivan says he can eat more than a kangaroo. ______

2 Read the text. Choose the right words and write them on the lines.

Pablo's Diary

OK, I wasn't very nice yesterday, but I [1] won't be mean again. Yesterday morning, Dad gave us a project on animals [2] ______ Patagonia. Jenny and I used the pictures and video that we took [3] ______ we were on the ship, but Jim and Su-Lin had to use books because we don't have wi-fi. I laughed at Jim about using books. (Not my best moment …)
Su-Lin had a great idea about going to the "End of the World Museum." Jenny and I thought we [4] ______ go, but Su-Lin was really kind and asked [5] ______ to go, too!
In the end, Jenny and I helped Jim and Su-Lin and we had time to go for a nice lunch. It was a great day out – and I was so terrible in the morning! I'll never [6] ______ at my friends' problems again.

1	won't	isn't	didn't
2	for	on	in
3	who	when	where
4	haven't	weren't	couldn't
5	us	we	our
6	laughed	laugh	laughing

3 Review the story.

I think the story is **great** / **good** / **OK** / **not very good**.

My favorite character is ______.

My favorite part is when ______.

1 Put the words in order. Write the sentences.

1 (worry Mom, I'll) (Don't) (after lunch.) (clean my bedroom)
Don't worry Mom, I'll clean my bedroom after lunch.

2 (morning, please?) (my bike this) (you repair) (Dad, will)

3 (we get back) (lunch when) (We'll make) (from town.)

4 (I'll) (blanket for) (you, Grandma.) (get a)

5 (message today because) (send us a) (he's lost his phone.) (He won't)

6 (the museum.) (They'll) (square behind) (meet us in the)

7 (after my dog) (Who'll look) (the store?) (while I go into)

8 (late for) (I hope we) (the movie.) (won't be)

2 Complete the conversations with the sentences in the box.

I'll call the doctor.	I'll give him some water.
I'll make you a snack.	I'm not sure. I'll text him.

1 Order the letters. Complete the puzzle.

1 womanns
2 solablnw
3 cpkteo
4 retwin
5 ownrabdos
6 vgleo
7 lafl
8 mursem
9 dsel
10 giksin
11 dpon
12 gripsn

1 S N O W M A N
2
3
4
5
6
7
8
9
10
11
12

What's the secret word? ______________

2 Look and read. Choose the correct words and write them on the lines. There is one example.

snowmen a sled foggy **skiing** gloves summer

snowballs pockets a snowboard a pond a storm fall

This sport may sometimes be dangerous because it's fast. You go down a mountain with snow. skiing

1 This season is the hottest and sunniest. ______________
2 We make these outside. They have a big body and a head. ______________
3 We wear these on our hands to keep them warm. ______________
4 We have these on our clothes. We put things in them. ______________
5 When there's a lot of snow, we can sit on this to go down a hill fast.
____
6 This is like a lake, but smaller. We can sometimes find one in a park.
____
7 This is like a skateboard, but it doesn't have wheels. We don't use it in hot, sunny places. ______________
8 This is the weather when it's difficult to see. ______________

1 Read and color.

brown	gray	blue
They took their umbrellas	He studied hard at school,	I don't have any gloves,

pink	black	purple
It started snowing this morning,	I'll make lunch	We're going to walk across the desert,

so he did well on his tests.	because we're all hungry.	because it was raining.
so we'll go sledding this afternoon.	so we'll need strong boots and water.	so I'll put my hands in my pockets.

2 Complete the sentences with *so* or *because*. Use a comma with *so*.

1 It was very hot , so I went for a swim.

2 I made a snowman ______ there was a lot of snow.

3 I'll be ten minutes late ______ I missed the 8:15 bus.

4 My parents went out ______ Grandma looked after me.

5 My chair's broken ______ we'll repair it this afternoon.

6 We're going ice skating ______ there's ice on the pond.

1 Label the diagram with the words in the box.

~~axis~~ equator Northern Hemisphere
North Pole Southern Hemisphere South Pole

1 axis
2 ______
3 ______
4 ______
5 ______
6 ______

SUN

2 Complete the text with the words in the box.

higher lower South ~~summer~~ sun winter

It's 1 summer in the **Northern** Hemisphere when the North Pole tilts towards the 2 ______. This means that the temperatures are 3 ______. At the same time, it's 4 ______ in the **Southern** Hemisphere because the 5 ______ Pole is tilting away from the sun. This means the temperatures are 6 ______.

3 Read about the Northern Hemisphere and write the seasons.

1 Spring begins in March. The temperature gets higher and there is sometimes a lot of rain. Flowers start to grow on plants, and many animals have babies in spring.

2 ______ begins in December. The temperature is low, and it may snow. Some trees lose their leaves.

3 ______ begins in June. The temperature is high, and there is less rain in some places. Lots of fruit is ready to eat.

4 ______ begins in September. It begins to get colder, and there is more rain. The leaves on some trees start to change color.

4 Correct the sentences about the seasons in Argentina.

1 Summer begins in June and winter begins in December in Argentina.

Winter begins

2 It is very hot in winter in the south of Argentina.

3 You can only see penguins in Argentina in winter.

4 You can only swim in the ocean in winter.

5 Complete the graph with the average temperature for each month where you live. Use the Internet to help you.

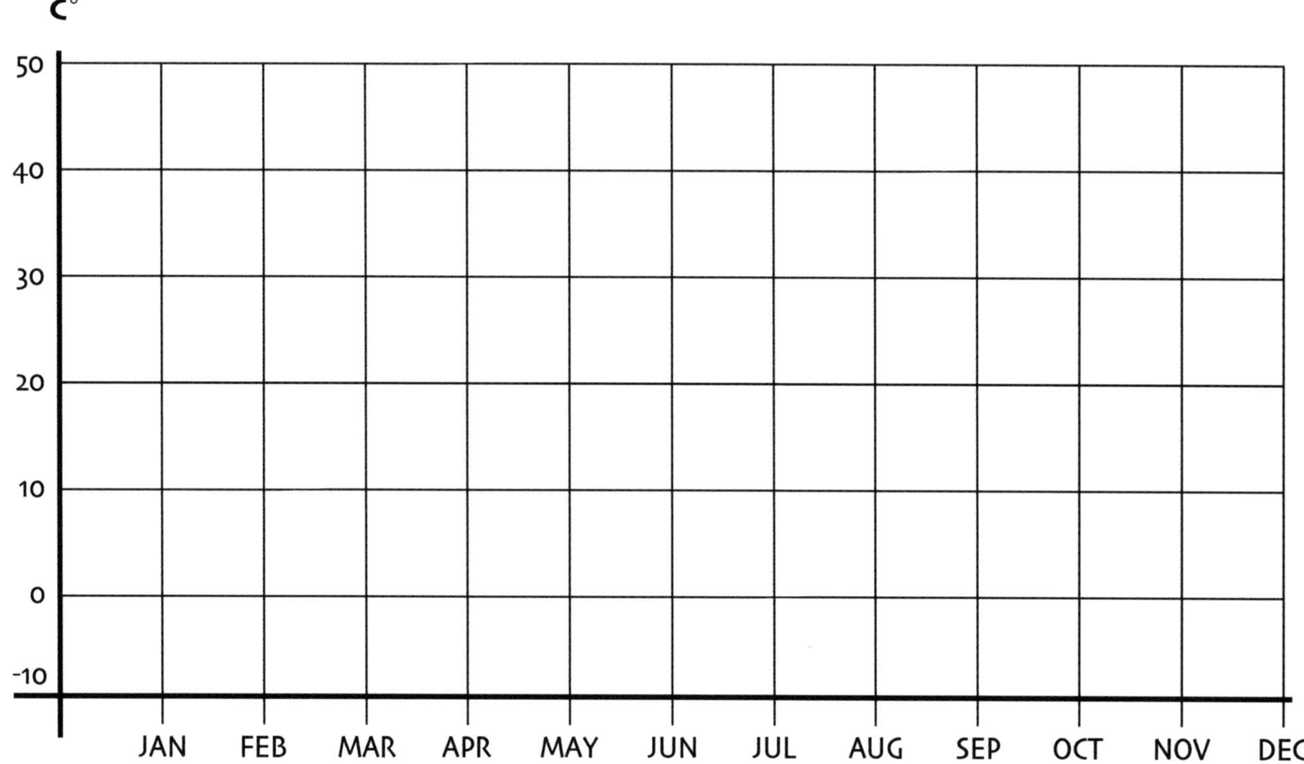

6 Look at your graph in Activity 5 and answer the questions.

1 Which months are the hottest?

2 Which months are the coldest?

1 Complete the sentences about *Tomás and the Snowman*.

1 Tomás and Valentín were from Patagonia, in Argentina.

2 Valentín was ______ years old.

3 Valentín knocked the snowman down because ______.

4 Tomás was sad because ______.

5 Valentín said sorry to Tomás and promised to make ______.

2 Are these sentences true or false? Correct the false sentences.

1 Tomás was older than Valentín. False: Tomás was younger.

2 The hill where the brothers played was in front of their house. ______

3 Valentín liked snowboarding. ______

4 The boys used a stone to make the snowman's nose. ______

5 Tomás and Valentín made more snowmen later that day. ______

3 Read the questions. Then discuss your answers with a partner.

1 Valentín knocked El Viejo down. Did he do the right thing or the wrong thing?

2 Have you ever made a member of your family sad? Why? What did you do?

4 5.14 Listen and check (✓) the box. There is one example.

1 What was Dad's favorite activity in the snow?

A ☐

B ✓

C ☐

2 Which is Valentín's favorite season?

A ☐

B ☐

C ☐

3 Which boots are Valentín's?

A ☐

B ☐

C ☐

4 What have the boys forgotten to pack?

A ☐

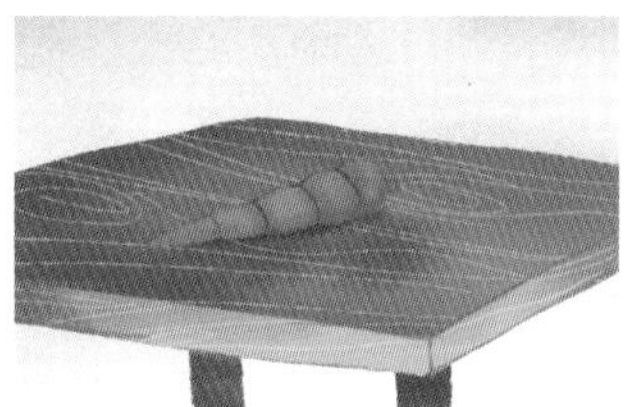

B ☐

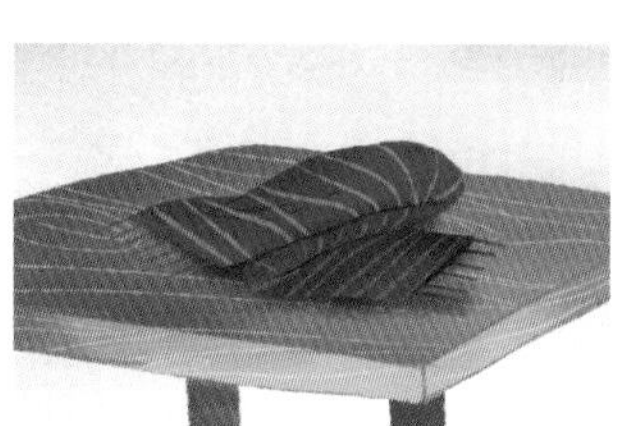

C ☐

5 What do the boys take to eat and drink?

A ☐

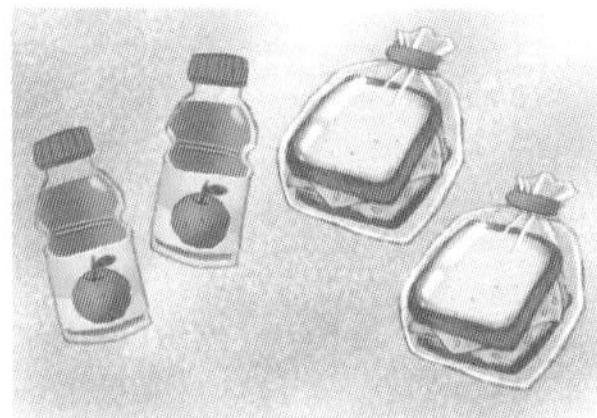

B ☐

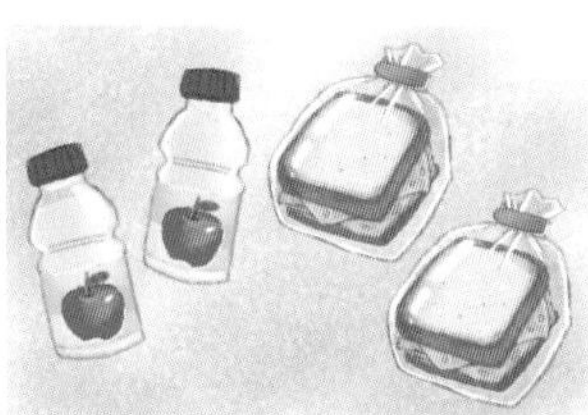

C ☐

6 What time did Mom tell the boys to come home?

A ☐

B ☐

C ☐

1 5.15 **Look at the notes about Harry's new DVD. Listen and make sentences to answer the questions.**

Harry's new DVD

What about	Spring animals
How long / DVD	70 minutes
Who / from	Grandma
Has / music	Yes
Like best	Butterflies

2 5.16 **Now ask questions about Sarah's new DVD. You will hear each answer, but you don't need to write.**

Sarah's new DVD

What about	?
How long / DVD	?
Who / from	?
Has / music	?
Like best	?

1 Read the instructions. Play the game.

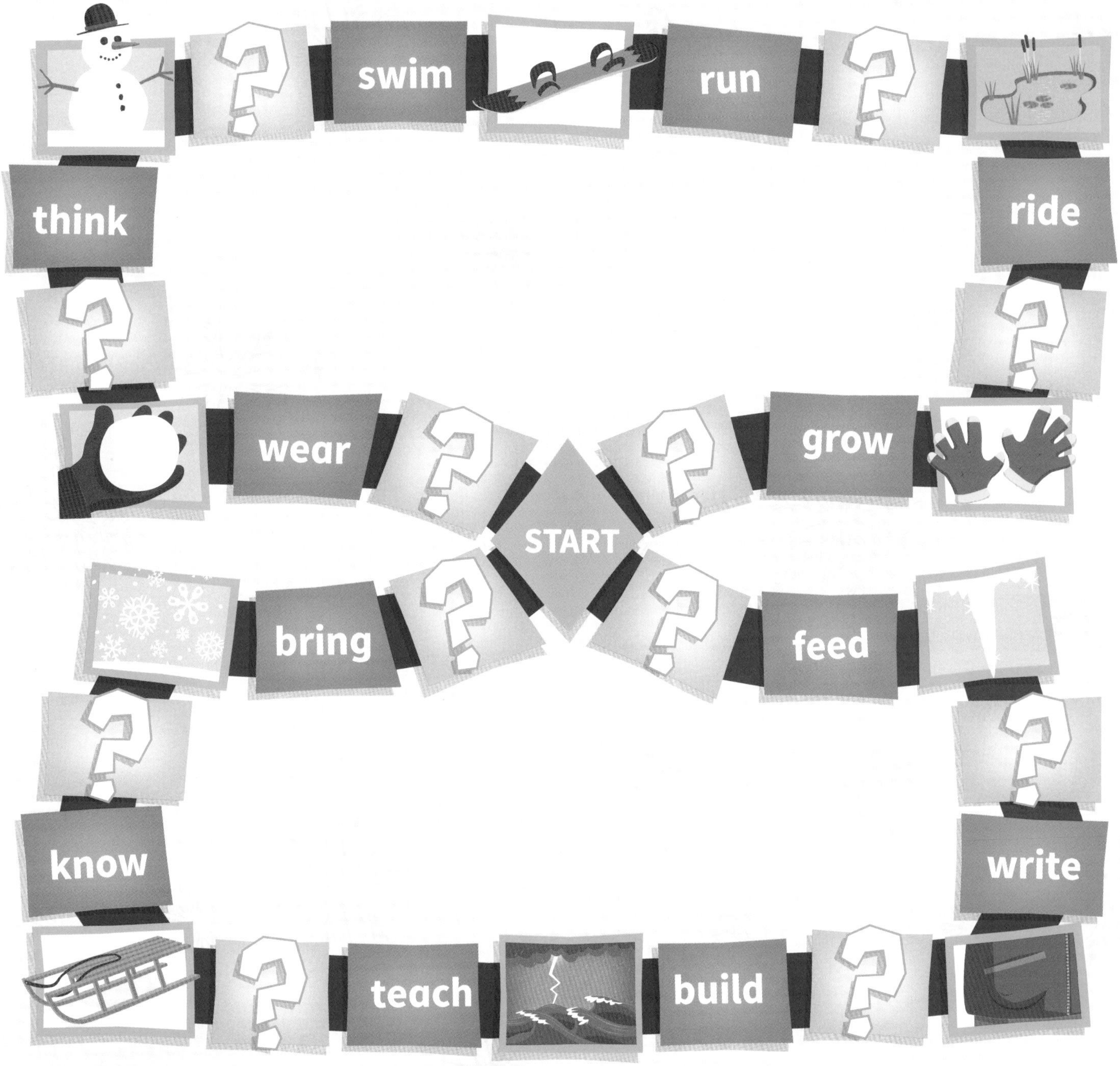

INSTRUCTIONS

Choose four pictures. Write the words in your notebook. You need to collect these.

Roll the dice and move across the board.

Collect your four words. Check (✓) them in your notebook.

On green spaces, say the word.

On ? spaces, answer the question on the card.

On orange spaces, say the past participle of the verb and spell it.

6 Working together

DIVERSICUS

My unit goals

- I want to ______________________________
  ____
- To do this, I will ______________________________
  ____
- I will say and write ____ new words.

My mission diary

How was it? Draw a face.

1

2

3

★

My favorite stage:

____

I can name jobs and places of work. ☐

I can use tag questions to check that a statement is true. ☐

I can use short questions to show interest and surprise. ☐

I can read, understand, and complete a factual text. ☐

I completed Level 4 Unit 6. ☑

Go to page 134 and add to your word stack!

1 Look and write the jobs. Find the words in the wordsearch and check your spelling.

manager

A Q W P I L O T N O Y S C
L P H O T O G R A P H E R
H T L L Z P X E T Y H N J
B U S I N E S S M A N G P
B M F C U Z O A E C X I R
V A M E K I E G C T K N O
Q N N O A A Y U H Y P E Y
C A X F B C U T A H K E O
O G W F T E N K N S U R P
O E Y I U R W A I T E R K
K R E C Y S G U C N O T L
W C S E N W I S T B R T I
A F I R E F I G H T E R K

2 Circle the different word.

1 pilot (drum) airport trip

2 manager office desk pillow

3 pop star song stage uniform

4 stream mechanic taxi truck

5 firefighter building brave corner

6 cave pond businesswoman stone

7 ambulance hospital nurse storm

8 waiter airport cook restaurant

Sounds and spelling

3 5.17 Listen and repeat. Underline the stressed word in each compound noun.

<u>movie</u> star bus stop pop star post office train station

4 5.18 Listen and repeat.

The pop star's playing rock music at the train station.
The police officer and the movie star are at the post office.

1 5.19 Read and write *yes* or *no*. Listen and check your answers.

1 They aren't in Australia, are they? ___no___
2 They invented K-pop music in South Korea, didn't they? ______
3 Jim and Jenny's dad has a robot in the kitchen, doesn't he? ______
4 Robots don't always look like people, do they? ______
5 They're designing robot teachers, aren't they? ______
6 The robot that Mrs. Friendly's looking at isn't playing the guitar, is it? ______
7 Ivan hasn't bought a kitten, has he? ______
8 Ivan's puppy can walk, can't it? ______

2 Complete the text with the words in the box.

friendliest	kitchen	looking	robots	~~South~~	strong	violin	Yesterday

Jim's Diary

We're in [1] ___South___ Korea at the moment, and we've seen some of the robots that they make. Sometimes people don't think about it, but there are lots of different kinds of [2] ______, and they can do lots of different things. People use them in the [3] ______, and to clean floors, and they're also very important for work. [4] ______ afternoon, we went to a place where they had some really interesting robots. There was one that could play the [5] ______, that my mom liked, and another one that could lift cars. Su-Lin said it was as [6] ______ as Ivan! I think the [7] ______ robot was a puppy, and so did Ivan! While we were [8] ______ at one of the biggest robots in the world, Ivan bought a robot puppy. His name's Mr. Barker. We couldn't believe it when Ivan came out of the building with Mr. Barker!

3 Review the story.

I think the story is **great** / **good** / **OK** / **not very good**.
My favorite character is ______.
My favorite part is when ______.

1 Read and match.

1 He isn't repairing the bike,
2 Your grandparents are taking care of your little brother,
3 She made sure it was the right answer,
4 We didn't send any messages,
5 You've met my cousin,
6 She's going to make a snack,
7 You can clean the kitchen,
8 You haven't brought in the shopping bags from the car,

a did we?
b have you?
c isn't she?
d can't you?
e aren't they?
f didn't she?
g is he?
h haven't you?

2 5.20 Listen and draw lines. There is one example.

Betty Sophia William

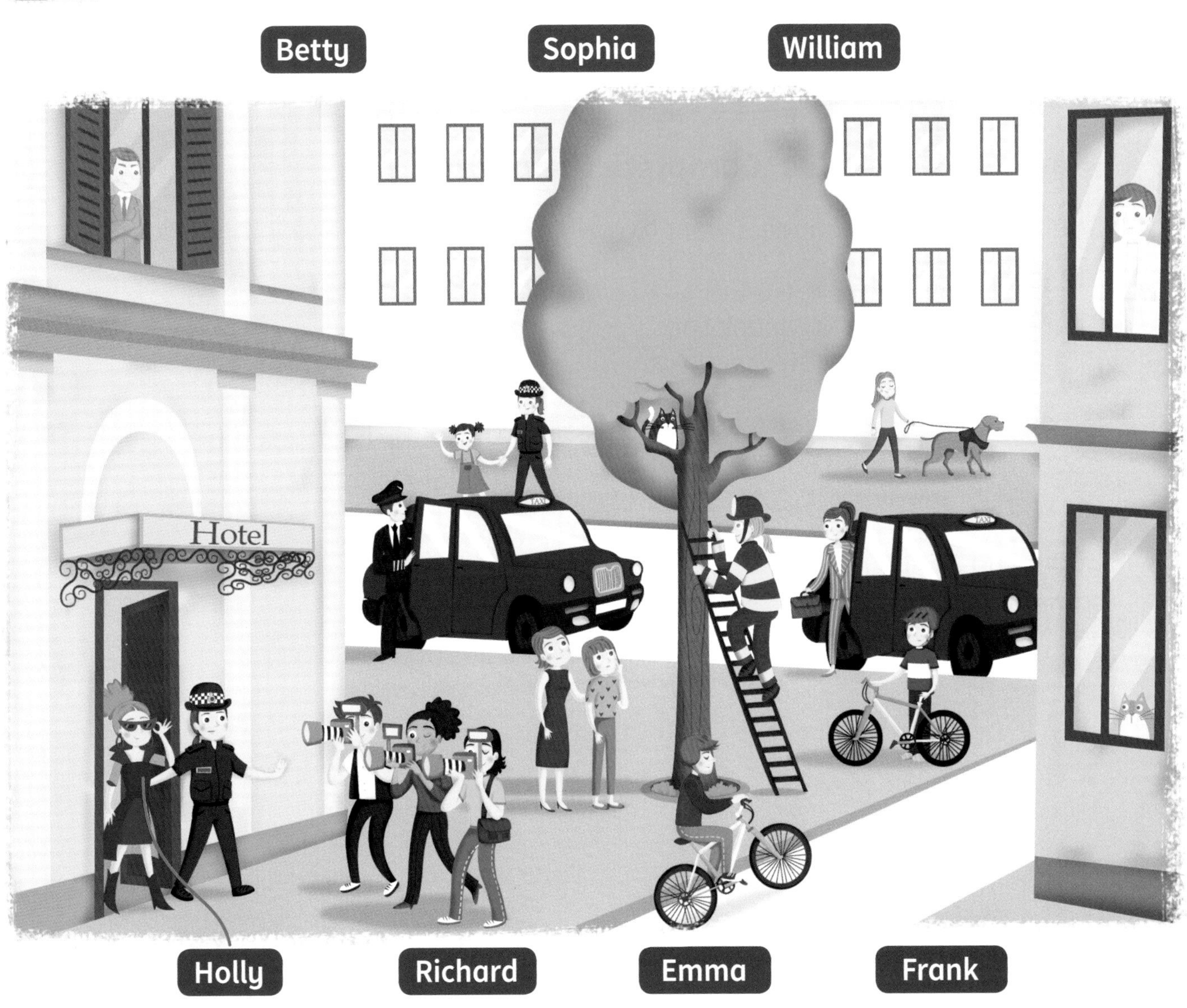

Holly Richard Emma Frank

1 Write the words in the correct picture.

boots ~~businesswoman~~ cabinet computer desk
engineer factory fire station gloves ~~helmet~~ manager
mechanic ~~office~~ ~~phone~~ pocket police station

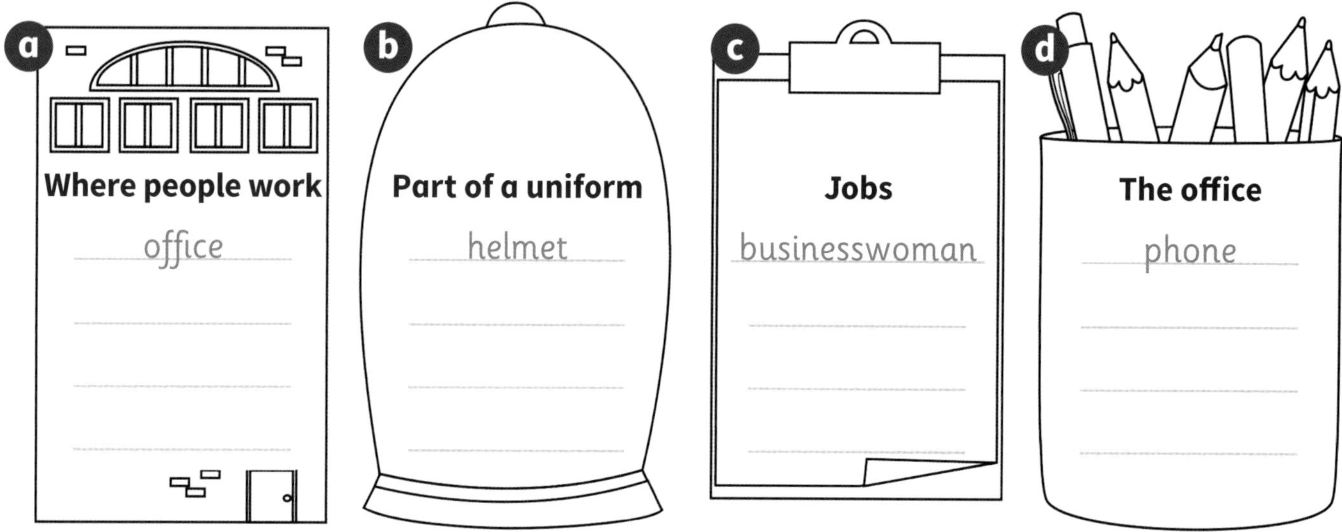

2 Read the sentences. Complete the puzzle.

1 At nine thirty, the managers went to a big office to have a …

2 There are lots of desks, telephones, and computers in this place of work.

3 My dad watches this on TV. It tells him about things that are happening in the world.

4 Buying and selling things is sometimes called …

5 Police officers usually work at the …

6 Robots make cars in a …

7 This is someone who stops other people doing bad things.

8 This is the big truck that firefighters use.

9 These are the special clothes people have to wear for some jobs.

1 M E E T I N G
2
3
4
5
6
7
8
9

Write a sentence using the secret word.

1 Complete the conversations with a short question.

2 Helen's Uncle Robert is a mechanic and she's visiting him at work to ask him about his job. Read the conversation and write the best letter (A–H) for each of Uncle Robert's answers.

1 **Helen:** Hello, Uncle Robert. Have you just repaired that red car?
Robert: D

2 **Helen:** That's good, because I'm going to ask you more questions!
Robert: ....

3 **Helen:** Your job. What have you just done to this car behind us?
Robert: ....

4 **Helen:** Have you? Do you usually do that for people?
Robert: ....

5 **Helen:** Oh, I see! How many cars have you worked on this week?
Robert: ....

6 **Helen:** I want to be a mechanic when I grow up.
Robert: ....

A Go away! Don't ask him now.
B Haven't you? I cleaned it yesterday.
C Are you? What about?
D Yes, and now I'm taking a break. **(example)**
E Not always, but that one's mine!
F Do you? Well, you can start today. You can help me clean my office.
G I've repaired about 12, I think.
H Oh, I've only washed that blue one!

1 Match the robots to the work they do.

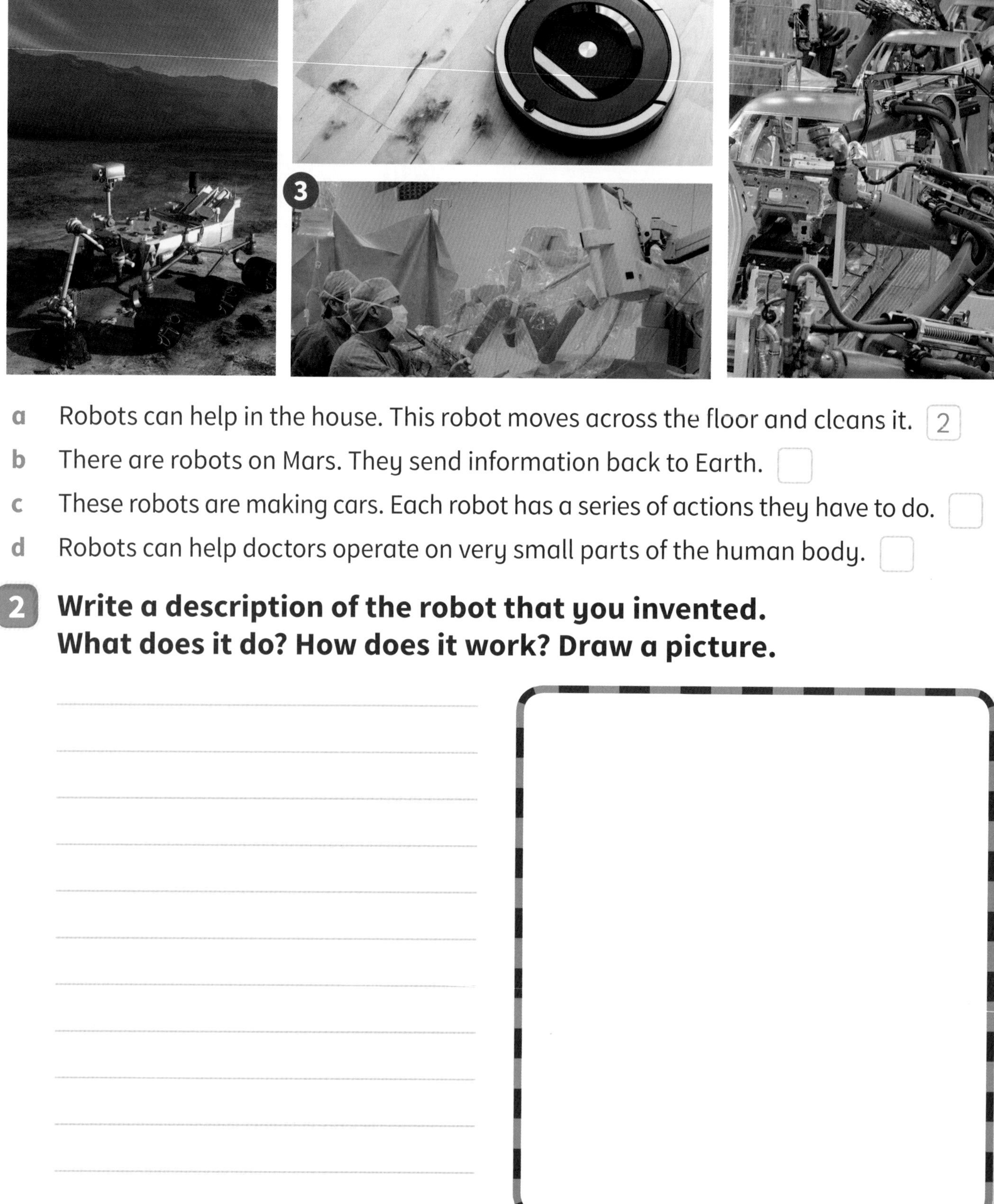

a Robots can help in the house. This robot moves across the floor and cleans it. 2

b There are robots on Mars. They send information back to Earth. ☐

c These robots are making cars. Each robot has a series of actions they have to do. ☐

d Robots can help doctors operate on very small parts of the human body. ☐

2 Write a description of the robot that you invented. What does it do? How does it work? Draw a picture.

3 Complete the descriptions of South Korean inventions with the words in the box.

~~clean~~ everything floor keep money music screen travel

1 This helps you clean the ______ and it works with water.

2 You can do ______ you want to do by touching the ______.

3 If you use this when you ______, you don't need ______.

4 You can ______ all your ______ here.

4 Read about the kimchi refrigerator and answer the questions.

When you open this refrigerator, you won't find any of the foods you usually see in refrigerators. There's no milk, no cheese, and no yogurt. This refrigerator is only for one food – kimchi, one of the most popular foods in Korea. It's a cabbage dish that is difficult to make, and very difficult to keep in good condition. Koreans eat kimchi with many different meals, and with the invention of the kimchi refrigerator, they can enjoy it all year. A lot of Koreans say that the kimchi refrigerator is the most important thing in their kitchen.

1 How is this refrigerator unusual? ______

2 Why is it important in Korea? ______

3 What do you think is the most important thing in your kitchen? Why?

______

1 Match the actions in the story to their consequences.

1 The children don't like Buddie. — d
2 Seo-joon says he'll help Buddie.
3 Seo-joon and Buddie spend a lot of time together.
4 Buddie learns to understand children.
5 Seo-joon's math improves and he's more friendly.

a They become good friends.
b The kids now like Seo-joon.
c All the children in the class now like Buddie.
d Buddie asks Seo-joon for help.
e Buddie offers to help Seo-joon with math.

2 Complete the story planner for *Buddie and Seo-joon's Adventure*.

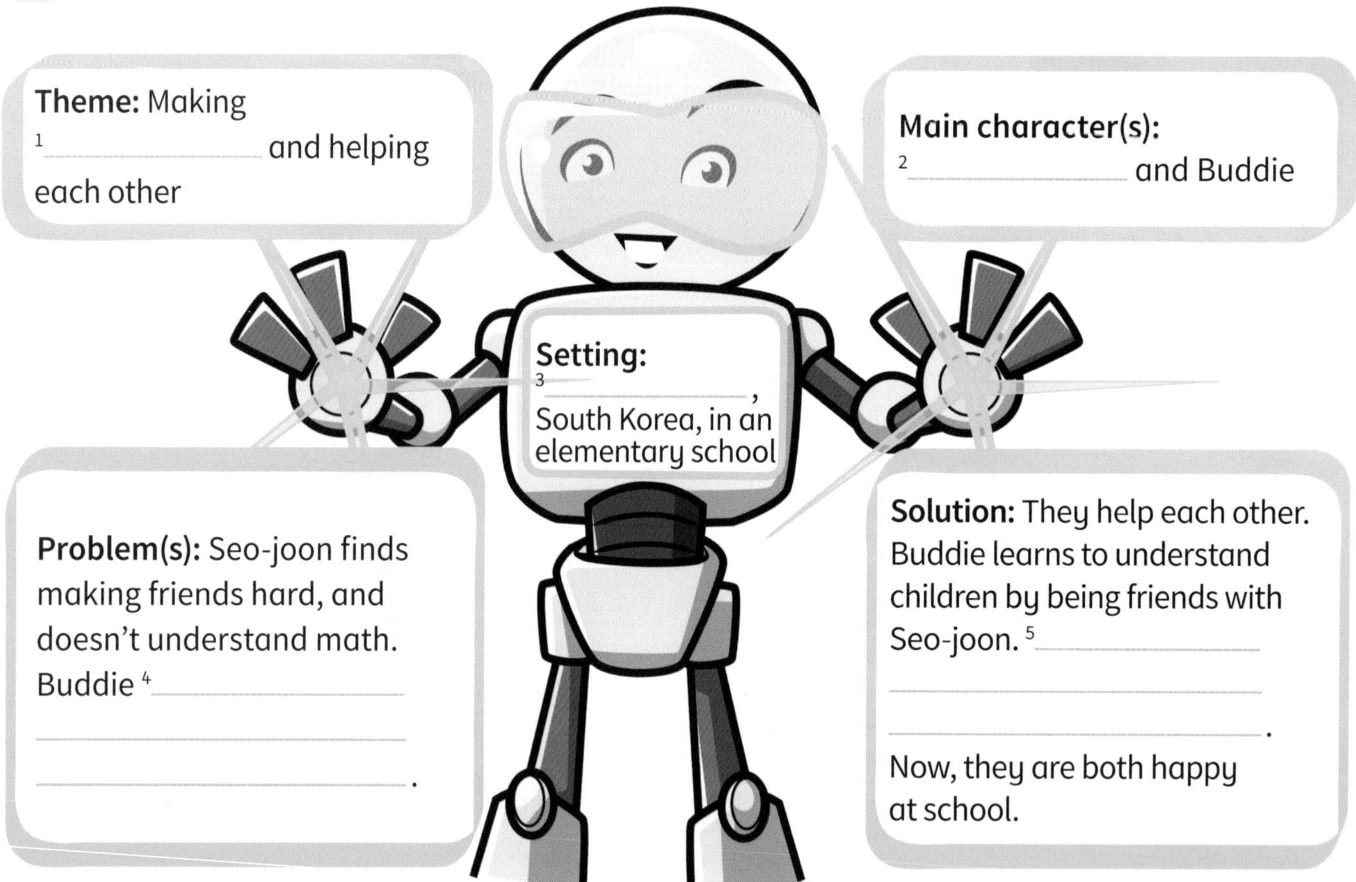

3 Read the questions. Then discuss your answers with a partner.

1 Do you think the principal sent Buddie back to the factory? How do you know? Do you think he made the right decision?

2 Why do you think Buddie took the children outside to study math? How was the lesson going to be different?

4 **Find the differences and make sentences in pairs.**

A

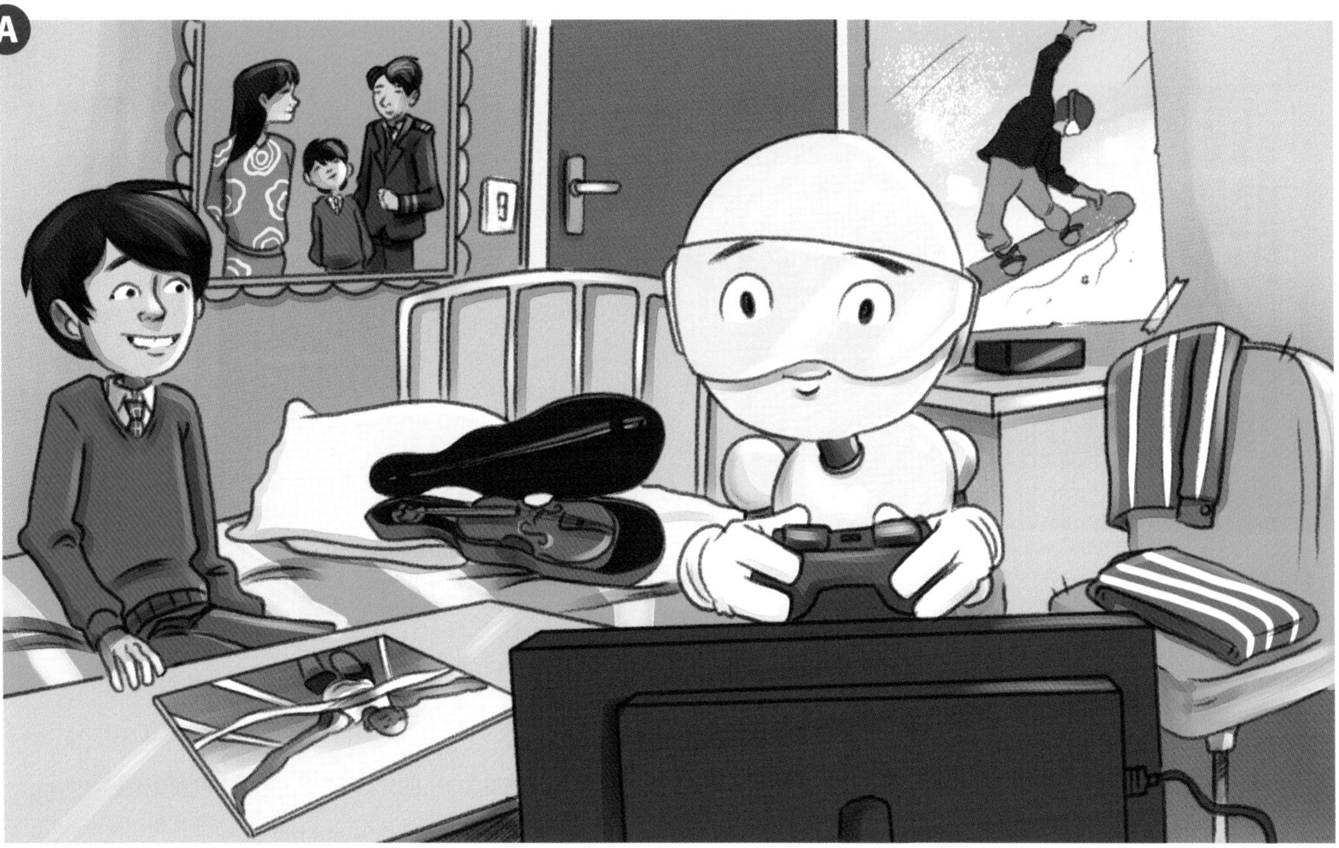

B

1 Read the text. Choose the right words and write them on the lines.

Reporters

Example Some people might ___think___ that being a reporter is an easy job,
1 but actually it is quite ________ to become a famous reporter. Many
2 reporters ________ been to college and they know how to
3 write about different subjects, ________ celebrities, sports, or cooking.
4 Reporters often have to ________ to meetings with their managers
to talk about changes in the newspaper. Many reporters work
5 ________ a photographer, and they enjoy being out of the office.
6 Reporters ________ have to wear a uniform, but they usually
have a laptop and a cell phone. If there is a very important story, they
7 ________ work for more than 12 hours a day. It's a busy job.
8 If you want to be a reporter, a ________ way to start is to write something
9 for a school newspaper or magazine. Later, you can ________ if you
10 want to work on TV or on the radio, or maybe your wish is to be ________
online reporter? That's a very popular kind of job for reporters right now.

Example think thought thinking

1	harder	hard	hardest	6	can't	don't	aren't
2	has	having	have	7	might	should	need
3	like	from	for	8	better	worse	good
4	went	gone	go	9	deciding	decide	decided
5	with	by	of	10	a	one	an

1 Read the instructions. Play the game.

INSTRUCTIONS

Roll the dice and move across the board.

On green spaces, say the word.

On ? spaces, answer the question on the card.

On purple spaces, say and spell the past participle of the verb.

Review ••• Units 5–6

1 Choose a picture. Give a definition. Your partner points to and says the word.

This person flies a plane.

A pilot!

1 
2 
3 
4 
5 
6 
7 
8 

2 Read the forum posts on Harry's blog. Circle the correct words.

Everyone likes **the same** / **a different** season.

Harry's blog

Today's question: What's your favorite season?

Hi! Today I'm writing about favorite seasons. I love spring! Last year we went camping in spring. Camping is a lot of fun, isn't it? We were making lunch by the tent and it was warm and sunny, but then there was a big storm! The weather can change very quickly in spring. I'll make sure I take an umbrella this year! What's your favorite season?

KatyM

Hi Harry! I love winter as there's a lot of snow. Meeting your friends to make snowmen is the best, isn't it? I think I'll go snowboarding this year because my friend Holly was talking about it last winter!

Betty09

Hello! My favorite season's fall. One day last year I was taking care of my sister. It was warm and sunny, so we repaired our bikes and went to the river. We were swimming when it started to rain! I love swimming in the rain, don't you?

RichardD

Hi! Summer's the best! My family's just moved to the beach. Lucky, aren't we? Yesterday, I was swimming in the sea all day because it was very hot. I'll go again tomorrow with my new friends, I think!

3 **Read the forum posts again. Complete the sentences with the correct online name.**

1 KatyM will go snowboarding.
2 ______ thinks summer is the best.
3 ______ was making lunch outside.
4 ______ has just moved to a new house.
5 ______ loves swimming in the rain.
6 ______ talks about trying a new sport.
7 ______ went camping last year.
8 ______ enjoys the snow in winter.
9 ______ repaired two bikes.
10 ______ will take an umbrella.

4 **Plan a forum post for Harry's blog.**

- What's your favorite season?

- What is the weather like in this season? ______
- What do you like doing? ______
- Where did you go last year? ______
- What will you do differently this year? ______

5 **Write your forum post for Harry's blog. Use your notes from Activity 4.**

CHECK!
Have you answered all the questions in Activity 4?
Have you used the format of a forum post?
Have you used the correct vocabulary and grammar?
Is your spelling correct?

7 Then and now

My unit goals

- I want to ______________________________
  ____
- To do this, I will ______________________________
  ____
- I will say and write ____ new words.

My mission diary

How was it? Draw a face.

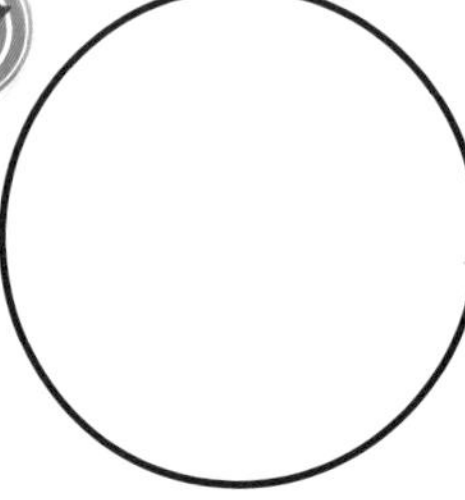

My favorite stage:

DIVERSICUS

I can name things in the home. ☐

I can describe objects. ☐

I can say what things are used for. ☐

I can read a story and answer questions. ☐

I completed Level 4 Unit 7. ☑

Go to page 134 and add to you word stack!

1 Order the letters and complete the crossword.

Across (→)

3 hoposam
5 heenopetl
7 surbh
8 yek
9 gridef

Down (↓)

1 ateg
2 nevo
3 paso
4 bomc
5 loitte
6 hefls

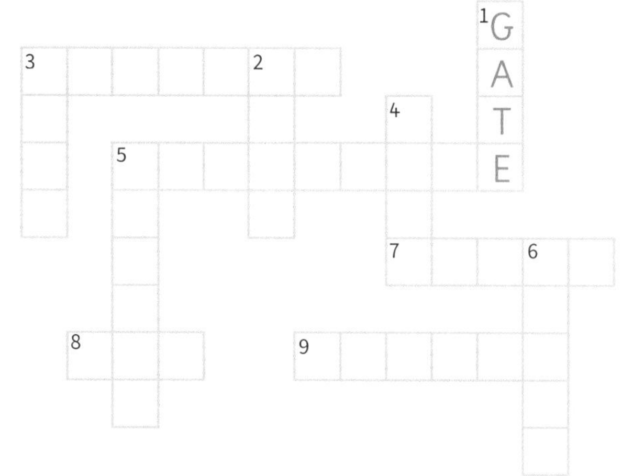

2 Match. Write the words.

1 ga gate ey
ga garden wel

2 sh ap
sh en

3 k ampoo
k ~~rden~~

4 to uth
to elf

5 so ~~te~~
so ilet

6 ov ing
ov er

Sounds and spelling

3 5.21 Listen and repeat. Circle the spelling of the *j* sound in each word.

fri(dge) engineer stage journey

4 Complete the words with the letters.

ge dge gi j

banda ge ______ bri ______ passen ______ r ______ ography
ma ______ cian pa ______ amas

1 Read and write *yes* or *no*.

1 Ivan's flown to meet the Friendly family. ___no___
2 He's borrowed Marc's car for four days. ______
3 Ivan would like to ride on a camel before he sees the old city. ______
4 Jenny's just fallen off a horse. ______
5 Jenny's broken her leg. ______
6 Jenny's cut her knee. ______
7 Jenny and Jim have forgotten their camera. ______
8 They've left their camera on the train. ______

2 Complete the text with the words in the box.

because	driven	gone	~~has~~	high	hurt	just	lying	wait

Jenny's Diary

Today [1] ___has___ taught me that, in the future, I'll do what grown-ups ask me to do. Jim and I have [2] ______ finished having lunch with Ivan, Mom, and Dad. They've [3] ______ to look around the old city, but I can't walk around because I've [4] ______ my leg. Ivan's [5] ______ from Cairo to spend time with us, and he wanted to ride a camel with Jim and me.

When we got there, the camels were [6] ______ quietly on the sand, and Ivan asked us to [7] ______ near them. While he was busy paying the man, I decided to get on a camel. They're very tall, and I was very lucky [8] ______ it didn't stand up... and then I fell off! It wasn't very [9] ______, but I fell onto some rocks and cut my knee. Next time, I'll listen to instructions more carefully!

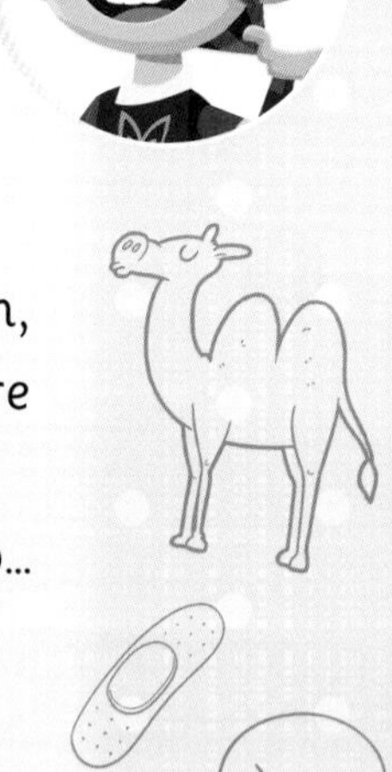

3 Review the story.

I think the story is **great** / **good** / **OK** / **not very good**.
My favorite character is ______.
My favorite part is when ______.

1 Circle eight more past participles in the wordsnake.

beenflowngivenolcomefeddonebritaughtmakknownmade

2 Complete the puzzle with the past participles of the verbs.

choose, chose, …
drive, drove, …
break, broke, …
leave, left, …
fly, flew, …

				1	H	U	R	T		
		2		O		N				
	3		T			D				
				4		E				
				5		R		V		
		6				S				
7						T				
			8			O	K			
			9		L	O				
			10			D				

hurt, hurt, …
find, found, …
forget, forgot, …
stand, stood, …
ride, rode, …

3 Complete the sentences with the past participles of the verbs.

1 Michael's just swum (swim) the 200 meter butterfly stroke in under two minutes. He's just won another Olympic gold medal!

2 Why are you tired? You've just ______ (sleep) for two hours on the sofa!

3 My little cousin's ______ (lose) his favorite teddy bear. We can't find it anywhere.

4 Grandpa and Dad have been at the lake for four hours, but they haven't ______ (catch) any fish yet.

5 We're drawing lots of pictures. They're going to be presents. I've ______ (draw) one for my friend and one for my mom.

6 Holly's already ______ (read) 200 pages of her new book, but she hasn't finished it yet. It's very long!

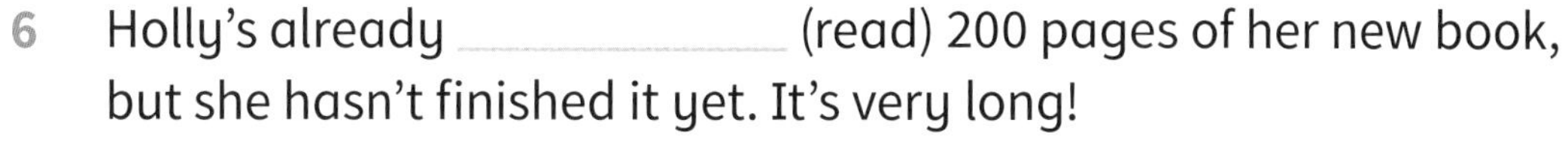

7 I love visiting my grandparents, but I hate it when they say "You've ______ (grow) a lot since the last time we saw you." They say it every time … and I visit them every week!

8 Richard isn't very happy. Sarah left her banana on the chair, and he has just ______ (sit) on it.

1 Complete the sentences with adjectives. Find them in the wordsearch and check your spelling.

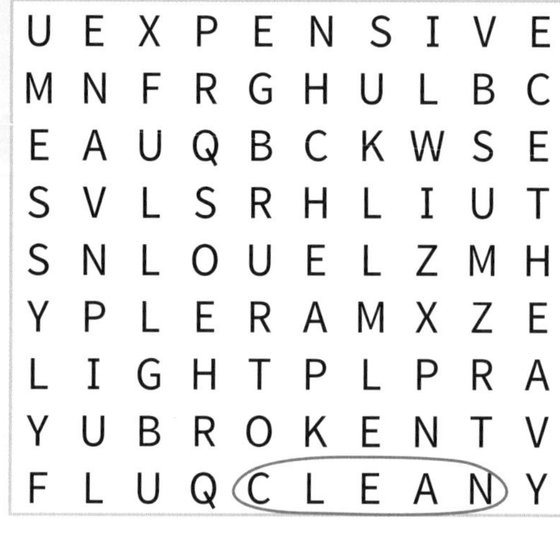

1 We put away all our clothes in the closet. Dad was really happy to see our nice, ___clean___ bedroom.

2 Be careful! There's too much coffee in that cup, so it's too ______________!

3 We need to repair the toilet because it's ______________.

4 Your room's very ______________. Please clean it before you go out with your friends.

5 Would he like some more lemonade? His glass is ______________.

6 She bought her camera for only 20 dollars. It was really ______________.

7 That's the most ______________ car in the world. You need a million dollars to buy it!

8 Can you please help Grandma with her suitcase? It's too ______________ for her.

9 Harry didn't go to soccer practice yesterday, which is very ______________ because he loves soccer. Maybe he hasn't been feeling well.

10 No, there isn't a problem with Holly's backpack. It's ______________ enough for her to carry.

2 Circle the correct words.

1 I'm looking for something very unusual. That isn't different ***too*** / ***enough***.

2 I like this game, and it's cheap ***too*** / ***enough*** for me to buy with my birthday money.

3 The books are ***too*** / ***enough*** heavy for this bag. It'll break.

4 I need to write my story again. It's ***too*** / ***enough*** messy to give to Mrs. York.

5 That watch is beautiful, but it's ***too*** / ***enough*** expensive.

6 Is this bag light ***too*** / ***enough*** to take on the plane?

7 Put your sneakers in Dad's suitcase. Yours is ***too*** / ***enough*** full.

8 Mom, do you think my bedroom is clean ***too*** / ***enough***?

1 Read and color.

green	orange	purple
What are scissors used for?	What's a toothbrush used for?	What are combs used for?

blue	black	yellow
What's shampoo used for?	What's soap used for?	What's a glass used for?

It's used for holding a drink.	It's used for washing your hair.	They're used for cutting paper.
It's used for brushing your teeth.	They're used for combing your hair.	It's used for washing your hands.

2 Complete the sentences about a trip to a museum with the words in the box.

~~cooking~~ to used catching for wash

1 We saw an old oven, which was used for cooking meat.
2 People used soap to ______ their clothes more than 1,000 years ago.
3 There was a big stone, and no one knew what it was ______ for!
4 They said eggs were used ______ pay for things instead of money.
5 We learned about the nets that they used for ______ fish.
6 We could use our phones ______ taking pictures outside, but not inside.

1 Are these sentences true or false? Correct the false sentences.

1 Simple machines have many moving parts.

False – Simple machines have only one or no moving parts.

2 Machines make our lives easier.

3 Complex machines have few or no moving parts.

4 People started to use sundials in the 14th century.

5 Clocks are simple machines.

6 A digital clock has hands.

2 Complete the sentences.

1 Early humans didn't hunt and work when it was dark .

2 The Egyptians used the ______ of tall buildings and the sun to tell the time.

3 People burned ______ to tell the time.

4 Every ______, you could hear a bell on a 14th-century mechanical clock.

5 Analog clocks have ______ .

3 Match the clocks that show the same time.

1 

2 

3 

4 

a 

b 

c 

d 

4 Look at problems 1–3. How did the ancient Egyptians solve them? Answer the questions. Use the words in the box to help you.

built	ramps	levers	pulled	rafts	brought

1 

2 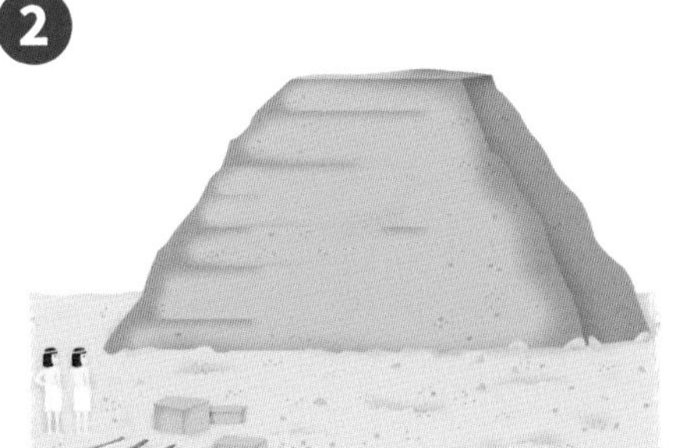

3 

1 What did they use to lift the rocks?

______

2 How did they get huge rocks to the top of the pyramid?

______

3 How did they get the rocks from a different part of the country to Giza?

______

5 Read the information about Egypt and complete the fact file.

The population of Egypt is over 80 million people. The official language is Arabic, but many people can also speak English and French. The capital city is Cairo, which has the largest population. Egypt is a very hot and dry country.

Parts of the Sahara Desert and the Libyan Desert are in Egypt. The River Nile, the longest in the world, goes through Egypt. Egypt is home to the Great Pyramid of Giza, which is one of the Seven Wonders of the World.

Country: ______

Population: ______ people

Capital: ______

Climate: ______ ______

Languages: ______, ______, ______

River: ______

Most famous monument: ______ ______

1 Circle the correct answers.

1 When Tut became pharaoh, his life was different because he
 a could make changes in his country.
 b liked having power.
 (c) wasn't happy any more.

2 When Tut was ten, he
 a decided to control Horemheb and Ay.
 b married a beautiful girl.
 c got some new sandals.

3 Horemheb and Ay said Tut's new sandals
 a were unusual.
 b could help him control his enemies.
 c were for walking on hot sand.

4 Tut fell down
 a when he was dancing with Ank.
 b so Horemheb threw away the sandals.
 c and hurt his leg.

2 Look at the pictures. Why is each item important in the story? Write a sentence about each picture.

1 ______________________________

____

2 ______________________________

____

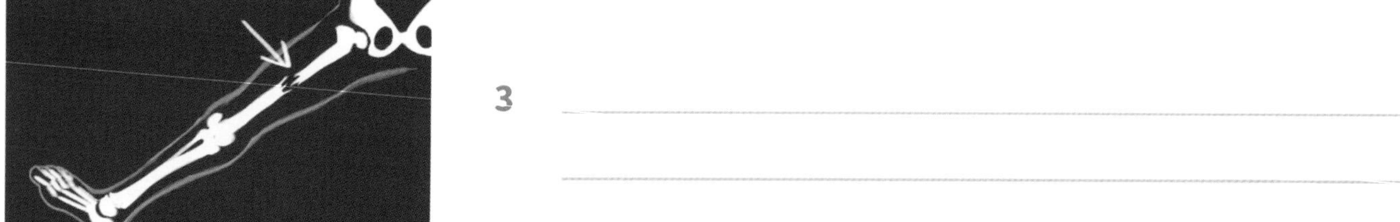

3 ______________________________

____

3 Read the questions. Then discuss with a partner.

Do you think Horemheb and Ay treated Tut fairly? Why / Why not?

4 5.22 **Where did Emma get each of these things? Listen and write a letter in each box. There is one example.**

C Bag	☐ Camel	☐ Comb
☐ Dress	☐ Rug	☐ Ring

A

B

C

D

E

F

G

H

1 **Look at the picture and read the story. Write some words to complete the sentences about the story. You can use 1, 2, 3, or 4 words.**

George's new rug

George hurried home from work on Thursday because his son was coming back from a trip around the world.

"It was an amazing trip, Dad!" said Frank. "I bought you this in Dubai." George opened the present. "A rug! Thank you!"

"It's unusual," said Frank, "and it's great for the hallway, isn't it?" George agreed, and they put the rug on the floor.

The next morning, Frank asked "Can I do anything to help?" George answered, "Well, could you paint the gate? There's some green paint in the basement."

After breakfast, Frank got the paint and went into the yard. It was a hot day and he left the door open, so their cat Betty followed him. Frank painted the back of the gate and then he went to get a drink. But sometimes Betty was naughty, so he put the paint on the shelf in the hallway.

Suddenly, a big dog came into the yard. Betty ran in and jumped on the shelf because she was frightened ... and the paint fell on the rug!

When George got home and saw the front of the gate, he was surprised. Then he saw the rug. "It was Betty!" said Frank. "And I couldn't finish the gate because we don't have any more paint!"

Examples

George came home from work quickly on ____Thursday____.

Frank had ____an amazing trip____ and visited lots of countries.

Questions

1 The present from Dubai was a ____________.

2 They put it on the floor in ____________.

3 On Friday morning, Frank wanted ____________.

4 Frank had breakfast and then he went to get the paint from ____________.

5 Betty went ____________ because the door was open.

6 The paint fell when the cat ____________.

7 Frank didn't paint all of the gate because there wasn't ____________.

1 **Read the instructions. Play the game.**

break FINISH

forget fall hurt

ride

leave meet

cut

catch stand

START hide find

INSTRUCTIONS

Roll the dice and move across the board.

On green spaces, say the word.

On orange spaces, say and spell the past participle of the verb.

On ? spaces, answer the question on the card.

Go up the ladder. Go down the rope.

8 Space travel

DIVERSICUS

My unit goals

- I want to ______________________

____

- To do this, I will ______________________

____

- I will say and write ____ new words.

My mission diary

How was it? Draw a face.

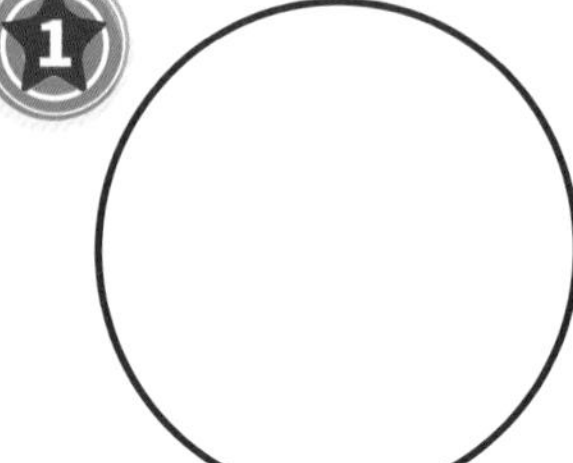

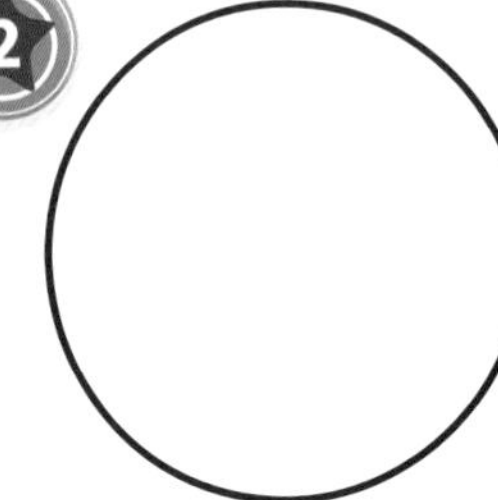

My favorite stage:

____

I can talk about space travel and investigation. ☐

I can make predictions and talk about future plans. ☐

I can use different tenses to talk about the past. ☐

I can read and complete a story. ☐

I completed Level 4 Unit 8. ☑

Go to page 134 and add to you word stack!

1 Read the sentences. Complete the puzzle.

1 An … travels in space.
2 The sun, moon, stars, and planets are in …
3 Earth, Jupiter, and Mars are all …
4 … is another word for spaceship.
5 We look at the stars with a …
6 … is another word for huge.
7 When something scares you, it's …
8 An … makes a car, truck, or bus move, and rockets have very big ones.
9 Pablo's astronaut is going to go into … space.

1 ASTRONAUT
2
3
4
5
6
7
8
9

Write a sentence using the secret word.

____
____

2 Read the times. Look at the clock and write the words.

1 It's five thirty. enormous
2 It's quarter after eight. ______
3 It's ten to nine. ______
4 It's ten after twelve. ______
5 It's twenty-five to ten. ______
6 It's five after eight. ______

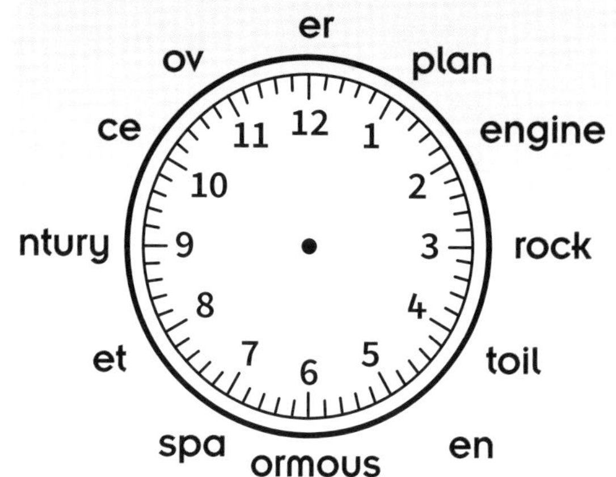

Sounds and spelling

3 5.23 Listen and repeat. Listen again and complete.

1 s p ace 2 _ _ ar 3 _ _ one 4 _ _ omach 5 _ _ ip
6 _ _ _ ipe 7 _ _ ot 8 _ _ _ eam 9 _ _ i 10 _ _ _ ange

4 5.24 Listen and repeat.

Stars are special strange spots in the sky.

DIVERSICUS

1 Circle the correct words.

1 Pablo has almost finished his **video** / **comic book**.
2 The **mechanic** / **astronaut** looks very big and strong.
3 Pablo's character is going to travel into **a deep ocean** / **deep space**.
4 Ivan thinks people **will** / **won't** eat more food.
5 The astronaut's going to use his **computer** / **oven** to get food.
6 Jim thinks we'll use planes and **trains** / **rockets** more.
7 Su-Lin thinks we'll use cars which will **sail** / **fly**.
8 Jenny thinks Pablo's comic book will be **boring** / **exciting**.

2 Read the text. Choose the right words and write them on the lines.

Pablo's Diary

This morning, we had a great conversation [1] ___about___ the future. Jim and Jenny think transportation [2] ________ be different. We'll use faster and cleaner trains and planes, and people [3] ________ use their cars on roads. We also talked about my new story. It's about an astronaut [4] ________'s going to travel into deep space. He's going to be big and strong, and he's going to go to new planets. He'll have a special spacesuit, [5] ________ he can do amazing things. Ivan thinks that in the future, people will eat more. He didn't like the idea of using a computer to get food! That's because he's always hungry and food is very important to [6] ________.

1 for about to
2 is was will
3 won't aren't don't
4 which who what
5 so while if
6 his he him

3 Review the story.

I think the story is **great** / **good** / **OK** / **not very good**.
My favorite character is ________.
My favorite part is when ________.

1 Find and write five sentences.

~~We're going~~	feed the	repair my bike	after seven.
I'll	going to	at quarter	this afternoon?
Mom, are we	them tomorrow	~~Grandma~~	in a minute!
We'll meet	be any	classes next	~~tomorrow.~~
There won't	~~to visit~~	cat	week.

1 We're going to visit Grandma tomorrow.

2 ______________________________

3 ______________________________

4 ______________________________

5 ______________________________

2 Complete the conversations with the sentences in the box.

Don't worry. I'll take it. ~~I'm going to drive there. I'll give you a ride.~~
Yes. I'll make her a cake! You're right. I'll close the window.

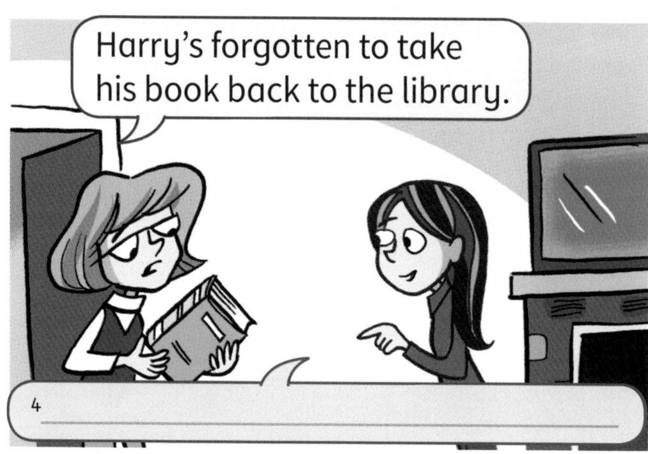

1 Read the sentences and complete the verbs.

1 I'll turn on ________ my robot dog, and he can get the ball!

2 People will e________ deep space next century.

3 Your hand's red. Did you t________ an unusual plant?

4 We're going to s________ with Grandma over the vacation.

5 You're going to t________ the music before you start studying, aren't you?

6 Are you going to s________ any money for your vacation?

7 Please e________ the space museum through the door on the left.

8 We've been in the air for hours! When's the plane going to l________, Dad?

2 Read the diary and write the missing words. Write one word on each line.

I've just [1] landed ________ on a new planet, and I've put a flag into the ground. I'm [2] ________ to bring some rocks and sand back to Earth. Scientists want to find out if there's any water, and if [3] ________ can live here. I think I'll [4] ________ for three days to [5] ________ the planet, but I have [6] ________ food and drink for two weeks, so I might be here longer.

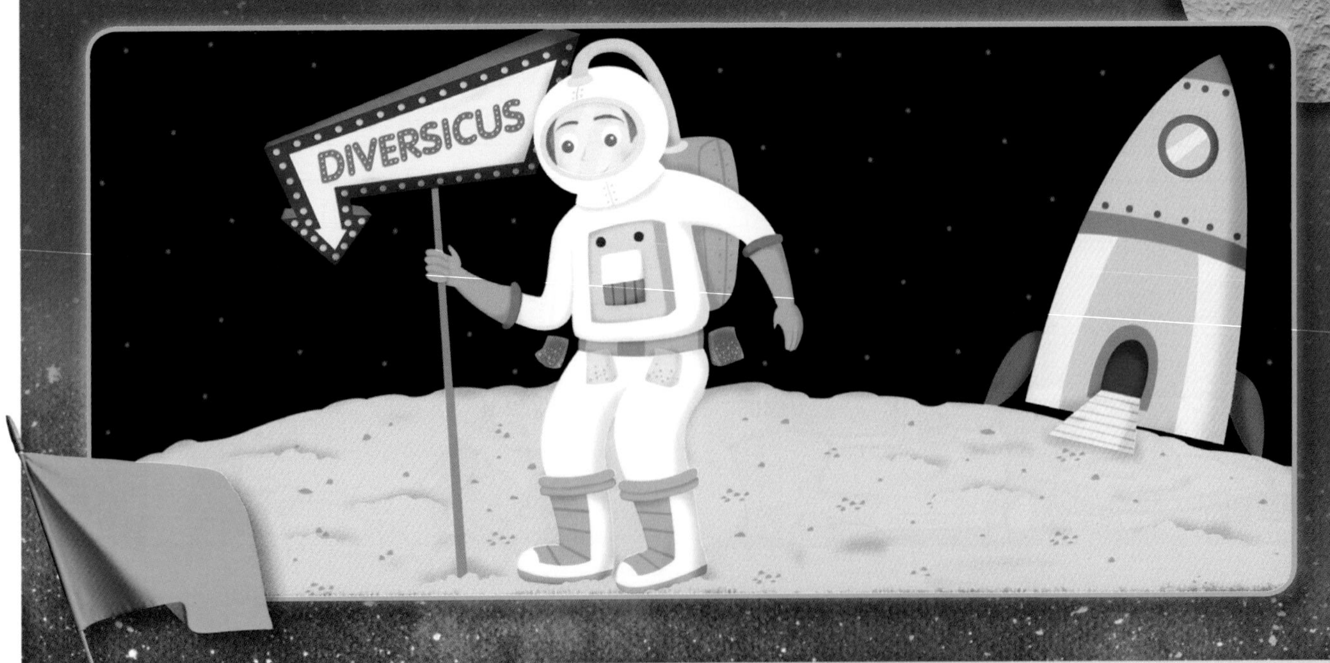

1 Oliver went to the circus last weekend. Read and put the sentences in order. Write the numbers.

a a pilot's uniform was singing beautifully on the stage, when ☐

b was wearing a fantastic costume with feathers. He caught the other acrobats ☐

c was amazing. There was a strongman who was carrying three people on his ☐

d suddenly a plane landed and she climbed in! One of the acrobats ☐

e Last weekend, we went to see a circus. When we entered the tent, musicians 1

f as they were flying through the air. It was the best show I've ever seen. ☐

g shoulders. He was dressed up as a firefighter. A woman who was wearing ☐

h were playing and we saw a beautiful stage with bright lights. The show ☐

2 Write questions with the past progressive and the simple past. Then invent answers.

1 What / he / do / when / his friend / arrive?
What was he doing when his friend arrived?
He was playing tennis when his friend arrived.

2 Where / they / go / when / they / meet / their teacher?

3 Where / they / explore / when / they / find / the pyramid?

4 What / she / do / when / her grandparents / arrive?

1 Read and write *Earth*, *Mars*, or *Both*.

1 It's called "the red planet." Mars
2 The diameter of the planet is 12,742 kilometers. ______
3 It has two moons. ______
4 It has weather and seasons. ______
5 You can see a lot of water on its surface. ______
6 There are 24 hours in a day on this planet. ______

2 Read the text and answer the questions.

In August 2015, astronauts on the ISS ate the first food grown in space. Normally, plant roots grow down into the soil where it is easy for them to take the water and nutrients. In space, because there is no gravity, the roots grow in all directions!

The plants grow in special containers. The containers have flexible walls so that the plants have space and can grow. There are bags of soil and nutrients inside the containers. Lights shine on the plants to give them the energy from light that they need.

The astronauts have grown lettuce, cabbage, and tomatoes from seeds. This is very exciting news because if we can grow plants on a space station, it might be possible to grow plants on the moon and on Mars.

1 When did astronauts eat the first food grown in space? In August 2015.
2 Why do roots grow in all directions on the space station?
______
3 Why are the walls of the containers flexible?
______
4 Which three things did they grow? ______
5 Why is this news so exciting?
______

3 Circle the correct answers. Use the Internet to help you.

1 Where is Italy?

a southern Europe **b** northern Europe
c western Europe **d** eastern Europe

2 What is the capital of Italy?

a Milan **b** Venice **c** Florence **d** Rome

3 How many sides of Italy are next to the sea?

a 4 **b** 3 **c** 2 **d** 1

4 What is the shape of Italy like?

a A square **b** A head **c** A hat **d** A boot

5 What is the most popular sport in Italy?

a Judo **b** Tennis **c** Soccer **d** Golf

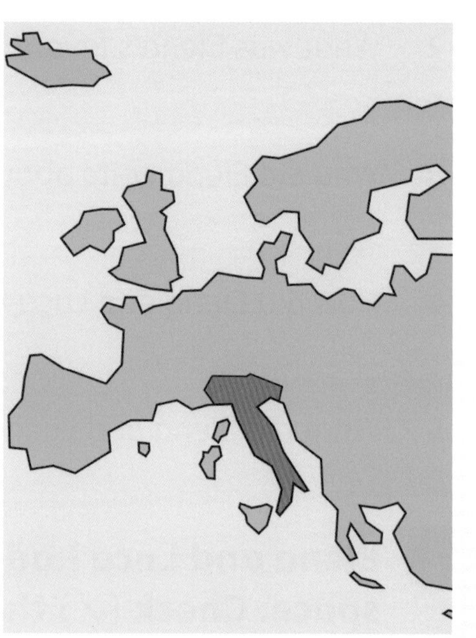

4 Complete the picture labels. Use the Internet to help you.

1 ______________ is a beautiful city with many canals.

2 You can see ______________ in Rome.

3 ______________ disappeared when a volcano erupted.

4 ______________
______________ was a famous artist who lived in Florence.

1 Answer the questions about *The Space Blog*.

1 Why did Elena and Luca go into space? They won a competition.

2 What was Elena's favorite thing about being in space?

3 Why did Elena write about food on the spaceship in Blog Post 3?

4 How did Elena and Luca feel when the engine wasn't working very well?

5 What did Elena and Luca have to do while the astronauts were fixing the engine?

2 Elena and Luca had to do lots of things before they went into space. Check (✓) the things in the list you think they had to do.

1 Swim underwater ☐
2 Watch different channels on TV ☐
3 Go to the doctor for a check-up ☐
4 Do a lot of exercise ☐
5 Sleep less than usual ☐
6 Learn about space ☐
7 Stay in bed all day ☐
8 Eat only chocolate cake ☐

SPACE
TRAINING CAMP

3 What special things do you think Elena and Luca took with them into space? Write three ideas and then share them with a partner.

I think they took a camera so they could take lots of pictures of Earth!

4 What would you take into space? Share your ideas with a partner.

5 **Look at the three pictures. Write about this story. Write 20 or more words.**

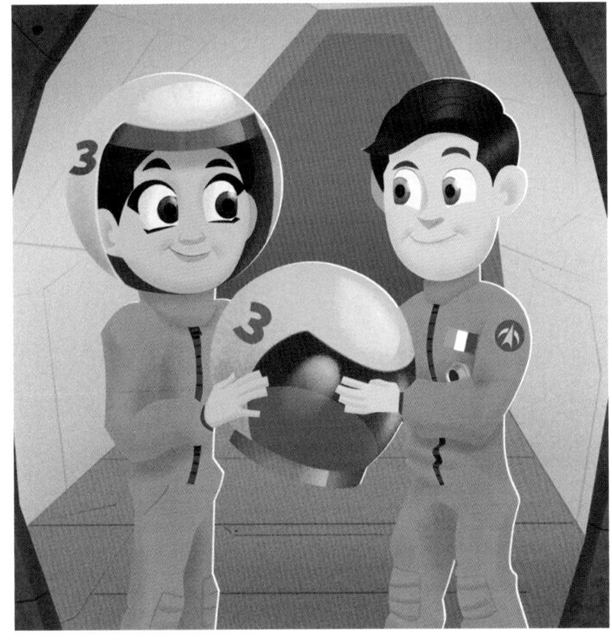

1 **Read the story. Choose a word from the box. Write the correct word next to numbers 1–5. There is one example.**

example				
~~space~~	deep	people	shelf	repairing
screen	ran	banks	flew	astronauts

Last Friday, Betty was preparing to go into ____space____ in an enormous rocket. First, she met the other astronauts in her team, Oliver and Helen. Betty checked their helmets. "We can't make a mistake because our trip is for two months," she told the team. Oliver suddenly remembered his gloves, so he (**1**) ____________ quickly back to his office to get them. The rocket was almost ready to leave!

At nine o'clock, they sat in their places. Betty wasn't worried because this was her tenth trip. She touched a (**2**) ____________ and turned on different machines. The engine started, and soon the team were on their way to an unusual planet called I-654-073K. "I feel sick," said Helen. It was only her second trip. She felt better after they (**3**) ____________ past the moon.

The team arrived. They explored the planet and collected some colorful rocks. The rocks helped Betty to explain why there weren't any (**4**) ____________ on I-654-073K.

There is going to be a party with scientists when the (**5**) ____________ come back, and Betty and her team are going to be on the news on TV!

2 **Now choose the best name for the story. Check one box.**

Helen Feels Sick ☐
Rocks from the Moon ☐
Good Job, Betty's Team! ☐

1 Read the instructions. Play the game.

INSTRUCTIONS

Choose four pictures. Write the words in your notebook. You need to collect these.

Roll the dice and move across the board.

Collect your four words. Check (✓) them in your notebook.

On green spaces, say the word.

On ? spaces, answer the question on the card.

On orange spaces, say and spell the past participle of the verb.

Review Units 7–8

1 **Choose a picture. Give a definition with *It's used to/for.* Your partner points and says the word.**

It's used for eating soup.

A spoon!

2 **Read Sophia's story. Find and write the words for feelings.**

Last night, I had a dream that I was an astronaut. I was in a rocket, and I was going to another planet. I remember I felt scared but also excited.

"You're going to arrive on the planet, and you're going to stay there for two years," another astronaut told me. I felt sad when I was saying goodbye to my family and friends.

When I arrived, I started to explore and I was surprised to find an enormous hole with something in it. "That's a spaceship," I thought as I looked down. I went back to my rocket to get my flashlight. I stood in front of the spaceship and touched the door.

Suddenly, someone (or something!?) opened the door, and it (or they) turned on a light. An unusual voice said, "Will you stay here and save us?"

"I smell cookies," I thought. "Is someone baking in there?" I felt happy, not afraid.

I don't remember the rest of the dream, but I was very hungry when I woke up! Dreams are strange, aren't they?

scared, ______________________________

3 Read Sophia's story again. Correct the sentences.

1 Sophia is an astronaut.

Sophia was an astronaut in her dream.

2 She was unhappy in her dream.

3 She felt sad when she was exploring the planet.

4 She found an empty hole.

5 She found the entrance and she opened the door.

6 She felt worried when she smelled the cookies.

7 She thinks dreams are boring.

4 Plan a story starting with *Last night, I had a dream that I was an astronaut.*

- Where were you going?
- How long are you going to stay there?
- How did you feel?
- What did you see/smell/hear?

5 Write your story. Use your notes from Activity 4.

CHECK!
Have you answered all the questions in Activity 4?
Have you used the format of a story?
Have you used the correct vocabulary and grammar?
Is your spelling correct?

9 Great bakers

My unit goals

- I want to ______________________________
- To do this, I will ______________________________
- I will say and write ____ new words.

My mission diary

How was it? Draw a face.

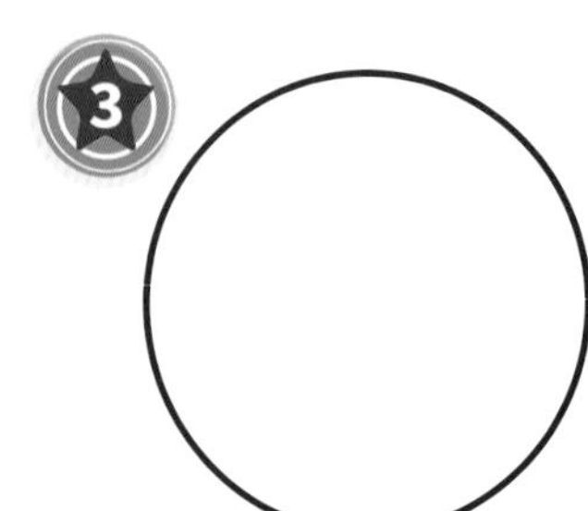

My favorite stage:

____

DIVERSICUS

- I can talk about mealtimes, snacks, and baking. ☐
- I can say what things look, feel, sound, smell, or taste like. ☐
- I can read and complete a text with the correct grammatical words. ☐
- I can say what makes me angry, sad, or happy. ☐
- I completed Level 4 Unit 9. ☑

Go to page 134 and add to your word stack!

1 Look and complete the crossword.

2 Match. Write the mealtime words and past participles

1	bo	bowl	rk	3	kn	oken
	bo	bought	oon		kn	rgotten
2	sp		~~wl~~	4	fo	~~ught~~
	sp		own		fo	ife

Sounds and spelling

3 Listen and circle the words with the *sh* sound in them.

5.25

snack delicious ocean station shampoo
chess sugar sure cheap shelf

4 Complete the words with the letters.

sh ci ti

1 space__ip 2 fire sta__on 3 musi__an

1 Choose words from the box to complete the sentences. You do not need to use all the words.

delicious expensive Grandpa like lots May ~~music~~ olives outside rice unusual

1 Grandpa thinks the ___music___ sounds nice.
2 They put on hats and sunblock because they're going to eat ________.
3 The sunblock smells ________ coconut.
4 Grandpa and Grandma are sitting on an ________ rug.
5 Jim tells Grandma how people eat ________ in South Korea.
6 ________ doesn't like olives.

2 Circle the correct words.

Su-Lin's Diary

What a great day we've [1]**had / have**! We're back home now and we had a party to say "goodbye" for the [2]**end / entrance** of the tour.

We've [3]**brought / sold** lots of things back from our trip, and we used [4]**any / some** of them for the party. We thought the music from Dubai [5]**tasted / sounded** wonderful. Mr. Friendly showed Jim and Jenny's [6]**parents / grandparents** the unusual rug that he found in Egypt. He was very pleased with it because it [7]**was / wasn't** cheap.

Jim and Jenny's grandpa tried to eat noodles with the chopsticks that Mom got in China, but he decided it was difficult ... but the [8]**funnier / funniest** moment was when he thought the olives were grapes because they looked like grapes. He didn't like them at all, and he said they tasted horrible!

Well, diary, this is the last day from this tour. Goodbye for now.

3 Review the story.

I think the story is **great / good / OK / not very good**.
My favorite character is ________.
My favorite part is when ________________.

1 Read and answer.

Katy was happy. That afternoon, a girl in her class was having a party, and she felt excited because she had an invitation. She was getting ready. While she was getting ready, she picked up her soap from the shelf in the bathroom. It looked like a rabbit, but it smelled like flowers. She loved it. While she was taking a shower, she also used her mom's expensive shampoo to wash her hair. The shampoo was called Butterfly Wings and it smelled like fruit and chocolate.

After her shower, Katy put on her costume. She dressed up like a piece of pizza.

Her mom smiled when she saw her and she said, "You look delicious, and you smell good enough to eat! It smells like you've used my shampoo!"

"Yes, I have," said Katy. "It makes me feel good. I feel like a queen."

"Yes, you look like the Queen of Pizzas," her mom laughed.

1 Who was having a party? A girl in Katy's class. ______

2 What did Katy pick up while she was getting ready? ______

3 What did her soap look like? ______

4 What did she use to wash her hair? ______

5 What did the shampoo smell like? ______

6 What did Katy put on after her shower? ______

7 What did she feel like? ______

2 Put the words in order. Write the sentences.

1 like oranges and | These cookies taste | delicious! | coconuts. They're

These cookies taste like oranges and coconuts. They're delicious!

2 was raining. | unhappy because it | looked | The children

______

3 like | This cheese | yesterday's socks! | smells

______

4 feels like | cat. | This blanket | a furry

______

5 whispering. | like people | wind sounds | That soft

______

1 Write the words in the correct column.

bake boil butter cheese clean up ~~cook~~ eggs flour fork ice cream
jelly knife ~~milk~~ mix oven rice scissors ~~spoon~~ ~~sugar~~ yogurt

Verbs	Dairy	Ingredients	Things we use
cook	milk	sugar	spoon

2 Put the sentences in order.

Ingredients
250 g soft butter 140 g sugar 1 egg yolk (the yellow part) 300 g flour lemon zest

a [ ] Clean up, make sure you leave a nice and clean kitchen, and enjoy the cookies.
b [ ] After 30 minutes, take out the mixture and cut it into the shapes that you want. The cookies can be circles, squares, or rectangles.
c [1] First, mix the butter and sugar in a large bowl. Use a wooden spoon.
d [ ] Put the cookies on a metal cookie sheet and put them carefully into the oven. Bake for 12–15 minutes.
e [ ] Second, add the egg yolk and lemon zest and mix together quickly.
f [ ] When the mixture is in the fridge, turn on the oven and heat it to 180°C./ 355°F.
g [ ] Then slowly add the flour and mix it all together. Use your hands to help you.
h [ ] Use oven mitts to take them out of the oven, and let them cool for 10 minutes.
i [ ] Put all the mixture in a plastic bag, and leave it in the fridge until it is cold.

1 Complete the sentences with the words in the box.

angry	bored	scared	happy	hungry	thirsty	tired	~~unhappy~~

1 Watching bad news on TV made my dad unhappy.
2 People who are mean to animals make me ______.
3 Our mom was baking bread in the kitchen. The smell made us ______.
4 Listening to her favorite pop music makes her ______.
5 The hot, dry desert made the explorer ______.
6 Traveling by car on a highway for a long time makes us ______.
7 Going on fast rides at the amusement park makes him ______.
8 Playing soccer all afternoon has made them ______.

2 Find six differences. Write sentences.

In picture A ,he's cleaned up the kitchen, but in picture B, he hasn't cleaned up it yet.

______

______

______

______

______

1 **Read about tea. Look at the tea bags 1–5. Where do sentences a–e go in the text? Write the numbers.**

Tea grows on large pieces of land called plantations. The best place to grow tea is on high land in the mountains because tea bushes need a lot of rain, and they don't like a lot of sun. 1

When the tea bushes are three years old, the plantation workers choose the smallest, youngest leaves from each plant. 2 Some plantations use machines to pick the leaves, but many plantations prefer people to pick them.

They send the tea to a factory. The leaves have a lot of water in them. Workers put the tea on large shelves, and leave them to dry in warm air. Now the leaves are about 60–70% water. 3 They put the broken leaves in a room for between half an hour and two hours. 4 The green leaves change to light brown and then darker brown. This makes kinds of tea that all taste different.

They use hot air to dry the leaves until they are only about 3% water. 5 These tea chests go to different factories where they make tea bags, or they put the loose tea into boxes to sell in stores.

- a ☐ In this room, oxygen changes the color of the leaves.
- b 1 The plants grow more slowly there, but the tea tastes better.
- c ☐ They pick the leaves carefully so that they do not hurt the plant.
- d ☐ Workers pack the tea into special boxes called tea chests.
- e ☐ Next, machines called rollers break the leaves.

2 **Compare the production of tea to the production of chocolate.**

1 Tea plants are bushes, but ______________________.

2 We use the leaves of the tea plant, but ______________________.

3 Tea plants need cool temperatures, but ______________________

______________________.

3 People in the U.S. like food from many different countries. Use the Internet to find out where these meals come from.

1 Paella comes from Spain.

2 Chicken korma comes from ________.

3 Pad Thai comes from ________.

4 Guacamole comes from ________.

5 Dim sum comes from ________.

6 Sushi comes from ________.

4 Complete the descriptions of these traditional foods from the U.S. Match them to the pictures.

1 ________ cookies were first made in the U.S. They're made of flour, sugar, butter, eggs, and chocolate chips, of course!

2 This is a piece of ________ pie. It's made with apples, cinnamon, nutmeg, and lemon juice. Some people like to eat it with ice cream on top.

3 A ________ is a sandwich made of cooked meat on a bread roll or bun. It's often served with cheese, lettuce, and tomato.

a 

b 

c 

1 Order the events from the gingerbread girl story.

a
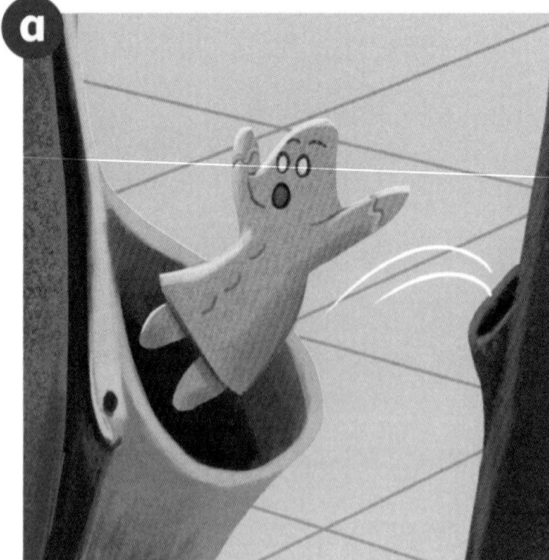
[ ] The gingerbread girl jumps into Mrs. Brett's handbag and escapes.

b
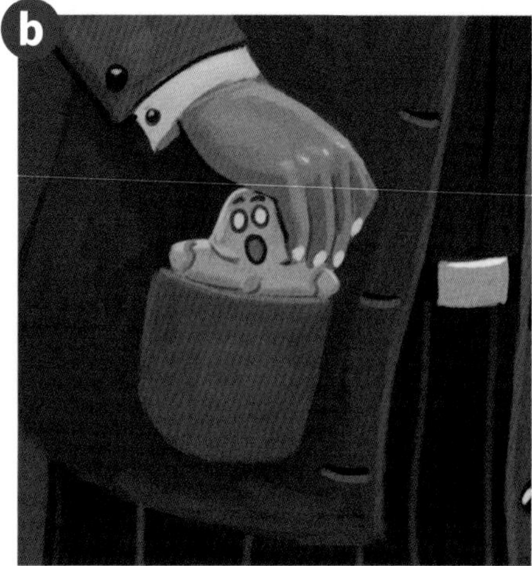
[ ] Mr. Brett puts a gingerbread girl in his pocket.

c

[ ] Bruno gives the gingerbread to the people at Spring Wood.

d
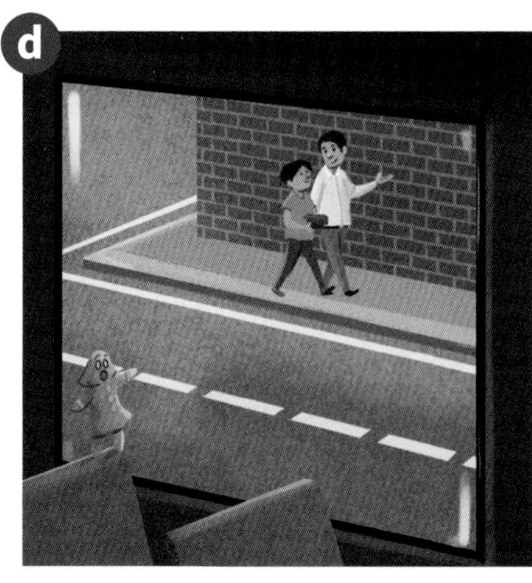
[ ] The gingerbread girl sees Bruno from the bus and runs to him.

e

[1] Bruno makes gingerbread people.

f

[ ] Mr. Brett comes to Bruno's house.

2 Write about something you made or did with love for someone. Who was it for? What was it? Draw a picture.

3 5.26 **Listen and draw lines. There is one example.**

Lucy

Charlie

Sarah

Robert

Katy

Helen

Nick

1 **Read the letter and write the missing words.**
Write one word on each line.

Example	We're ___having___ an amazing time in the mountains.
1	We've made some jelly, and tomorrow we're going ________ visit a village to see some bees. We're going to learn how they make honey!
2	Yesterday, we met a friend of Mom's while we ________ walking in
3	the mountains. He's a cook here. He invited ________ to his restaurant to make some cookies. They smelled delicious when they were
4	baking in the oven. They tasted better ________ the ones we usually buy in the supermarket. Later, we cleaned up the kitchen and walked to our hotel in the square. The walk made us hungry,
5	________ Mom and I ate an enormous pizza.

1 Read the instructions. Play the game.

FINISH

?

You didn't clean up the kitchen after you made a sandwich. Miss a turn.

?

I have to fix it because it's …

I can't pick up the suitcase because it's too …

?

I love the taste of pizza. It's …

?

?

I need to eat. I'm very …

You put salt instead of sugar in the apple pie. Go back 2 spaces.

?

You put sugar instead of salt in your paella. Go back 2 spaces

You cleaned up after lunch. Go forward 4 spaces.

?

I'd like some water, please. I'm …

?

He isn't kind, he's …

?

You've forgotten to turn on the oven. Go back 4 spaces.

S

The opposite of full is …

START

The opposite of unpopular is …

?

Everyone loves your cookies. Go forward 2 spaces.

INSTRUCTIONS

Roll the dice and move across the board.

On **green** spaces, say the word.

On **?** spaces, answer the question on the card.

On **purple** spaces, complete the sentence with an adjective.

Review unit

Units 1–3

1 Play the game.

1 Flip a coin to move spaces. If it's heads, move 2 spaces. If it's tails, move 1 space.
2 Read the sentence, and say if it's *True* or *False.*
3 If your sentence is *False*, move back one space.

START

1 January comes before February.	2 You might go skiing in the desert.	3 Ivan isn't stronger than anyone.	4 Mrs. Friendly may play the violin.
8 You may go hiking in the woods.	7 The beetles might play in a band.	6 You may swim in the ocean.	5 December comes before November.
9 The camel might not drink water every day.	10 There might be a lot of cars on the highway.	11 Butterflies are insects.	12 You might use a tent in the ocean.

FINISH

2 Look at Activity 1. Write the number for each picture.

3 Look, read, and complete the sentences.

Andrea is thinking about what she may do this year ....

go fishing	go hiking	go skiing	play volleyball

1 On January 17th, she might ____________ in the mountains.

2 She may ____________ in the stream on the last day of April.

3 She might ____________ at the beach on the first day of July.

4 On October 8th, she may ____________ in the woods.

4 Think about what you might do this year. Write. Then tell a partner.

1 ____________________________

2 ____________________________

I might explore a cave in August.

I may go ice skating in December.

5 Read and color.

1 Color the animal words **red**.

2 Color the natural place words **blue**.

3 Color the trip words **purple**.

4 Color the month words **yellow**.

5 Color the pronouns **orange**.

6 Color the verbs **green**.

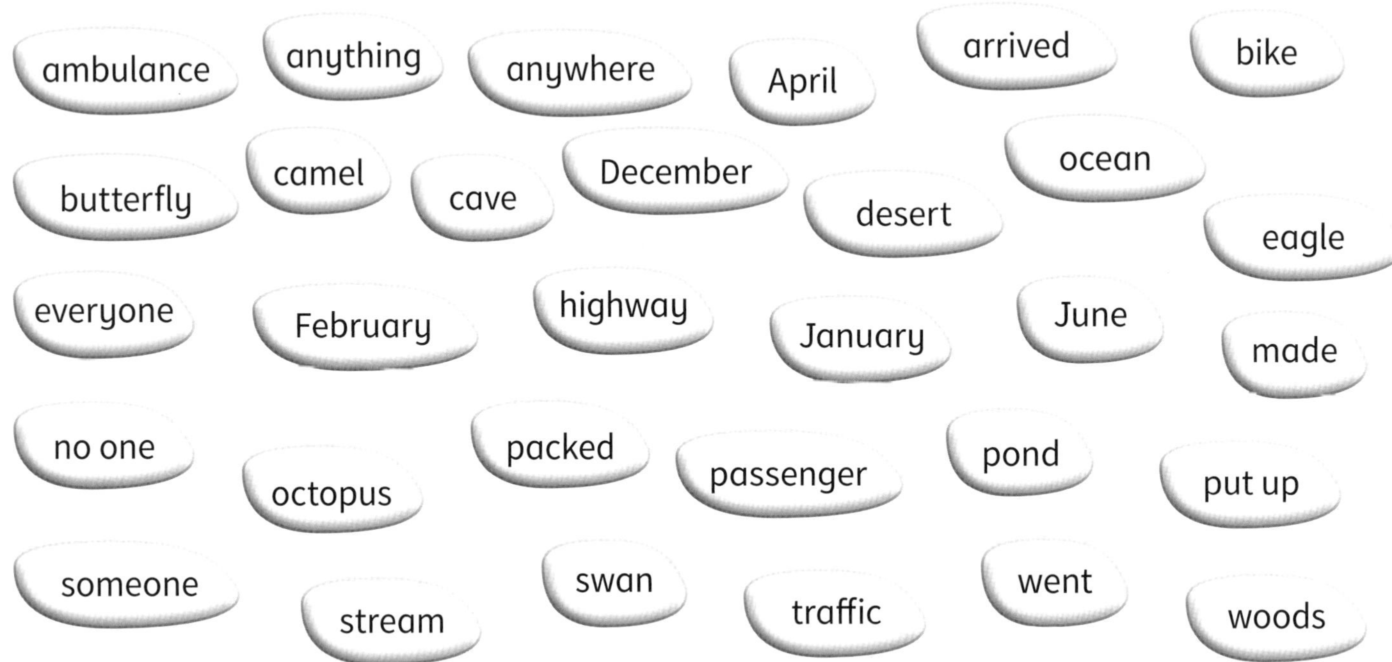

6 Find and cross out the mistakes. Then write the correct words. Use the words in Activity 5 to help you.

1 There were a lot of cars on the pond. ____________

2 He rode his boat in the park. ____________

3 The fire truck took the boy with the broken leg to the hospital. ____________

4 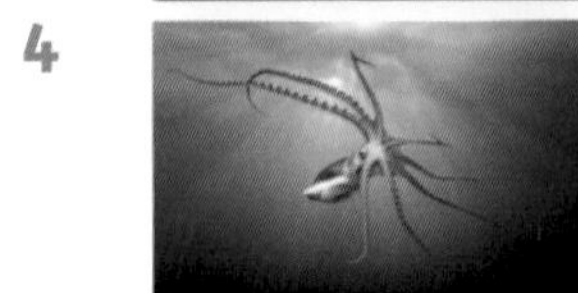 We saw an octopus swimming in the desert. ____________

7 Write the words in the correct order.

1 / because / I / loud / like / music / don't / it's / the / too / . /

____

2 / win / enough / He / . / wasn't / he / fast / didn't / because /

____

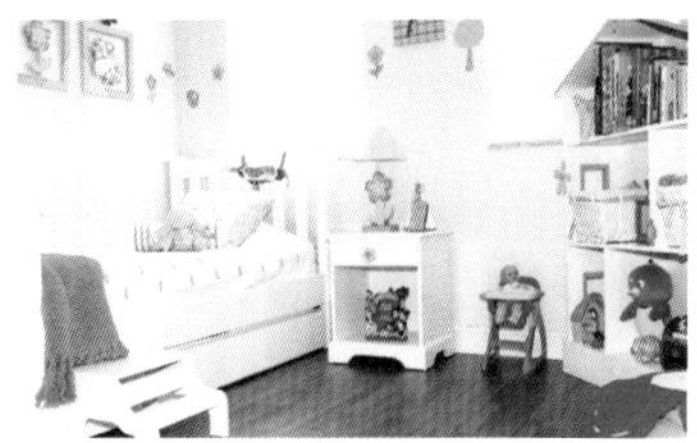

3 / messy / too / I / was / because / it / room / my / . / cleaned /

____

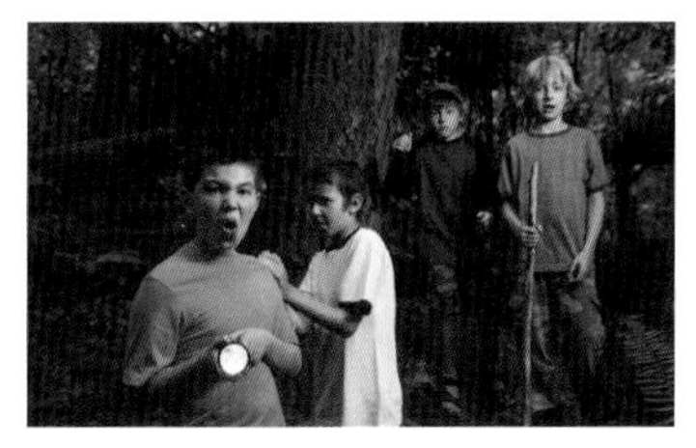

4 / enough / a / used / light / because / flashlight / it / wasn't / . / They /

____

8 Read and complete the chart. Then ask and answer with a partner.

	Have you ever … ?	Me		My Partner	
1	played chess	Yes ☐	No ☐	Yes ☐	No ☐
2	been in a race	Yes ☐	No ☐	Yes ☐	No ☐
3	won a prize	Yes ☐	No ☐	Yes ☐	No ☐
4	flown in a plane	Yes ☐	No ☐	Yes ☐	No ☐
5	taken a taxi?	Yes ☐	No ☐	Yes ☐	No ☐
6	ridden in an ambulance	Yes ☐	No ☐	Yes ☐	No ☐
7	seen a camel	Yes ☐	No ☐	Yes ☐	No ☐
8	seen an octopus	Yes ☐	No ☐	Yes ☐	No ☐
9	been to a desert	Yes ☐	No ☐	Yes ☐	No ☐
10	been in a cave	Yes ☐	No ☐	Yes ☐	No ☐
11		Yes ☐	No ☐	Yes ☐	No ☐
12		Yes ☐	No ☐	Yes ☐	No ☐

Have you ever played chess?

No, I haven't. Have you?

Units 4–6

1 Play the game.

1. Flip a coin to move spaces. If it's heads, move 2 spaces. If it's tails, move 1 space.
2. Read the sentence, and say if it's *True* or *False*.
3. If your sentence is *False*, move back one space.

START

1 A firefighter will put out the fire.	2 It was cold outside, so I wore a T-shirt and shorts.	3 A caterpillar won't change into a butterfly.	4 A pilot will fly the plane from London to New York.
8 I had a toothache, so I went to the dentist.	7 The turtle was running.	6 It will snow in the desert.	5 The leaves on the trees will change colors in the fall.
9 It was snowing outside, so I built a snowman.	10 A mechanic won't fix your car when it's broken.	11 It won't be hot in the summer.	12 The reporter was asking questions.

FINISH

2 Look at Activity 1. Write the number for each picture.

3 Which word is not like the others? Read and circle.

1 dentist passenger police officer firefighter mechanic

2 a.m. p.m. Friday hour minute

3 fire snowball sled snowman ice

4 spring April fall winter summer

5 fog storm warm foggy festival

6 police station factory office desert fire station

4 Use the words from Activity 3 to complete the chart.

Jobs	Seasons	Time	Weather	Winter	Work Places
dentist					

5 Draw lines to match the sentences to the short questions.

1 All the animals at the zoo were sleeping.
2 Elena set up a tent in the desert.
3 I made a fire to keep warm.
4 Jim made lunch for us.
5 We're going to look after the baby.
6 You'll win the competition.

a Did she?
b Did you?
c Were they?
d Will I?
e Did he?
f Are you?

6 Write the tag questions.

aren't you? didn't they? doesn't she?
will he? will we? won't you?

1 You're a firefighter, ____________________
2 She writes for the newspaper, ____________________
3 They went to the police station, ____________________
4 You'll meet my brother at the party, ____________________
5 He won't forget to pack a jacket, ____________________
6 We won't be late for school, ____________________

7 Ask and answer with a partner.

You take the bus to school, don't you?

Yes, I do. You walked to school today, didn't you?

No, I didn't. I rode my bike today.

Oh, did you?

8 Read and answer the questions.

Katy's *Busy* Day

Katy is tired because she had a busy day. She had a lot of homework and small jobs (or chores) to do. Look at Katy's "To Do" list, and read about what she did today.

Done:	Katy's "To Do" List:	Start:	Finish:
✓	Water the flowers and plants.	2:30 p.m.	2:45 p.m.
✓	Clean bedroom.	3:00 p.m.	4:00 p.m.
✓	Fold laundry.	4:00 p.m.	4:30 p.m.
✓	Wash the dinner dishes.	6:00 p.m.	6:20 p.m.
✓	Take out the trash.	6:20 p.m.	6:30 p.m.
✓	Do homework.	6:30 p.m.	8:30 p.m.

1 What was Katy doing at 2:30 p.m.?

She was watering the flowers and plants.

2 What was she doing at 3:00 p.m.?

____

3 What was she doing at 6:00 p.m.?

____

4 What was she doing at 6:20 p.m.?

____

9 Look at Katy's "To Do" list in Activity 8. Answer the questions.

1 How long was Katy watering the flowers and plants? *For 15 minutes*

2 How long was she folding and putting away the laundry? __________

3 How long was she doing her homework? __________

Units 7–9

1 Play the game.

1 Flip a coin to move spaces. If it's heads, move 2 spaces. If it's tails, move 1 space.
2 Read the sentence, and say if it's *True* or *False.*
3 If your sentence is *False*, move back one space.

START

1 A fridge is used for cooking rice.

2 Mr. Friendly bought a camel when he was in Egypt.

3 Astronauts explore in the desert.

4 When I smell pizza, it makes me hungry.

5 A knife is used for eating soup.

6 Grandpa Friendly thinks that olives look like grapes.

7 An oven is used for baking cookies.

8 Mars is sometimes called the "Blue Planet."

9 A key is used for opening the door.

10 It's unusual to have snow in the summer.

11 A rocket is used to go into space.

12 Mr. Friendly has never ridden on a camel.

FINISH

2 Look at Activity 1. Write the number for each picture.

3 Read. Then answer the questions.

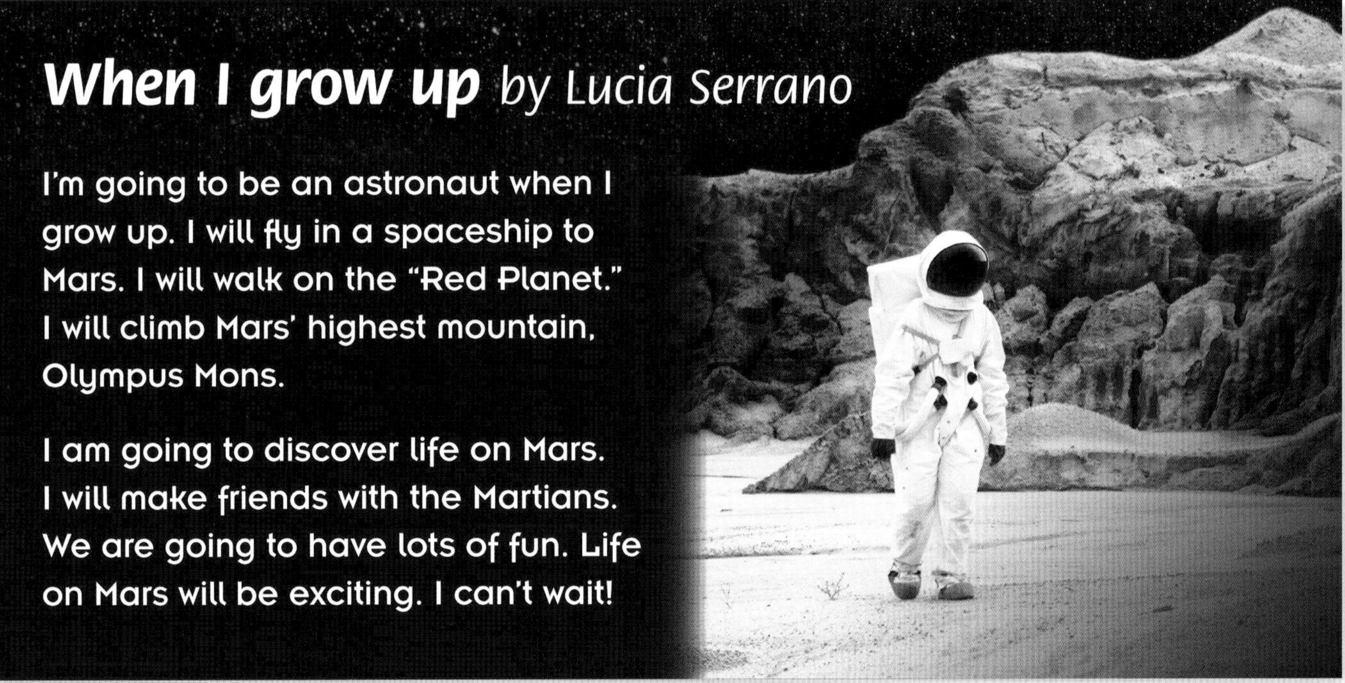

1 What is Lucia going to be when she grows up?

2 What is she going to discover?

3 Who will she make friends with?

4 What does Lucia think life on Mars will be like?

4 Finish the sentences to write a story.

1 I was exploring on Mars when

2 I was climbing Olympus Mons when

3 I was walking back to my spaceship when

5 Read. Then look and number the pictures in the order of the story.

Dan and Stan's Camping Adventure

Dan and Stan explored the mountain and found a place to camp. It was a beautiful spot. It was next to a stream, and there were lots of trees. They set up their tents and rolled out their sleeping bags. Then it was noon, and it was time for lunch.

Dan made a fire and cooked hamburgers. The smell of the hamburgers cooking over the fire made Stan hungry. When lunch was ready, Stan was so hungry he ate three hamburgers. After lunch, Stan was full and tired, so he took a nap. When Stan was napping, Dan went fishing in the stream.

Dan was sitting next to the stream and waiting for the fish to bite when he heard a loud noise. It sounded like a monster. It made him feel scared. He turned around and saw a big, brown bear. Dan couldn't move because he was too scared. He watched as the bear walked into the stream, grabbed a fish, and ate it. When the bear finished eating, it walked back into the trees. Dan couldn't believe his eyes.

Dan wanted to catch fish like the bear. He walked into the stream and grabbed a fish with his hands. He caught it! Then he grabbed another fish and caught that one, too. Now, he had two fish for dinner tonight. Stan would be happy.

6 Read the story in Activity 5. Then draw lines to connect the sentences.

1	Dan and Stan explored the mountain and	a	he caught fish like the bear.
2	They set up their tents and	b	he ate three hamburgers.
3	Then it was noon and	c	he saw a bear.
4	Stan was really hungry, so	d	found a beautiful place to camp.
5	When Stan was napping,	e	rolled out their sleeping bags.
6	Dan was fishing when	f	Dan made lunch.
7	Dan caught two fish because	g	Dan went fishing in the stream.

7 Read and complete Dan's letter to his mom. Use correct verb tenses.

feel look smell sound taste

Dear Mom,

Thank you for the cookies you sent in the mail. They're so good. I ate five already. They [1] __________ like the ones Grandma makes. Did you use her recipe?

I'm camping in the mountains with Stan. We are in a beautiful spot. It [2] __________ like a painting. There are lots of trees and a stream. The water in the stream is clean and clear, and it [3] __________ like a cool bath.

I was fishing in the stream yesterday when I saw a bear. I heard it first, and it [4] __________ like a monster in the trees. It scared me, but it didn't hurt me. It caught a fish with its paws, ate it, and then went back into the woods.

I tried catching fish like the bear, and I caught two fish! Stan cooked the fish over the fire, and when it was cooking it [5] __________ like the most delicious food in the whole world!

Write soon!

Dan

1 Write your favorite new words.

Home Booklet

Kathryn Escribano

with Caroline Nixon and Michael Tomlinson

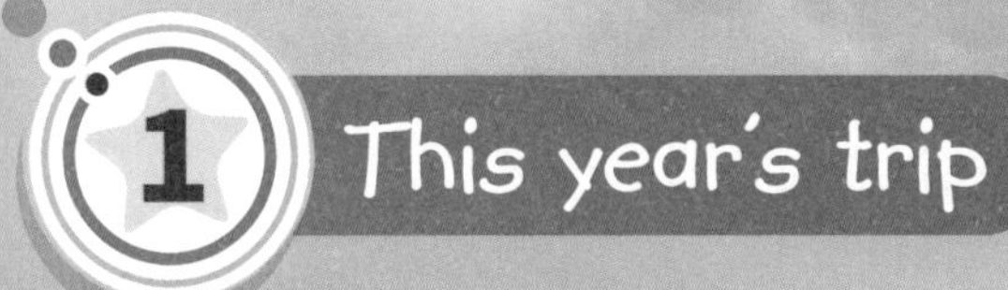

1 This year's trip

Birthday math!

When's Katy's birthday? Do the math and find out!

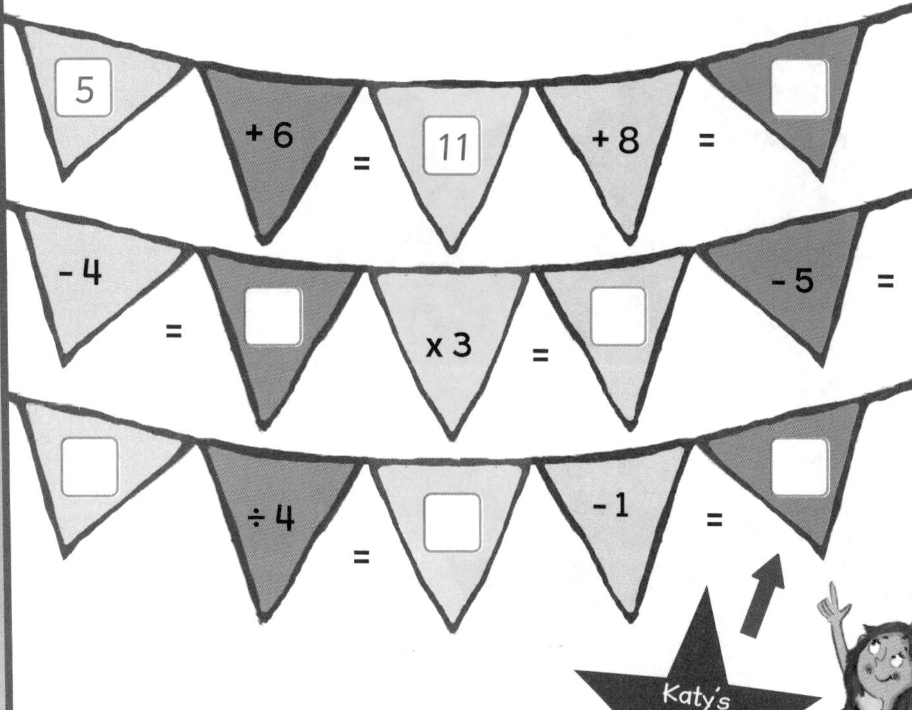

Katy's birthday is in the **eighth** / **ninth** / **tenth** month.
The name of this month is ________________.

Did you know?

The word "calendar" comes from the Latin word *Kalendae*. It means "the first day of the month."

What word does your birthday month come from?

Funny English

In your dreams ...

You can say "in your dreams" when you think something is impossible.

I think all the stores are open January 1st.

Yeah, **in your dreams!**

Is there a similar phrase in your language?

Guess what it is

ambulance ~~bicycle~~ highway platform taxi train station

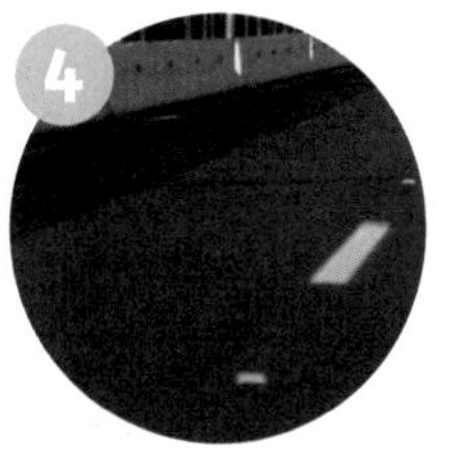

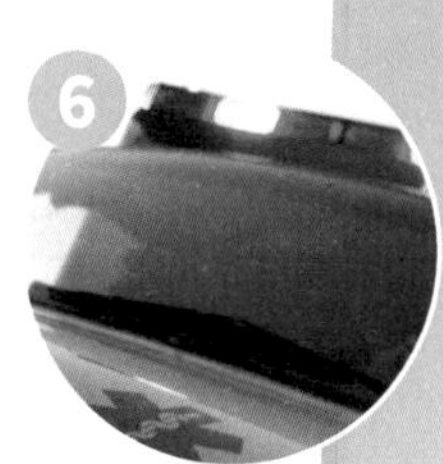

1 *It may be a bicycle.*

2 ______________________

3 ______________________

4 ______________________

5 ______________________

6 ______________________

Window to the World

Burj Al Arab is a luxury hotel on an artificial island in Dubai. It looks like a huge ship sail → ⛵ . There's a restaurant under the sea and a helipad (a space for a helicopter) → Ⓗ .

In 2005, two famous tennis players played on the hotel helipad. Who were they? Find out!

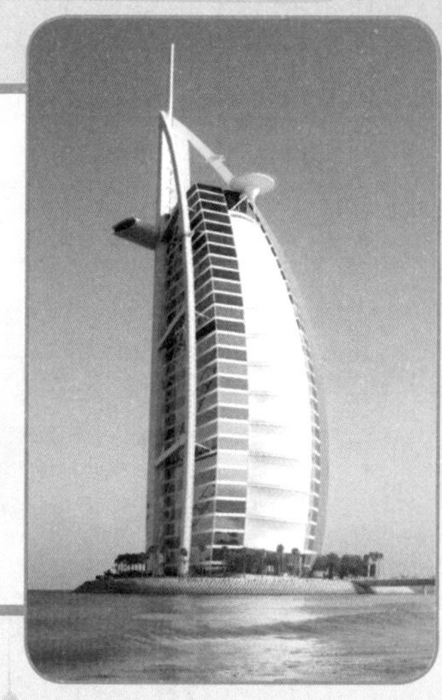

Home mission

Design a luxury hotel.

- Ask three people at home for ideas. What does the hotel have? What does it look like? Where is it? You can use the words in the box.

gyms movie theaters restaurants stores swimming pools

- Draw your hotel, name it, and describe it.

This is the "Silver Hotel." It has two swimming pools and four restaurants. There are …

Our beautiful planet

Natural world word search puzzle

Find 11 more words. Circle the animal words blue and the natural places green.

j	s	t	r	e	a	m	l	w	p	o
t	u	r	t	l	e	s	e	o	h	c
o	l	c	c	h	i	w	c	o	i	t
c	l	a	n	d	e	a	a	d	a	o
e	x	v	o	r	o	n	m	s	n	p
a	d	e	s	e	r	t	e	n	c	u
n	f	t	n	e	a	g	l	e	s	s
l	a	v	i	b	e	e	t	l	e	e

Funny English

It's raining cats and dogs!

You can say "It's raining cats and dogs!" when it's raining a lot.

Let's stay at home. It's raining cats and dogs!

What do you do when it's raining cats and dogs?

Window to the World

Some words that Australians use are different from the words that people use in the U.K.

What do these Australian English words mean?

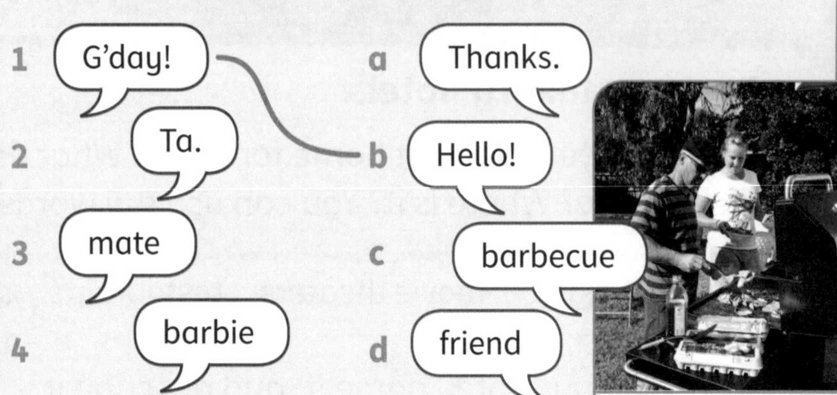

an Australian "barbie"

Are there different words for the same thing in your language?

Picture instructions

- Read the instructions and find, circle, and write three more mistakes in Michael's picture.
- Read the instructions again and draw the picture in your notebook.

Instructions

On the right, draw three trees. In the sky above the trees, draw four butterflies. On the left, draw a stream and a swan swimming in it. Next to the stream, on the grass, draw six stones. At the back, draw three hills, and draw a cave in the second hill.

1 *There aren't enough trees.*

2 There are too many ______.

3 ______

4 ______

Home mission

With people at home, match the places and animals from Australia to the descriptions. What is your favorite place? What is your favorite animal? Ask the people at home what they prefer.

a emus **b** koalas **c** Kangaroo Island **d** Uluru

1 These marsupials sleep for more than 20 hours a day! ☐

2 These are the largest birds in Australia. ☐

3 Another name for this huge red rock formation is Ayers Rock. ☐

4 Koalas, penguins, and kangaroos live there. ☐

What is your favorite place?

It's Kangaroo Island.

3 Let's celebrate!

Have you ever ... ?

- Circle *Yes* or *No*. Then count your points and read your result.
- **Yes** = 2 points **No** = 1 point

- **Have you ever visited another country?** Yes / No
- **Have you ever traveled by plane?** Yes / No
- **Have you ever eaten food from another country?** Yes / No
- **Have you ever spoken to someone from another country?** Yes / No
- **Do you like learning about other countries?** Yes / No
- **Have you ever watched a movie from another country?** Yes / No

Points

- **10–12 points:** You've had lots of experiences about different countries. You've been lucky!
- **7–9 points:** You've had some experiences about different countries. Why don't you look for more?
- **6 points:** You haven't had many experiences about different countries yet, but there may be some in the future. Enjoy them when they come!

Window to the World

Capoeira is a Brazilian activity with dance, music, and martial arts. People often play capoeira in a circle called a "roda."

Are there any sports or activities that come from your country?

What do the crazy words mean?

volleyball

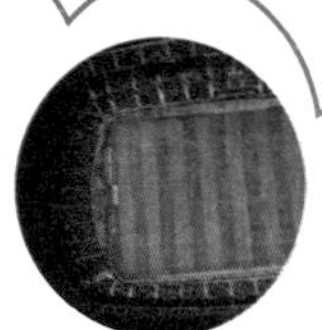
chess

stadium

violin

drum

instruments

- stadrum: *stadium + drum = a stadium where you play the drums*
- volleyments: ______________________
- instruchess: ______________________
- vioball: ______________________
- volleydium: ______________________
- drumlin: ______________________

Funny English

It rings a bell.

If something "rings a bell," you can remember it, but not fully.

*Your name **rings a bell**. Did we play volleyball last year?*

Is there a similar phrase in your language?

Did you know?

Chess comes from India. People first played chess 1,500 years ago!

What's the English name for your favorite chess piece?

Home mission

Who sings best at home? Ask three people to sing *Happy Birthday* (or another song that you like). Then sing the song yourself. Give everyone a score out of ten and see who's the winner!

4 Time of our lives

Emma, David, or Holly?

My name's **Emma**. I was born in Los Angeles, but now I live in Boston. I'm ten and I've played tennis since I was seven. I love sports! I don't have a pet. Last July, I went to Colombia with my family. I met my cousins there. It was great!

I'm **David** and I'm ten. I was born in Boston in the house where I live now. I have a dog, Tess. I've had Tess since I was four, and I love taking care of her. I play the drums. I began when I was six. I love music!

My name's **Holly** and I'm nine years old. I've lived in Boston all my life but in two different houses. Two years ago, I began to play the violin, and a year ago I started tennis lessons. I like music and sports, but I don't like preparing for exams!

1 ___David___ has always lived in the same house.

2 ____________ has played tennis for three years.

3 ____________ has had a pet for six years.

4 ____________ is learning to play an instrument and a sport.

5 ____________ has been to a different country.

6 ____________ has played tennis for a year.

Funny English

race against the clock

You "race against the clock" when you do something quickly because there isn't enough time.

This homework is due tomorrow. I'm ***racing against the clock*** *to finish it!*

When was the last time you raced against the clock?

Did you know?

Bogotá is one of the highest capital cities in the world.

What is the highest city in your country?

What was the time?

Read Katy's note and look at the pictures. Can you draw the hands on Katy's clocks?

Yesterday was a busy day! While I was sleeping, Michael was having breakfast. While I was cleaning my room, Michael was preparing for his math exam. And while Michael was repairing his bike, I was looking after my brother.

1 

2 

3 

a 

b 

c 

Window to the World

Colombia is famous for its coffee. Have you ever seen a coffee plant?

Look at the picture of the coffee beans. What fruit do they look like? Circle.

Coffee beans look like **strawberries / mangoes / grapes.**

What food or drink is your country famous for?

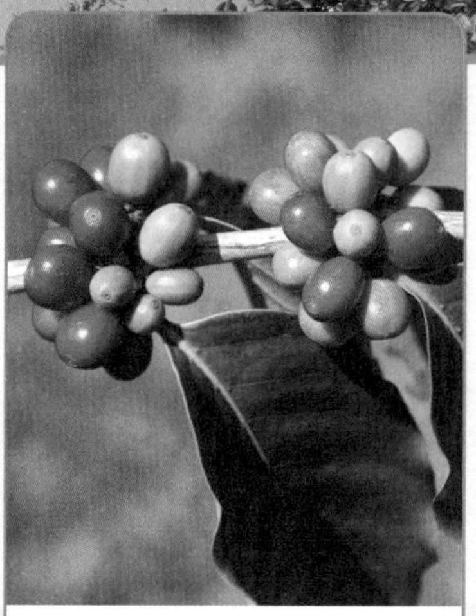
coffee beans on a coffee plant

Home mission

Look at the times from Michael's clocks and write three more times. Write what you were doing yesterday at these times. Then ask someone at home and write their answers. Were you doing the same thing at any of the times?

8:10 in the morning   4:25 in the afternoon   5:45 in the afternoon

What were you doing yesterday at ten past eight in the morning?

I was taking a shower.

5 Let it snow!

Storyboard

- Choose a number between two and six.
- Start on "spring" and move around the board. Cross out the words you stop on. For example, if you choose number 3, cross out "fall" and then "foggy."
- Keep going around the storyboard, moving the number of squares you have chosen. Jump over the crossed out words and cross out new ones. When you have one word of each color, make a crazy sentence!
- Repeat the game. Choose a different number each time.

It's spring and there's ice. Michael says "I'll swim in the pond."

START →

	spring	summer	fall	winter	
I'll make a snowman.					warm
I'll go to the beach.					foggy
I'll swim in the pond.					storm
I'll go skiing.					ice
	Katy	Jim	Michael	Betty	

Did you know?

Argentina's name comes from the Latin word *argentum*, that means "silver." It's the only country in the world named after a metal.

What's the origin of the name of your country?

Window to the World

The Perito Moreno Glacier (*Glaciar Perito Moreno*) is in the southwest of Argentina. It's one of the most beautiful places to visit in Patagonia. A glacier is a huge body of ice.

Do glaciers move? Find out!

Match the joke parts

Why did the melon jump into the pond?

Why was the math book sad?

Why do birds fly south in winter?

Why did Katy throw the clock out of the window?

Why didn't the skeleton go to the dance?

Because it's easier than walking!

Because it had many problems!

Because he had noBODY to go with!

So it could become a WATERmelon!

So she could see time fly!

Choose your favorite joke and draw it in your notebook. Show it at home!

get cold feet

You "get cold feet" when you become too scared to do something you wanted to do.

*I wanted to learn snowboarding, but I **got cold feet**!*

Have you ever gotten cold feet?

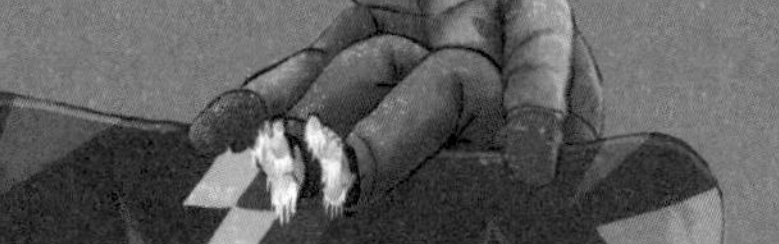

Do you change your clocks in spring and fall? What happens to the light in the mornings and evenings when the clocks change? Is changing the clocks a good idea? Ask three people at home.

Do you think changing the clocks in spring is a good idea?

Yes, I think it is.

Break the jobs code

Use the code to write the jobs. Then write the code for three more jobs.

	A	B	C	D	E
1	a	b	c	d	e
2	f	g	h	i	j
3	k	l	m	n	o
4	p	q	r	s	t
5	u	v	w	x	y

1 1E – 3D – 2B – 2D – 3D – 1E – 1E – 4C = engineer

2 4A – 2D – 3B – 3E – 4E = ______________

3 3C – 1E – 1C – 2C – 1A – 3D – 2D – 1C = ______________

4 ______________

5 ______________

6 ______________

Window to the World

Taekwondo is a South Korean martial art with high kicks and jumps. Its name comes from the Korean words *tae* = foot; *kwon* = fist → and *do* = way of. Taekwondo means "the way of the foot and fist."

Another martial art from South Korea starts with the letter *H*. What's its name? What does the name mean?

snowed under

You are "snowed under" when you have too much work.

*My aunt needs help. She's **snowed under** with work!*

What can you do if you feel snowed under?

What are they saying?

Write the sentences. Then match the short questions to the sentences.

already / my / I've / prepared / school uniform

~~I / my / before / cleaned / room / I / to bed / went~~

not / I'm / the / watching / soccer match

cake / the / I / eat / didn't

a Didn't you?
b Have you?
~~c Did you?~~
d Aren't you?

1

I cleaned my room before I went to bed. c

2

3

4

Home mission

Ask four people at home what they wanted to be when they were children. Compare their answers with the jobs they have now. Is anyone doing the job they wanted to do when they were young? What would you like to be when you grow up?

What did you want to be when you were a child?

I wanted to be a pilot. I loved planes!

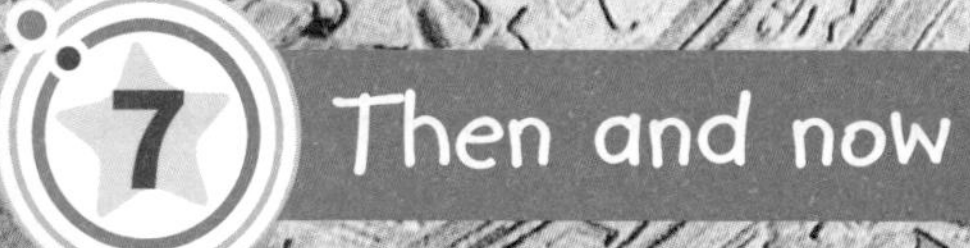

Things in the home sudoku

Write the missing words. The same word can't be on the same line → ↓ or in the same rectangle.

comb		brush			key
	refrigerator			____	
oven			soap		____
____		____	____		
____	____		____	____	____
			____	____	

Did you know?

People started using combs about 5,000 years ago. The ancient Egyptians made combs out of wood.

Do you have a comb? What color is it?

brush up

If you "brush up on" something, you study and practice it.

*I'm going to **brush up on my English** before my trip to New York.*

Do you have to brush up on something this week?

ENGLISH

Crazy definitions!

- Play and write definitions. You need a die, a pencil, and paper.
- Check (✓) or put an ✗ in the box.

What's a refrigerator used for? It's used for brushing your hair. ✗

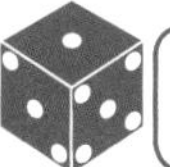

- What's a refrigerator used for?
- What's a brush used for?
- What's an oven used for?
- What's a key used for?
- What's shampoo used for?
- What's a telephone used for?

- It's used for brushing your hair.
- It's used for cooking food.
- It's used to keep food fresh.
- It's used to wash your hair.
- It's used to open a door.
- It's used to speak to someone in another place.

Window to the World

About 5,000 years ago, the ancient Egyptians started to use hieroglyphs to write. A hieroglyph is a picture that represents a sound or a word. The people who wrote were called "scribes," and they started learning to write hieroglyphs when they were six.

Can you write your name using the hieroglyphs in the chart?

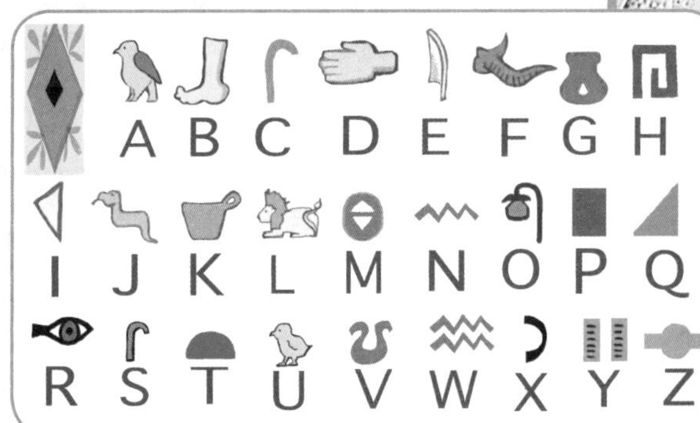

Home mission

Use the hieroglyphs chart on this page to write the names of four people at home. Then show them the names. Can they guess whose name is whose?

I think this one is my name.

Yes, it is!

8 Space travel

Amazing rocket

Circle eight more space words in the rocket. When you find an extra letter, write it below. What's the mystery word?

The mystery word is s__________________.

Window to the World

The ancient Romans named most of the planets in our solar system. Only one planet got its name from the ancient Greeks. **What planet is it?**

Find out and circle it.

Mercury Venus Earth Mars
Jupiter Saturn Uranus Neptune

Funny English

once in a blue moon

You do something "once in a blue moon" when you don't do it very often.

My grandma turns on the TV ***once in a blue moon.*** *She doesn't like it.*

What do you do once in a blue moon?

Space calculator

- You need a calculator, a pencil, and paper.
- Read the instructions and do the math. Remember to total the sum after each stage. What are you in space to discover?

1 Your spaceship has the number 1569. Put this number on your calculator.
2 You are going to go into space on December 28, so add 1228 → **1569 + 2805**
3 Your spaceship has three parts, so multiply by 3 → **1569 + 1228 x 3**
4 It's time to leave and count down! So subtract 10 → **1569 + 1228 x 3 – 10**
5 You're traveling with two astronauts, so multiply by 2 → **1569 + 1228 x 3 – 10 x 2**
6 There are eight planets in our solar system, so add 8 → **1569 + 1228 x 3 – 10 x 2 + 8**
7 The International Space Station is 350 kilometers above the earth, so add 350 → **1569 + 1228 x 3 – 10 x 2 + 8 + 350**
8 350 kilometers is 218 miles, so add 218 → **1569 + 1228 x 3 – 10 x 2 + 8 + 350 + 218**
9 After two days, you get to the ISS, so multiply by 2 → **1569 + 1228 x 3 – 10 x 2 + 8 + 350 + 218 x 2**
10 You go around the Earth 16 times a day: that's 64 times in four days. Add 64 → **1569 + 1228 x 3 – 10 x 2 + 8 + 350 + 218 x 2 + 64**
11 You fall asleep and dream that you're 40! So add 40 → **1569 + 1228 x 3 – 10 x 2 + 8 + 350 + 218 x 2 + 64 + 40**

- Write the result of your sum here: ____________
- Now, use this chart to break the code and write the word. The word is ____________.

0	3	4	8	7
s	h	o	e	l

- Use the word above to complete what you are in space to discover.
I'm in space to discover black ____________.

Home mission

Play the planets game.

- With people at home, practice this sentence to remember the order of the planets in English. The first letter of each word is the first letter of each planet.

My **V**ery **E**nthusiastic **M**other **J**ust **S**erved **U**s **N**oodles!

- Close your Home Booklet. Can you all say the names of the planets in order?

What's wrong?

Look at the ingredients to make English scones. Look at the picture. What's wrong?

English scones

225 grams of flour

¼ teaspoon of salt

3 teaspoons of baking powder

50 grams of butter

25 grams of sugar

150 milliliters of milk

1 egg

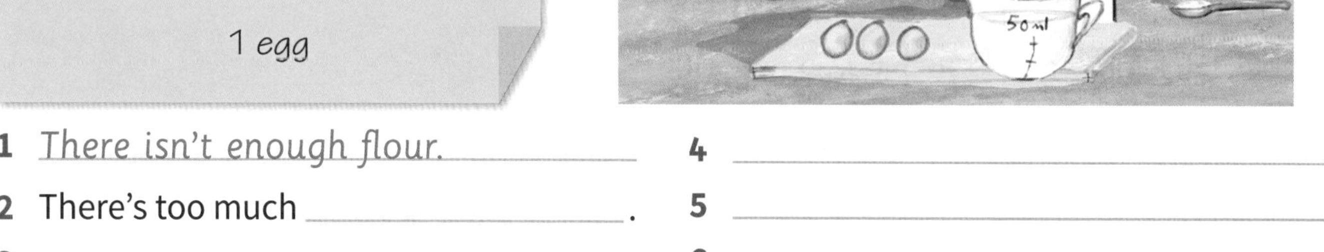

1 *There isn't enough flour.*

2 There's too much ______________.

3 ______________

4 ______________

5 ______________

6 ______________

Window to the World

"Slang" is informal words and phrases that people use. Cockney rhyming slang comes from the east of London and uses words that rhyme. For example, *cookies and cheese* means *knees* (*cheese* rhymes with *knees*).

What do these phrases mean? Circle the correct word. It has to rhyme!

Jam tart means **spoon** / **heart**.

Plates of meat means **feet** / **legs**.

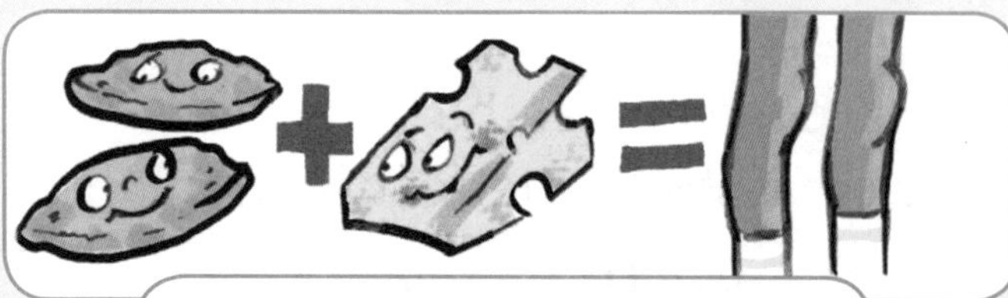

cookies and cheese = knees

a piece of cake

Something is "a piece of cake" when it's very easy.

I did my homework in ten minutes because it was a piece of cake!

What's a piece of cake for you?

Emotions pizza!

Complete each piece of pizza with your ideas. You can use these words:

makes me ... angry excited happy hungry sad scared thirsty

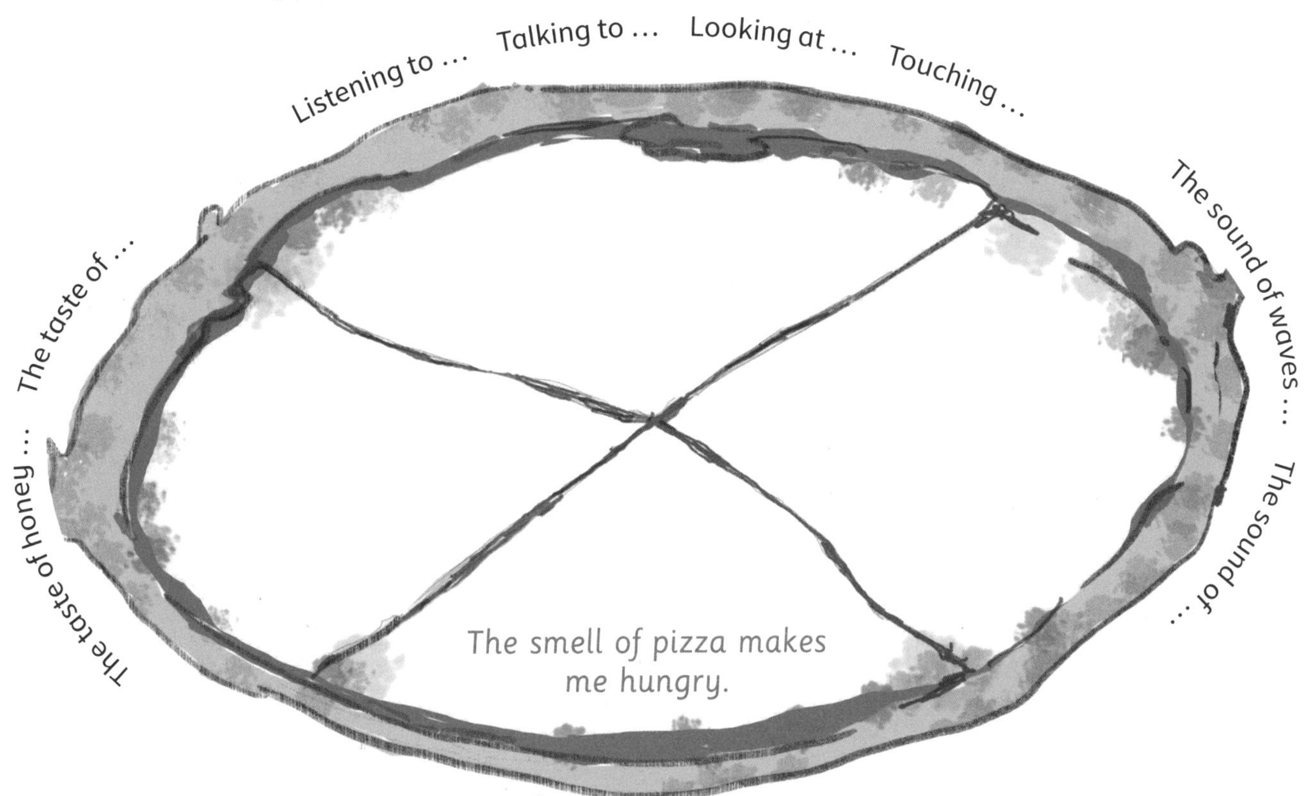

Home mission

What does your favorite sandwich have in it? Write your answer. Then ask three people at home and compare their answers with your own. Are any of the ingredients the same?

What does your favorite sandwich have in it?

It has cheese, olives, and ...

What sandwich makes you hungry? Make it and enjoy it!

Did you know?

The inventor of the sandwich was British. His name was the Earl of Sandwich. He wanted to have a quick lunch, so he asked for "a piece of meat between two pieces of bread."

Find out about a snack from your country. Who invented it?

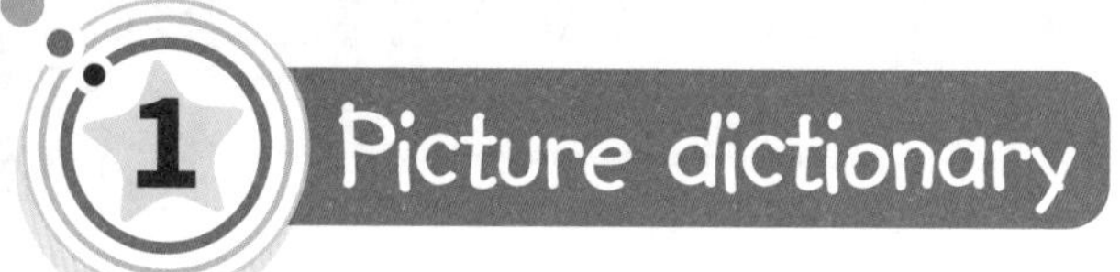

Ordinal numbers

1st	2nd	3rd	4th	5th	6th
first	second	third	fourth	fifth	sixth

7th	8th	9th	10th	11th
seventh	eighth	ninth	tenth	eleventh
12th	13th	14th	15th	16th
twelfth	thirteenth	fourteenth	fifteenth	sixteenth
17th	18th	19th	20th	21st
seventeenth	eighteenth	nineteenth	twentieth	twenty-first
22nd	23rd	24th	25th	26th
twenty-second	twenty-third	twenty-fourth	twenty-fifth	twenty-sixth
27th	28th	29th	30th	31st
twenty-seventh	twenty-eighth	twenty-ninth	thirtieth	thirty-first

When's your birthday?
Think of three people at home. When are their birthdays?

Months

Jan	Feb	Mar	Apr	May	Jun
1	2	3	4	5	6
January	February	March	April	May	June
Jul	**Aug**	**Sep**	**Oct**	**Nov**	**Dec**
7	8	9	10	11	12
July	August	September	October	November	December

What's your favorite month?

Journeys

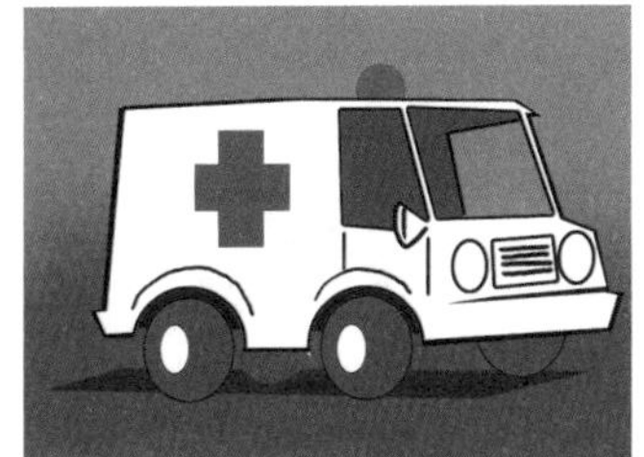

ambulance

bicycle

highway

passenger

platform

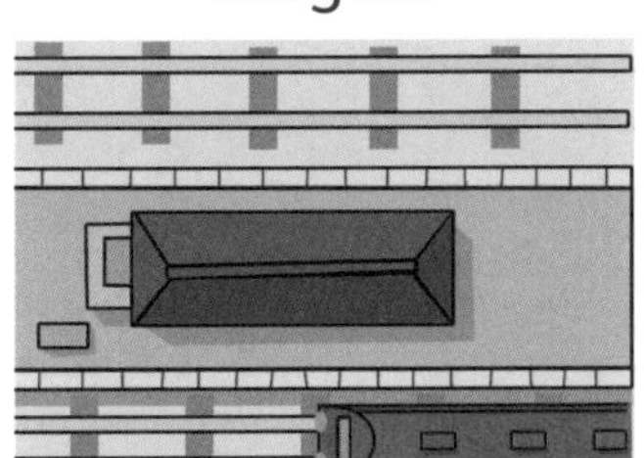

train station

taxi

traffic

Can you think of five more journey and transport words?

The natural world

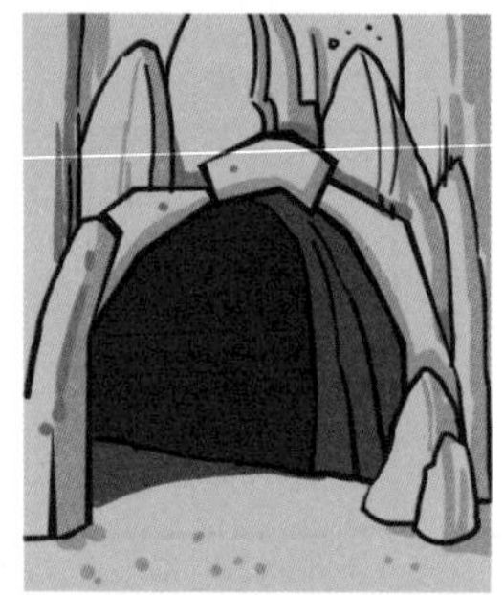

cave

desert

environment

fire

hill(s)

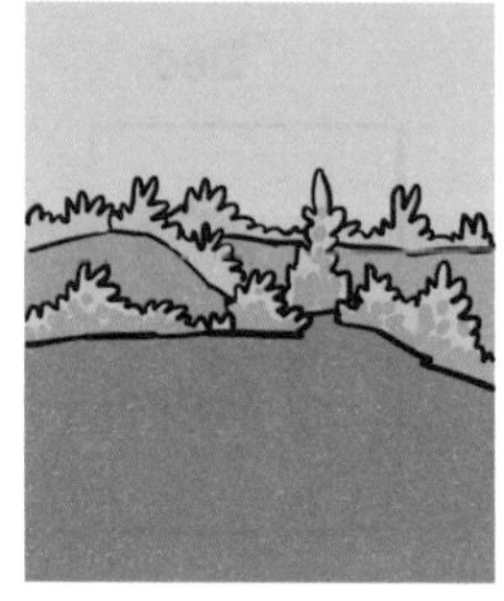
land

ocean

stone

stream

woods

Imagine your ideal natural place. What can you see there?

Animals

beetle

butterfly

camel

creature

dinosaur

eagle

extinct

octopus

swan

turtle

Where can you see these animals? What animal is extinct?

Competitions

chess

game

prize

crossword puzzle

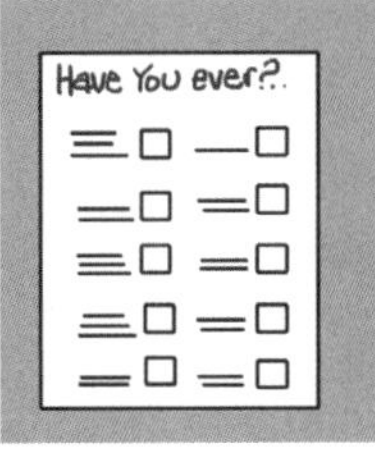

quiz

race

score

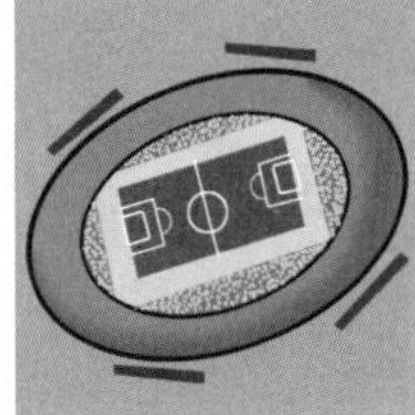
stadium

team

volleyball

winner

Have you ever played on a team?

Music and festivals

concert

drum

festival

flag

instrument(s)

musician

pop

rock

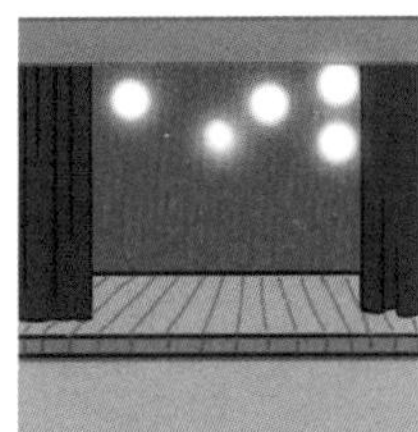
stage

song

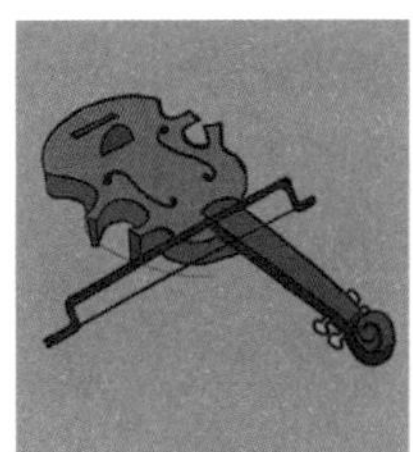
violin

whistle

What's your favorite type of music? What can you see at festivals in your country?

Verbs for offers, promises, and requests

clean

get

take care of

make sure

meet

make

repair

send

What things did you do last week? Choose five.

Telling the time

five after three

ten after three

a quarter after three

twenty after three

twenty-five after three

twenty-five to four

twenty to four

a quarter to four

ten to four

five to four

a.m.

p.m.

What were you doing at … ? Choose five times.

Seasons and weather

spring

summer

fall

winter

fog/foggy

ice

storm

warm

What's your favorite season? Do you see storms in your country?

In winter

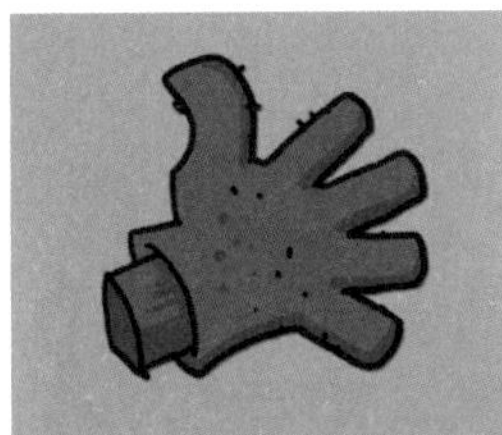
glove

pocket

pond

skiing

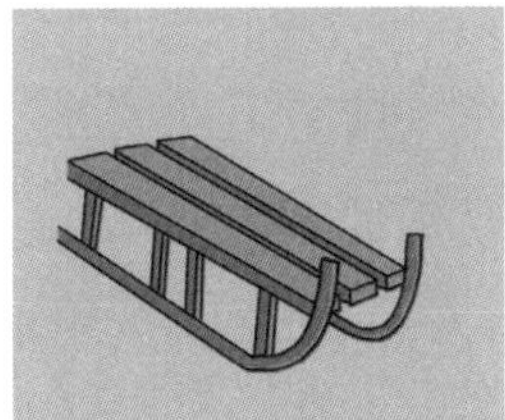
sled

snowball

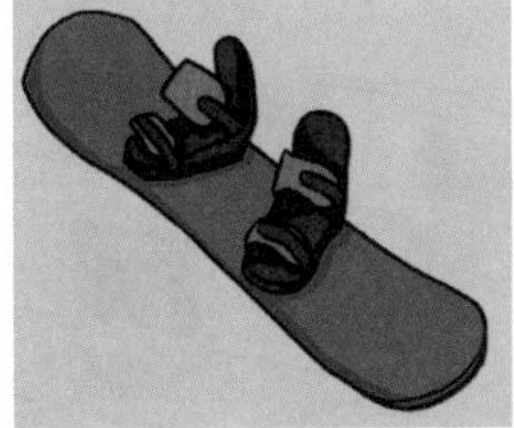
snowboard

snowboarding

snowman

What will you do this winter? Say five things.

Jobs

businessman/
businesswoman

engineer

firefighter

manager

mechanic

pilot

police officer

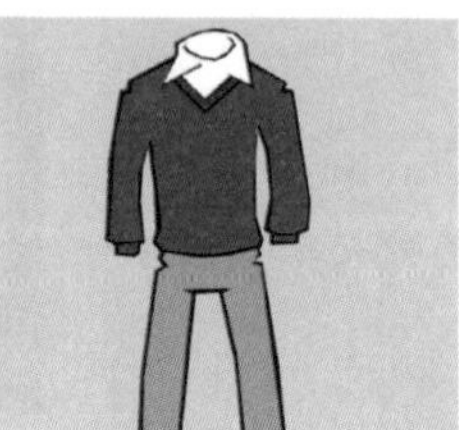
uniform

Can you think of five more jobs?

World of work

factory

fire engine

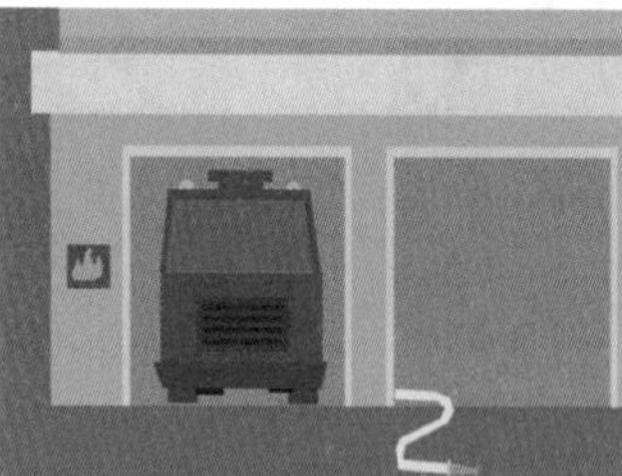
fire station

meeting

news

newspaper

office

police station

What work places are in your town?

Things in the home

brush

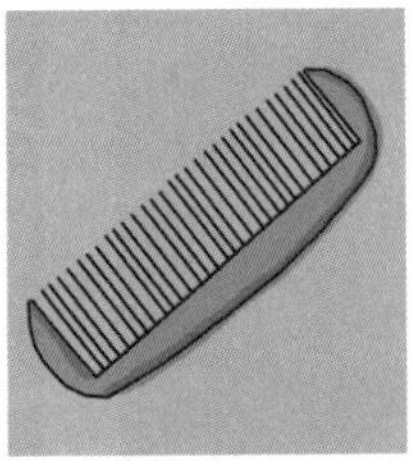

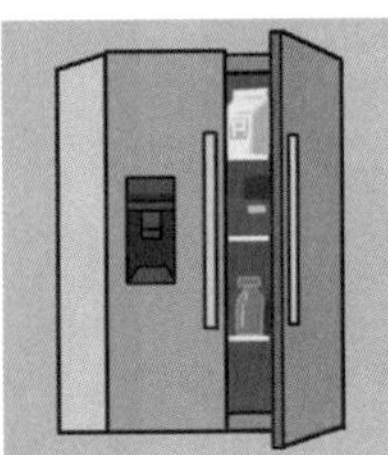
comb

fridge

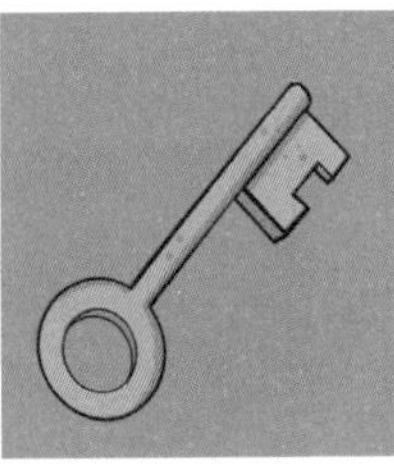
gate

key

oven

shampoo

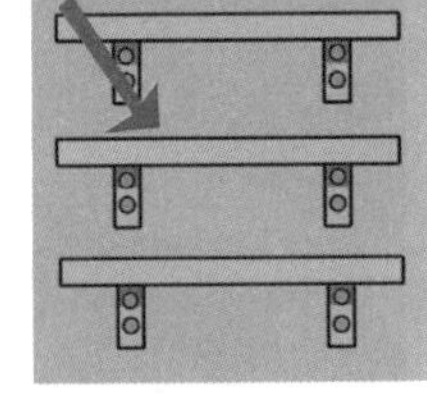
shelf

soap

phone

toilet

Where can you find these things at home?

Adjectives to describe objects

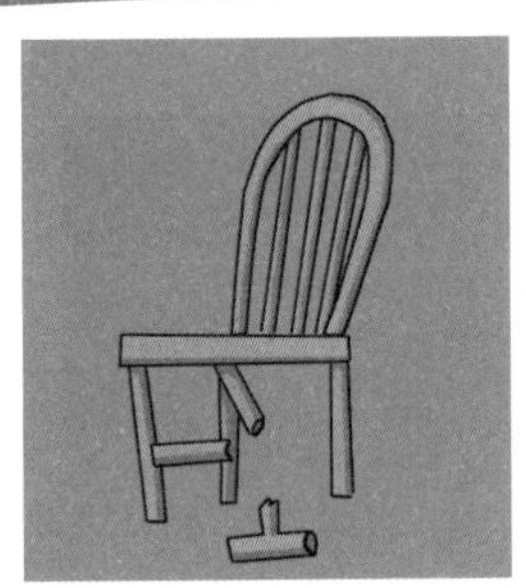
broken

cheap

expensive

empty

full

heavy

light

neat

messy

unusual

Think of an object, place, or animal for each adjective.

In space

astronaut

deep

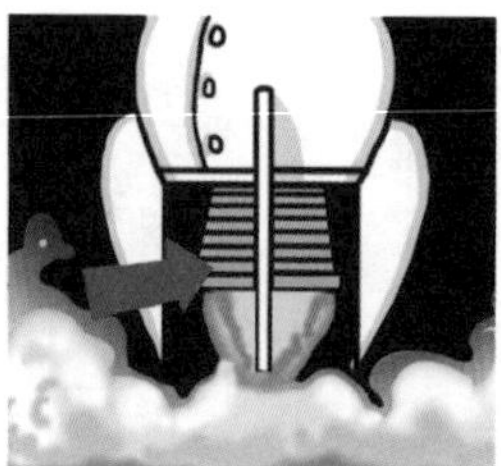
engine

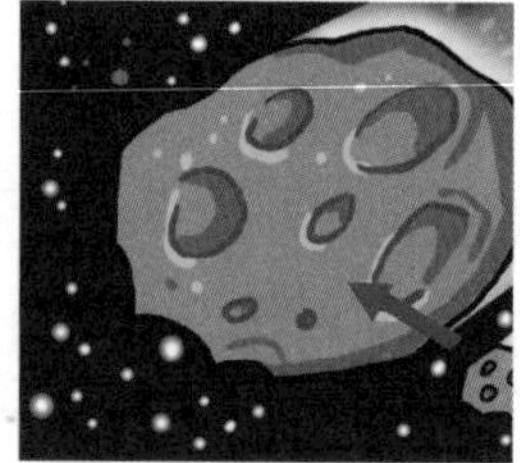
enormous

frightening

planet

rocket

space

spaceship

telescope

What space word is also a job?

Adventure words

enter

entrance

exit

follow

land

save

stay

touch

turn off

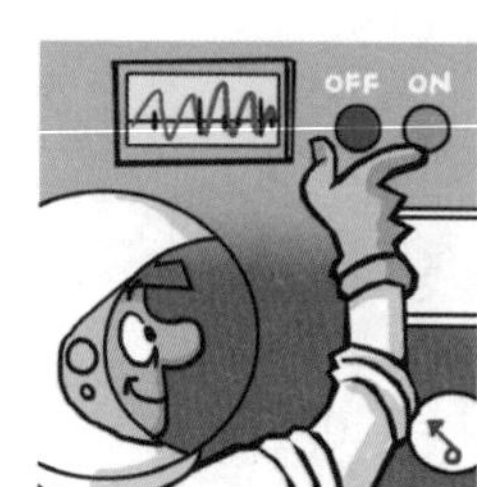

turn on

Choose five words. How do you do them?

Mealtimes and snacks

delicious

fork

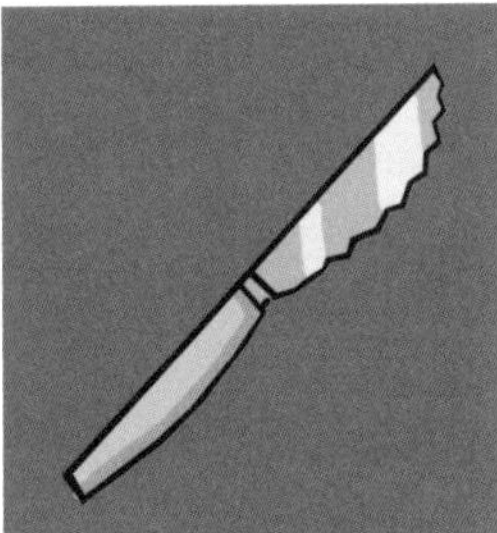
knife

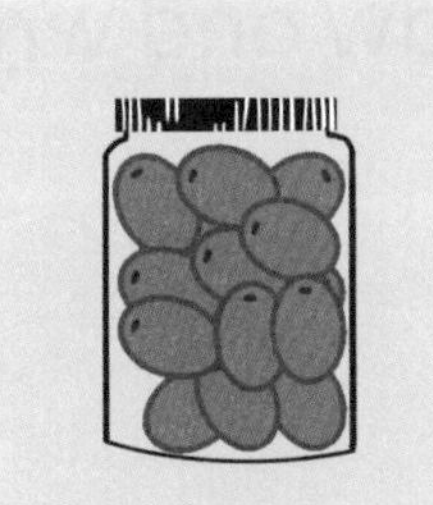
olives

pepper

piece

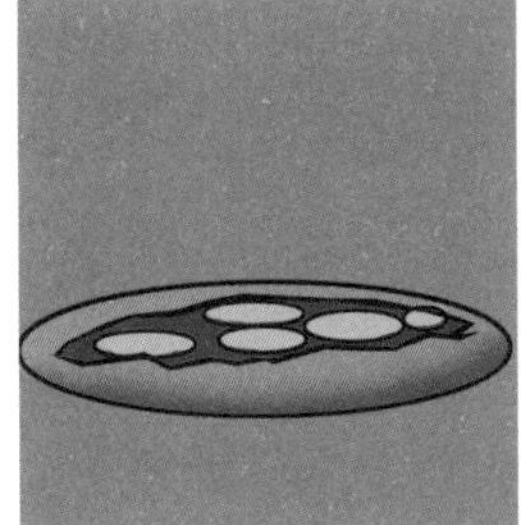
pizza

salt

snacks

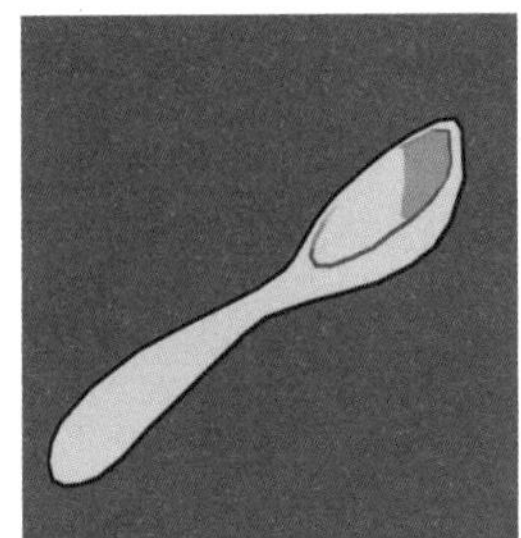
spoon

What are your favorite snacks?

Cooking

bake

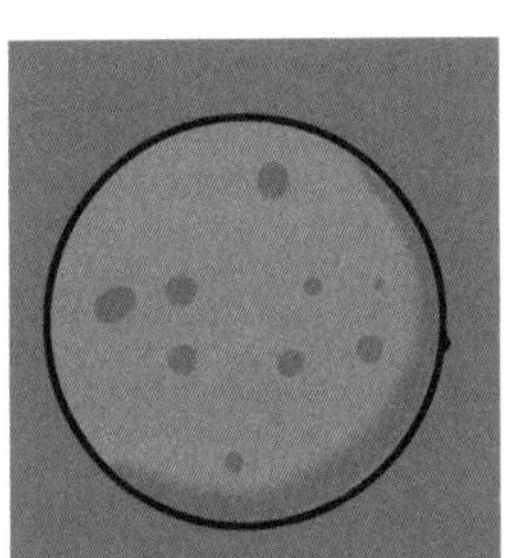
cookie

butter

stove

egg

flour

honey

jelly

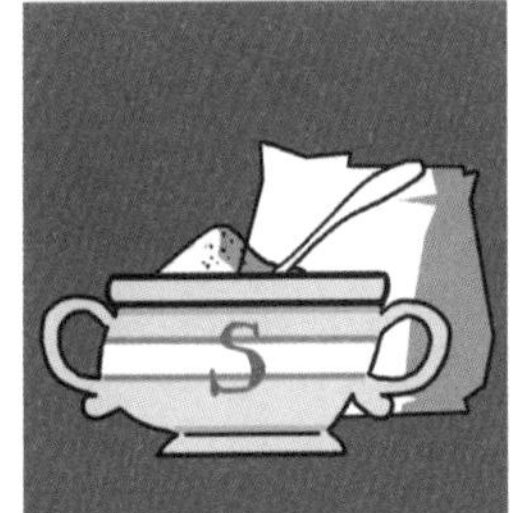

sugar

wash the dishes

What do you need to make cookies? Say five things.

Draw and write words you know in English.

Draw and write words you know in English.